Managing by Measuring

Managing by Measuring

How to Improve Your Organization's Performance Through Effective Benchmarking

Mark T. Czarnecki

AMACOM
American Management Association

New York • Atlanta • Boston • Chicago • Kansas City • San Francisco • Washington, D.C.
Brussels • Mexico City • Tokyo • Toronto

Library of Congress Cataloging-in-Publication Data

Czarnecki, Mark T.
    Managing by measuring : how to improve your organization's
performance through effective benchmarking / Mark T. Czarnecki.
        p.   cm.
    Includes index.
    ISBN 0-8144-0390-5
    1. Benchmarking (Management)   2. Organizational effectiveness.
I. Title.
HD62.15.C95   1998
658.5'62—dc21   98-35080
                                                                            CIP

Printing number

10   9   8   7   6   5   4   3   2   1

Contents

Collection Platform • Measuring Systems Effectiveness •
Identifying Changes to Systems • Conclusion

Preface

Managers today have an increasingly large amount of information available to them to aid in their decision-making process. Since competitors will have the same information available to them, no one can afford to ignore information that might be of use. Managers cannot simply rely on the mistakes of others to help them win the game. They must be constantly searching for new information, but they must also have some means of making sense of the information rapidly in order to continue to be productive. The purpose of this book is to show how companies can move to more scientifically managed business practices and to more stable markets through measuring themselves, measuring competitors, and measuring the markets.

Though measurement was first popularized in manufacturing environments through Total Quality Management programs, professionals from all areas of the corporation, in both the manufacturing and service sectors, are involved with measurement today. The research conducted for this book reveals that measurement functions can be housed in an executive area (such as corporate quality), a manufacturing area (such as a total quality department), a human resources function, or in any business process. This book is for any professional who wants to know more about starting and maintaining a measurement program.

The number-one complaint among process owners struggling to implement a new program is that it sounds good in theory but is impossible to apply to real life. While recognizing that corporate situations differ greatly, and only process owners who truly understand the corporation can apply theories appropriately, I wanted to write a practical manual.

Case studies and charts scattered throughout this book give the reader a snapshot of techniques being used in real life. As part of the research for this book, The Benchmarking Network, Inc. conducted surveys of over twenty companies of varying sizes in different industries to find out how prevalent certain measurement practices were in today's

corporate environment. The participants represent a significant population of workers in the United States (about two million). The Benchmarking Network also made use of extensive publicly available information to
compile a complete picture of measurement today.

Of course, I've also formulated opinions of what works best, based
on extensive conversations with the participants. It is my goal to give
readers an outline of steps necessary to implementing a strong measurement program while allowing them to formulate their own opinions
about detailed implementation.

To share your comments or for further information about Mark Czarnecki's speeches, seminars, or benchmarking studies, call 1-800-569-5044
or e-mail mczarnecki@ebenchmarking.com. Further information is also
available on The Benchmarking Network, Inc. web page at www.bench-
markingnetwork.com. Or you can write Mark Czarnecki, President, The
Benchmarking Network, Inc., 4606 FM 1960 West, Suite 300, Houston, TX
77069.

Acknowledgments

A special thank-you to all the companies that participated in the study that served as a basis for this book:

- Alcoa Fujikura, Ltd.
- Amoco
- AT&T
- AT&T Universal Card Services
- Bank America
- Blue Cross/Blue Shield, Michigan
- Boeing
- Chevron
- Citicorp
- Federal Mogul
- Florida Power and Light
- Intel Corporation
- Johnson Controls
- Kellogg
- NCR
- Nucor Corporation (Nucor Steel Division)
- Phillips Petroleum
- Public Service Electric and Gas
- Ryder Systems, Inc.
- Sears
- Texas Instruments
- The Steelcase Company
- United Services Automobile Association (USAA)

Thank you also to all The Benchmarking Network, Inc. staff who assisted me in the production of this book, including Joel Bowley, Fred Dorin, John Howell, and Eric Toces, and especially to Molly Elliott, who coordinated The Benchmarking Network book assembly and production on my behalf.

Managing by Measuring

1

The Measurements-
Oriented Corporation

Introduction

If you picked up this book, you probably are already thinking about implementing a measurement program in your corporation. But measurement takes on different faces in different corporations. Some focus on ongoing measurement while others focus on measurement for specific improvement efforts. Some measure customers; others measure manufacturing operations. Only you can determine what you want to measure, how you want to measure it, and who will benefit from the results.

In a measurements-managed corporation, measures are tools of management. Management selects measures that focus the priorities of the organization on numerical representations of the business process, which can be translated into day-to-day actions. While measurements must be actionable, they must also be linked to the highest levels of strategy in the organization. Management can then refocus attention away from daily activities to more strategic initiatives, assured that process owners will be able to make strategically sound decisions based on measurement information.

The intent of this chapter is to focus attention on measurement itself—impetus for measurement, benefits of measurement, basic categories of measurement, audiences for measurement, and uses of measurement. Case studies have been provided to allow the reader the chance to observe the use of measurement in real companies.

The Quality Movement: Impetus for Measurement

Much of the measurement activity in the United States began with the quality movement in the 1950s. Quality was defined slightly differently

1

by each of the three American gurus—Dr. W. Edwards Deming, Dr. Joseph Juran, and Philip B. Crosby. To Crosby, quality is conformance to requirements. Juran defines quality as fitness for use. Deming describes quality as a predictable degree of uniformity and dependability at low cost and suited to the market. Each of these definitions requires extensive measurement for its achievement. How else would one know when quality is achieved than by measuring conformity and customer expectations?

Therefore, the initial focus of quality was necessarily on structure. For example, Deming's fourteenth point is to create a structure in top management that will impact every day on the other thirteen points. Juran specifically recommends that a council be formed to guide the quality improvement process. He states that problems can be thought of as projects and that all improvements be made project-by-project. Each of these structures lends itself quite handily to an integrated measurement program. Direct measures, cost of quality, and statistical measures are all a necessary part of a Total Quality Management (TQM) program.

The Malcolm Baldrige National Quality Award was developed as an annual effort to recognize U.S. companies that excel in quality achievement. The award promotes:

- Awareness of quality as an increasingly important element in competitiveness
- Understanding of the requirements for quality excellence
- Sharing of information on successful quality strategies and the benefits derived from implementation of these strategies (benchmarking)

Unfortunately, in the late 1980s and early 1990s, the Baldrige award and the American quality movement began to move away from its emphasis on structure and measurement. Much more emphasis was put on more qualitative factors such as the use of specific manufacturing processes. The award received a lot of negative press when several winners suffered heavy declines shortly after receiving the award. In the late 1990s, the award criteria were redefined to refocus on quantitative management tools.

For example, the Malcolm Baldrige National Quality Award promotes benchmarking by allocating over half of the points to the process of comparing performance among organizations. A parallel renewed interest in corporate measurement has occurred recently as many companies are recognizing a need for measurement, both as a part of a quality system and as a smart business strategy.

More detail on the award criteria can be found in Appendix A. The award examination is designed not only to serve as a reliable basis for making awards but also to permit a diagnosis of each applicant's overall quality management. After going through the categories, items, and areas to address in the Baldrige criteria, most organizations find that they do not have sound and systematic methods in place, or that they have not deployed the principles of TQM to all parts of their organization, or that the methods they tried did not produce the level of performance they wanted (or have the positive influence on their customers they expected). The Baldrige criteria can serve as a great jumping off point for a measurement program.

Benefits of Measurement

The benefits of measurement, though numerous, can be hard to quantify. Most are indirectly linked to the measurement program and depend upon not making mistakes that would have been made otherwise. For example:

- The company that measures customer opinions is more likely to come out with successful products or services.
- The company that measures quality and efficiency of manufacturing processes will be able to achieve higher quality and efficiency goals.
- The company that measures employee satisfaction is likely to have higher employee retention rates.

Measurement focuses attention on specific aspects of your business and allows you to achieve goals within those aspects through a greater understanding of each aspect's needs. It is also a communications tool—a manager communicates a sense of importance of a particular dimension of the business to employees through what is chosen for measurement.

Monitoring a Changing Marketplace

Corporations are finding themselves in a rapidly changing environment. Though the nature of industries has always evolved, the level of technology available to businesses today has greatly increased the pace at which business realties change. Businesses need internal measurement to help them manage themselves effectively, but must rely on extensive external measurement to help them face the uncertainties inherent in venturing beyond their traditional roles to new and unexplored areas.

In recent history, this venturing led to the growth of and reward for a "cowboy" form of management. Executives established battlefronts a la John Wayne and "led the charge" with little more than winning the current battle for a strategic vision. This "ready, fire, aim" form of management has led to a number of corporate corpses that, for the most part, were unnecessary. Billions of dollars have been invested and wasted due to the lack of information about corporate capabilities and true risks and costs.

For example, in the 1980s, the oil field equipment industry geared up in places like Texas. A temporary decrease in oil supplies created a shortage for U.S. product, thereby raising prices. The industry responded by pumping product out to fill the need. Meanwhile, back in the plants, management had little or no understanding of costs, margins, cycle times, or in short, what was really going on. As history has it, oil prices dropped, triggering a wave of bankruptcies, largely due to the fact that the companies began to increase production beyond true market demand.

In fact, many were selling oil field equipment below true cost and creating a market perception of even lower costs. These mistaken perceptions became the problem. Information in the form of measures would have placed a floor on pricing by providing early warning signs of market trouble and encouraging many oil companies to switch production before they were stuck with excess inventory.

A few well-financed companies have overcome these weaknesses in the decade that followed the downturn. The companies we find in the oil industry today are characterized by their:

1. Long-term focus
2. Understanding of the nature of their markets
3. Understanding of what is happening in their organizations through measures

It is comparatively easy to quantify what would have been the value of measurement once mistakes are made. One of the primary reasons corporations are turning to measurement today is to avoid mistakes such as those that occurred during the 1980s in the oil industry. Though the details of the story change in each industry, the underlying theme that information—when properly analyzed—is the key to avoiding mammoth mistakes does not change.

Studying the Success of Measurement-Managed Companies

A recent study by Wm. Schiemann & Associates Inc. of Somerville, New Jersey, summarized why measurement-managed companies outperform non–measurement-managed companies in four main points: agreement on strategy, clarity of communication, focus and alignment efforts, and organizational culture. Each of these attributes, though not quantifiable by itself, is generally believed to be beneficial to the proper management of the corporation as a whole. What follows is an excerpt from this study as printed in *Management Review*:

Wm. Schiemann & Associates

■ *Agreement on strategy.* Only 7 percent of our measurement-managed companies reported a lack of agreement among top management on the business strategy of the organization. In the same study, 63 percent of the non–measurement-managed organizations reported disagreement. The act of translating vision or strategy into measurable objectives forces specificity. It helps to surface and resolve those hidden disagreements that often get buried when the strategy remains abstract, only to rise at some later date to haunt an organization.

■ *Clarity of communication.* We asked managers how well their business strategy was communicated and understood from top to bottom at their organizations. Sixty percent of managers in measurement-managed organizations rated favorably how well the strategy was communicated throughout the organization, while only 8 percent of managers from non–measurement-managed organizations reported that their organization's strategy was well-communicated and understood.

Good communication demands a clear message. If the strategy itself is unclear, insisting on measures of strategic goals can force clarity, as it has at Sears. "There was a real gap between the strategy and what it meant on a day-to-day, operational basis," explains Sears' vice president of quality at the Merchandising Group, Richard Quinn. This left employees uncertain about how they could contribute. So Quinn and other senior executives added a number of "wraparound elements" to the strategy and then tied the key strategic goals to performance measures. "This helped to clarify our strategic thinking and bring to life what we want to become and how to get there," concludes Quinn.

Measurement also provides a common language for communication. "People talk about how they're being measured," says Quinn. "It is almost the language in which communication occurs in an organization." Consistent with the notion of a common language, 71 percent of managers from measurement-managed organizations reported that information within their organization was shared openly and candidly, compared with only 30 percent in non–measurement-managed companies.

■ *Focus and alignment efforts.* Effective organizations are organic, integrated entities in which different units, functions and levels support the company strategy—and one another. Not surprisingly, our measurement-managed organizations reported more frequently that unit performance measures were linked to strategic company measures (74 percent versus 16 percent for non–measurement-managed companies) and that individual performance measures were linked to unit measures (52 percent versus 11 percent, respectively).

For example, at Steelcase North America, a $2 billion manufacturer of office furniture, the company strategy is reviewed each year and modified as appropriate. Business unit and functional strategies are then developed. John Gruizenga, senior vice president for architectural products, points out that as strategy cascades down the organization, performance measures are established to link up with the strategic performance expectations of the entire company. "This alignment of effort ensures that the corporate strategy is carried throughout, right to tactics and individual performance measures," Gruizenga says.

Measurement-managed companies were also more likely to link multiple measures to compensation. Forty-seven percent of measurement-managed companies had measurements in at least three performance areas linked to compensation, while only 9 percent of the non–measurement-managed companies had measures in as many as three areas linked to compensation.

■ *Organizational culture.* Call it culture, tone, or style, but a number of mechanisms are at play in every organization to create a set of collective attitudes and behaviors that either sustain or impair competitiveness. Take teamwork. When compared to non–measurement-managed counterparts, managers of measurement-managed companies more frequently reported strong teamwork and cooperation among the management team (85 percent favorable ratings on teamwork versus 38 percent for non–measurement-managed companies).

We also asked respondents the extent to which employees in their organization self-monitored their own performance against agreed-upon standards. Forty-two percent of the measurement-managed companies reported excelling in this regard, compared with only 16 percent of their non–measurement-managed counterparts.

Finally, increased willingness to take risks appears as an additional feature for building success in measurement-managed organizations. Fifty-two percent of managers from measurement-managed companies said employees in their organization generally were unafraid to take risks to accomplish their objectives, compared with only 22 percent of the non–measurement-managed companies.[1]

Each of these benefits that can be directly linked to measurement is a stepping-stone to improved corporate performance. All of the benefits cited by Wm. Schiemann & Associates are generally considered to be good intermediate goals for a strong corporation. While one must always keep the ultimate goal in mind (typically return on investment for shareholders), measurement provides a tool to smooth operations along the path to success.

What Is Measurement?

Corporations have been measuring their performance for quite a long time. Measurement in the 1950s was characterized by the stopwatch on the factory floor. Since then, measurement has expanded from the manufacturing arena to every facet of the business. The issue was then, and still is today, one of choosing measures that accurately portray business reality without consuming vast resources in time or money.

Measurements are comparisons. The raw numbers are of no value without some baseline to compare them to. Internal measurements are kept consistent in order to compare them year after year for either improvement or consistency.

Measurements designed for external comparison give a snapshot of where the corporation stands vis-à-vis the market. They tell the company where there is room for improvement and what the company's greatest concern for staying competitive should be.

Many would argue that it may not be fair or even relevant to compare the performance of one company to that of another. For example, within the steel industry there are large discrepancies in cost structure. The largest companies in the industry produce steel the old-fashioned way—from iron ore. The most successful companies reprocess steel from scrap. How do you compare the management of two companies in what appears to be the same industry, but which operate in entirely different ways within the industry?

The answer is by breaking the companies into smaller pieces or corporate processes that are similar. The issue of external measurements will be covered more thoroughly in chapters 6 and 7, but suffice it to say that corporations are being compared on a daily basis. Stockholders demand maximum profitability for their dollar. Customers require high innovation and reliability. Bondholders and other holders of corporate debt require maximum return for the risk category. Corporations need to be prepared for these competitive comparisons by keeping an eye on the external marketplace themselves.

The following section deals with stakeholders and types of measurement to consider when designing a comprehensive, comparative measurement program.

Measurement Stakeholders

A measurement program must always focus on the needs of stakeholders in the corporation—or those individuals who have a significant interest in the corporation. From the shareholders to the employees to the customers—all have different perspectives on measurement. What follows is a brief outline of corporate stakeholders and how measurement programs can meet their needs.

Shareholders/Lienholders

Shareholders and lienholders are relying on the representations made by corporate management to protect their interests in and make the corporation grow. Shareholders are typically most interested in measures of financial success of the company as a whole. Corporations must monitor their operations in the exercise of their fiduciary responsibilities. Starting after the great stock market crash of 1929, government stepped in and required more thorough financial reporting. It required management to report its financial position to shareholders in a manner consistent with other companies and to have third parties review the books on behalf of the shareholders. This triggered a fifty-year cycle that drew management to internal financial measurement and eventually led to management relying on financial data to run the company.

Employees

Employees are concerned with the overall health of the corporation, financial and otherwise. But they are also individually concerned about their position in the corporation. Corporations today have established very complicated psychological contracts with their employees. A part of that contract is the assumption that employees are going to be compensated for excellent performance. This can be in the form of periodic raises, bonuses, and promotions to the best employees; assignment of the most desirable jobs to the best performers; or commissions or other incentive plans. To that end, corporations have established performance appraisal systems. The systems are typically based on a combination of measures of performance and subjective opinions of immediate supervisors. Often salary survey data are also incorporated. Many employees, however, feel that they are not being adequately evaluated on their productive performance. While it may seem relatively easy to measure the contribution of a factory line worker, the magnitude of the complexity of the employee measurement process can be appreciated when one is challenged to measure the productivity or contribution of an indirect contributor, such as a communications professional.

Customers

Customers are typically concerned with the value of the product or service received. Calculating that value can be a difficult undertaking. Customers want the best product or service for the lowest cost, but perception of "best" and even the perception of cost can vary significantly by industry and customer segment. The best product or service may be the most technologically advanced, the easiest to use, the most reliable, the one with the most helpful sales associates, or the one that goes with your decor. Cost is also more complex than the sales price. It can include time required to obtain the product or learn about the product, cost of accessories, or costs associated with repair. In order to get a complete picture of the value of your product or service from the customer's perspective, you will need to be involved in measuring the customer. Chapter 6 explains customer measurement in more detail.

Community

As a stakeholder, the community may value environmental measures, measures of corporate contributions to the community, or measures of your impact on the welfare of the local citizens. Oil refineries, for-profit prisons, and many others find a need to monitor community expectations on a regular basis. The more controversial the business, the more important these measures become.

Executives

Each corporation must set internal goals and aspirations. These are usually incorporated into the overall corporate strategy. Companies use measures to link aspirations to daily activities and to track their progress on the road to their goals.

Process Managers

Managers of individual processes are typically focused on those measures that effect them operationally. Manufacturing will have a set of unique measures, as will marketing, sales, human resources, engineering, among others.

Dimensions of Measurement

Just as there are many groups for whom measurement is important, there are several types of measurements you will want to collect. Companies typically gather measures in four basic areas:

1. Quality
2. Productivity
3. Cycle time
4. Control

A *quality* measure is a clearly quantifiable figure derived from one of two sources. One source is to measure how many failures have occurred in a function or process. The figures derived are expressed as a "rate per." For instance, companies that measure the error rate in accounting may express that measure as "the number of errors per thousand paychecks." A number like that is obtainable. Records can be reviewed to determine if employees are pointing out errors in their paychecks or if there was a processing problem known to the payroll department. At this point, it will be possible to compare relative error rates among organizations to determine which is better at producing an error-free paycheck.

The second source of a quality measure is the customer. Customer perceptions are measurable. Many organizations have adopted a "customer satisfaction" rating as their guide for redefining their products and services. Over the past few years, some of these customer satisfaction statistics have become widely advertised.

Surveys by J. D. Power and Associates have become widely used by automakers, airlines, and other organizations. These surveys use a combination of scales that indicate customer attitudes toward products and services. The responses to these surveys can compare relative performance against other competitors as well as changes in satisfaction levels over time.

Many customer satisfaction surveys use a numerical scale such as one to five, with one being poor service and five being excellent (or vice versa). The actual scaling for customer satisfaction processes has been a subject of much debate. The choice of a scale will be discussed in Chapter 6, but the most important thing is to be consistent with regard to scales used so that data is comparable over time.

Many customer satisfaction surveys go beyond the basic quality of the product and probe the associated service level. The concept of service level looks beyond quality to incorporate the speed (cycle time) in which the product or service can be delivered. Service levels vary widely among organizations. In the restaurant business, service is measured in minutes while manufacturers may measure service in days from order to fulfillment. The organization that can provide a high-quality product in a shorter cycle time is better able to respond to rapidly changing competition.

Consider the depth of services when you develop service-level measures. Some accounting organizations supply high-level summary reports to their managers; others will carry the same financial statements with a complete analysis of operations. The organization that delivers more information will often satisfy more of the customer's needs than the organization that does not. The trick is to reach the right customer needs with minimal cost and effort.

Service features are typically identified during customer interviews. Customers are asked to assign values to each feature. The measurer converts these features and capabilities into numerical scores for comparison purposes. The result is a single numerical score of customer need fulfillment that can be used to identify where the gaps exist.

Many companies emphasize *productivity* in their process measurement. Measures of productivity are usually expressed as a "cost per." For example, cost per product manufactured or benefits cost per employee would be considered productivity measures. Productivity reflects the efficiency of a process and generally is a calculation of output/input.

Productivity measures are typically more comparable between companies than raw cost data is. The ratios inherent in productivity measures provide scale adjustments that make organizations of different sizes comparable.

Cycle time is an indicator of how long it takes for a product or service to be prepared. Cycle time represents the elapsed time between the start of a process and the delivery of its final defined outputs. To measure cycle time, it will be necessary to have a clear definition of where activities start and end. For example, time to release a new product to market can start with the initial concept or with the go/no-go decision.

Control tells management whether the process is replicable. Are people doing the same thing time after time? The answer to this question seems critical to the overall success of the effort. Measurements are not just a scorecard but a management tool. Watching failure rates jump up and down sends a clear message about whether people are doing the same thing over and over. How can you get different results by doing the same things?

Using Multiple Measures

A single measure is usually not a good predictor of overall performance. Therefore, a family or group of measures spanning several dimensions of performance is a more effective approach.

In the payroll department, companies may initially choose a measure of productivity that is defined as cost per paycheck. They might go out and find two or three other companies that can give the operating statistic stated in common terms. One of those companies may pay all its employees monthly. As a result, its "cost per paycheck" measure may be higher, but it may actually represent better overall performance.

Companies typically embrace an entire family of measures to lessen the impact of a single measure. Some of these other measures may include cost per employee, cost per pay period, cost to correct a paycheck, and cycle time to produce payroll. Your measures may also focus on head count by defining full-time equivalents assigned to payroll.

Each of these measures is likely to give you an indication of "best" performance. Companies find it important to understand all of them.

An example of the types of measures a company might maintain in the accounts receivable (A/R) area can be found in Figure 1-1. These are the measures maintained by the Credit Research Foundation of Columbia, Maryland. Notice how the measures fall into the categories of quality (1,2,11), cycle time (6,7), and productivity (3,4,5,8,9,10,12,13).

Sources of Data for Measurement

Sources of data for measurement play a big role in the integrity and accuracy of the data. Certain data sources, though, are more expensive or difficult to implement. Measurement programs are forced to make trade-offs between precision and the practicality of collecting data. Too much attention to precision is overly time-consuming and will ultimately cause you to overanalyze the numbers. Therefore, the best course is to develop reasonable comparisons and focus on large differences or gaps and how to improve operations around those gaps.

Measurement systems can generally be segregated into four types based on the source of the data:

Figure 1-1. Sample industry measures for accounts receivable (A/R).

1. Collection effectiveness
2. Bad debt to sales
3. Active customer accounts per credit and collection employee
4. Annual operating costs per employee
5. Credit and collection costs per sales dollar
6. Days sales outstanding
7. Best possible days sales outstanding
8. Annual check turnover per cash application
9. Annual transaction turnover per cash application
10. Annual transaction turnover per accounts payable employee
11. Annual deductions (adjustments) turnover per cash application and deduction specialist
12. Annual operating cost per transaction
13. Annual operating cost per employee

Source: Credit Research Foundation of Columbia, Maryland.

1. *Direct measurement systems* are usually used when there is a unit of production or an event that is captured in an automated system such as a computer. The count is very reliable because it counts events that are actually happening. These are the best kinds of measures because they can be easily compared between organizations and promote high confidence in the results.

An example of direct measurement from the manufacturing arena is "number of units produced." In this case, a computer system can be queried and a count can be made of units produced. Some sources of this kind of information include:

- Line product in statistics
- Packaging material units consumed
- Shipping data
- Invoicing data

2. *Indirect measurement systems* are used when the actual data is not collected at the time the event occurs. An example from one study required the count for the number of photocopies produced in a facility. Machines were replaced during the year; therefore, no reliable count was possible. As a surrogate, the number of sheets of copier paper purchased was known. This number was considered more reliable when taken from receiving reports than the other estimates that could be produced. This

indirect method is usually not as good as the direct method because it depends heavily on the accuracy of the alternate data source. In this case, some of the receiving records may have been missing certain data that had to be reconstructed. Alternately, some of the paper could have been used in other ways, such as in laser printers or as scrap paper.

3. *Statistical samples* can be used to develop estimates where whole data is incomplete. In the event that there are a large number of transactions for which there are no summaries, it may be necessary to perform statistical sampling to determine an approximate measure. For example, a company that wishes to determine an error rate in its marketing database may choose to test a small random sample rather than inspect the entire database. The inspection of the entire database is warranted only if the sample indicates an unacceptable error rate. Statistical samples are subject to the usual sampling error that occurs due to:

- Insufficient sample size
- Poor sampling techniques
- Sampling risk

Statistical samples can be useful tools to answer some of the simple questions that come up during a comparative study that are not regularly collected in your organization.

4. *Interviews or surveys* to gather metric information are used as a last resort. Some companies have resorted to face-to-face interviews to determine measurements when other sources were unavailable.

Interviews are most helpful when the measures are perceptual. As we discussed, when customer measures are employed, the use of interviews can be helpful in identifying some of the factors of value to the customer. Perceptual measures contain inherent imprecision and bias. Nevertheless, perceptual information is still valuable, since it can be linked to nonquantifiable behaviors and can suggest improvements in quality, cycle time, productivity, and control.

Uses for Measurement

In the research performed for this book, two main uses for measurement prevailed—to support corporate improvement efforts and as part of a performance appraisal process. While not mutually exclusive, the purpose of measurement appears to impact the nature of the measures gathered.

Improvement-Based Measurement

Improvement-based measurement tends to focus on creating a common language for improvement efforts, communicating measurement results, and understanding organizational dynamics. Improvement-based measurement can be ongoing or a one-shot deal. Many companies use ongoing measurement processes to springboard into improvements while others institute measurement when they begin to notice the need for improvement.

The following case study about improvement efforts at Sears was developed out of a research study conducted as a basis for this book. The study included both a scan of business articles that touch on measurement and a proprietary corporate performance benchmarking study that surveyed measurement practices at over twenty corporations of various sizes. My hope is that through the case studies you will be better able to see how measurement theory can be put into practice at real companies.

Sears

Sears is a company that up to the 1980s was characterized by success through size. More recently, intense competition from companies like Wal-Mart has forced Sears to find a better message. Now, as a company coming out of a turnaround situation, Sears sees the role of measures as integral to its long-term strategy.

Sears has established an improvement program that links customers, employees, and shareholders through a set of winning measures. The program recognizes three "compellings" as being key indicators of company success—a compelling place to shop (customer focus), a compelling place to work (employee focus), and a compelling place to invest (shareholder focus). Sears proposed that the key to change would lie in the customer- and employee-focused areas, presuming that investors would follow (see Figure 1-2).

While the underpinning of this program is a simple idea, the implications and the implementation are not. With a simple concept, the rest of the program can be organized. Sears focused on the three areas defined by the three "compellings" to expand its program into specific performance measures.

The first step in measurement implementation was to develop and communicate the message of measurement. Sears had to develop a culture that values and understands measures and integrates the results into the organization. Sears instituted a program of educating the employees

Figure 1-2. Key performance indicators.

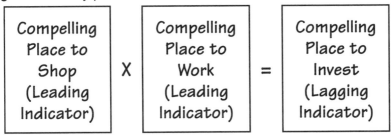

Source: Sears Roebuck and Co.

that measurement was key to open communication, competition, and rewards that would ultimately create value for customers (see Figure 1-3).

Based on the three core goals stated in the framework of the improvement program and the mission statements that were developed from them, Sears created a set of more detailed core objectives that include messages about what kind of company Sears wants to be. For example, one customer-oriented objective was great merchandise at a great value while an employee-oriented objective was to provide an environment for personal growth and development. Performance indicators (or measures) were then established to monitor the objectives. For example, customer satisfaction was seen as an indicator of great merchandise at a great value. Figure 1-4 outlines Sears' integrated message in more detail.

The performance indicators were measured by both objective and subjective factors. Objective factors are those measures that are supported by hard numbers. Subjective factors include items such as customer satisfaction that are more dependent on perception.

Because the measures that Sears chose touched all parts of the cor-

Figure 1-3. Value statement for employees.

Simplifying and Integrating Our Message

Our Shared Beliefs

Our People Add Value
We value each person's uniqueness and contribution. We respect the dignity and potential of all our people and encourage their growth. We treat each person fairly and honestly, and we communicate openly. We face the competition as a team and share in the rewards of our success. Our people and their ideas are what ultimately create value for our customers.

Source: Sears Roebuck and Co.

Figure 1-4. Detailed core objectives and performance indicators.

	Three Compellings		
	Compelling Place to Shop	Compelling Place to Work	Compelling Place to Invest
Objectives	■ Great merchandise at great values ■ Excellent customer service from the best people ■ Fun place to shop ■ Customer loyalty	■ Environment for personal growth and development ■ Support for ideas and innovation ■ Empowered and involved teams/ individuals	■ Revenue growth ■ Superior operating income growth ■ Efficient asset management ■ Productivity gains
Total Performance Indicators	■ Meeting customer needs ■ Customer satisfaction ■ Customer retention	■ Personal growth and development ■ Empowered teams	■ Sales growth ■ Sales/square feet ■ Inventory turnover ■ Operating income margin ■ Return on assets

Source: Sears Roebuck and Co.

poration, various departments needed to be coordinated for data gathering. Accounting and finance, store operations, and other departments were all involved in the measurement process.

Measurement means nothing if it does not impact behavior. The next step for Sears was to convert the short "sound bites" of inspiration they had been feeding to employees into fundamental changes in what the employees did on a typical day. This was no small task since Sears is a store chain with more than 800 locations, a half dozen specialty stores (Sears Hardware, NTB, etc.), part-time workers, and a culture that has historically experienced a sense of entitlement. The answer was to develop a leadership model that addresses:

- Communication with workers
- Training for critical skills
- New team models
- Problem-solving guidance
- Improvement in communication models

Since a large portion of the workforce worked part-time, Sears believed that the way to real change was to change behaviors in key personnel, then allow those behaviors to cascade to the rest of the organization as employees observed their coworkers.

In addition to employee communication, Sears sought to change employee attitudes through three key areas that can be controlled by management:

- Job supervision
- Job structure
- Job context

Sears identified ways in which employees' managers could affect their attitudes about the job and the company through these three aspects. For example, the manager's customer service orientation, a piece of job supervision, directly affects employees' attitude about the job and eventually their behaviors. Figure 1-5 illustrates this concept in more detail.

The core premise behind Sears' change initiative was to demonstrate the link between individual employee satisfaction and the ultimate delivery of services to the customer, and how this link can be measured. Sears identified employee attitudes about both the job and the company that may not always be controllable but that can be measured.

Sears initially hired a consulting firm to measure both worker and customer attitudes. As a first step, employees' attitudes about their jobs were identified by the consulting firm on an individual and aggregate basis. Stores were able to compare their employee attitudes to aggregate numbers to determine their progress. This is tracked internally today.

Key opportunities for improvement in highly strategic areas became

Figure 1-5. Managerial concepts with highest impact on associates' behaviors.

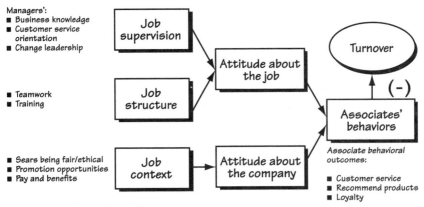

Source: Sears Roebuck and Co.

apparent to management through the reporting structure and allowed management to focus on key gaps to close. Since fixed scales are applied on an individual, local, and national basis, scores can be compared to internal benchmarks. Internal measures were aimed at producing involved and empowered employees, but Sears recognized that there were multiple steps to that goal. Figure 1-6 is a graphical depiction of what management believed to be the three steps: (1) establishing a foundation for an environment for personal goals and development, (2) encouraging new ideas, which leads to (3) involving and empowering associates. Management believed the establishment of a foundation was key to achieving the ultimate change goals.

Sears developed a parallel model for external measures (see Figure 1-7). The foundation under the customer is to get the right merchandise at the right prices. Excellent customer service people then provide the second-level foundation. Finally, an enjoyable place to shop can be reestablished, leading to the ultimate goal of customer loyalty.

Figure 1-6. Three steps to employee empowerment (internal measures).

Source: Sears Roebuck and Co.

Figure 1-7. Steps to customer loyalty (external measures).

Externally Focused Measures

Source: Sears Roebuck and Co.

Impact on Sears

Since Sears established measurable indicators of its change process, the company was able to trend performance over time at the individual level and at the group level. This gave managers a check on their progress and told them when goals were met.

So what was the payoff? Sears successfully demonstrated the link between associates' attitudes and bottom-line results. In the company's retail environment the following is true:

- Improving associates' attitudes about their jobs and the company by 5 units increases the customer impression by 1.3 units; increasing the customer impression 1.3 units has a direct effect on revenue of 0.5 percent; and a 1.3 unit increase in customer impression and a 1 unit increase in customer retention drives revenue by 0.9 percent.
- The demonstrated results from this analysis mean that the relationship is valid and that the measurement program is working.

Next Steps for Sears

While measurement at Sears was instituted to begin an improvement process, the measurement program does not end with the turnaround. Sears recognizes the importance of maintaining ongoing measurement to make sure that none of the improved areas slip back into old habits. Sears will also need to continue to refine the measurement program as market realities change and specific goals of the company change. Many of the company's improvement-oriented measurements will transfer into an appraisal system as well, since Sears is already measuring employees extensively.

Appraisal-Oriented Measurement

Performance appraisal-oriented measures are rooted in the need to understand, communicate with, and reward employees. They tend to focus on managing employees, communicating strategies into performance goals, and applicability to individual reward and recognition systems. Three short case studies follow that outline corporate approaches to measurement. Sprint and National City Bank of Kentucky provide classic examples of appraisal-oriented measurement. The Sprint case study was originally published in *Training & Development* and the National City Bank case study is from an article in *Business First–Louisville.*

Sprint

In 1990, the Sprint Corporation was made up of business units with different human resources (HR) systems for performance planning and assessment, and no common culture or language for communicating Sprint's vision, values, and mission to employees. Now, Sprint uses the LINK Performance Management System with a common language for integrating business objectives, employee-development plans, 360-degree-evaluation instruments, and educational courses.

The system includes seven Sprint core dimensions and twenty-nine subdimensions that share a language and value system for describing Sprint's work and culture. The Sprint dimensions are defined through job analyses, employee and executive interviews, and external industry data. They are the foundation of all training, performance management, selection, career development, and assessment within Sprint.

The LINK system operates continuously in a cascading format. Before the new calendar year, executives announce their business plans. Then, four to six key business objectives are identified for each associate aligning the Sprint dimensions and subdimensions to support the accomplishment of the objectives. Each associate creates an individual development plan with input from a 360-degree instrument. The LINK process also involves two interim reviews, one annual performance appraisal, and a yearly salary adjustment. This aspect is unique in that compensation is based on whether an employee attains his or her objectives as well as how those objectives are met.[2]

National City Bank (of Kentucky)

National City Bank uses job descriptions in combination with goals and objectives as the basis for performance appraisals. Performance is rated on a scale of one to five with opportunity to rate overall performance through an open-ended comment section. Raters are encouraged not to give all employees high scores, but to rank them so that merit increases can be distributed based on performance.

Together, the manager and the employee create a development plan. This can open lines of communication, but it can also be difficult to reconcile the manager's and employee's perception of performance. Employees are coached throughout the year based on the previous year's development plan so that there are no surprises at the time of the appraisal.[3]

Conclusion

Each company chooses a measurement system that is most effective for its specific business circumstances. The key message to be understood before embarking on a measurement program is that information is power. Other messages are that:

- Measurement influences employee behavior.
- Measurement improves employee decisions.
- Measurement identifies areas to be improved.
- Measurement points to new developments.

Therefore, measurement should always be linked to corporate strategic goals, but there are multiple ways to measure a corporation or business process.

2

Organizing to Collect Measures

Introduction

The first step in measurement is always the hardest. Often there is a management mandate to institute a measurements program with little direction as to how to do it. This chapter will focus on how one (1) links measurement to corporate strategy, (2) develops a mission and methodology for measurement, and (3) assembles an organization for identifying and collecting measurement data.

Link Measurement to Strategy

The first step is always strategic. If the CEO isn't already involved in the measurements program, it's time to get the top executive involved. If measurements don't reflect the goals and aspirations of the corporation, they are of little value and may actually do damage by steering employees toward undesirable behaviors.

The executive team must define long-term goals for the corporation. Think of these goals in terms of the various stakeholders discussed in Chapter 1. Ask yourself, "How do we want our (shareholders, customers, employees) to view our company?"

Now you can "drill down." Remember how Sears started with a high-level goal (e.g., compelling place to shop) and established more detailed objectives that had to be obtained to reach the high-level goal. Select about a half dozen stepping-stone objectives.

Each of these objectives should be measurable. Brainstorm multiple ways of measuring these objectives. Try to make sure your measures fall into multiple categories of quality, cycle time, productivity, and control so that the measures paint a balanced picture. You may have to go through multiple iterations of this process before you arrive at a solid set of measures. Each time, bounce your ideas off executive management and process owners to get a good idea if these measures will motivate the right behavior.

Getting the organization involved is, of course, the key to the success of the measures program. The following case study examines how ARCO Transportation Co. related its performance appraisal system to key corporate values, making it more meaningful to employees. It was originally published in *Training*.

ARCO

ARCO Transportation Co. (ATC) is a $1 billion division of Atlantic Richfield Co. Over the past two years, ATC developed an organizationwide performance dimension model that now applies to all of its 1,725 regular, full-time employees.

The process began with the company's executive team. Senior managers defined a set of thirteen prototype performance dimensions they believed would lead to corporate success in the 1990s. The dimensions reflected ATC's values and its performance philosophy. The executives also provided specific examples for each dimension.

The thirteen original performance dimensions were reviewed and reworked by a larger group of managers who met in Ojai, California, in the summer of 1990. The Ojai group generated a revised set of dimensions and turned them over to a task force composed of a broad cross-section of employees. This task force, with help from ATC's training department and consultants from the Hay Group, worked the dimensions into their final form during the fall of 1990.

In the end, ATC adopted a set of ten performance dimensions. The final set that was developed included the following ten performance dimensions:

1. Action
2. Teamwork
3. Creativity
4. Communication
5. Decision making
6. Leadership
7. Proficiency
8. Accountability

    9. Adaptability
10. Development

The dimensions are intended partly to communicate company values. But they also will help integrate ATC's various human resource processes; they will serve as the foundation upon which HR activities stand.

The real value of a performance dimension model is realized in its application. The first application at ATC came in the form of a revamped performance appraisal process for all employees. The performance review form was rewritten to include the ten dimensions. The old form consisted of three parts. A section called Performance Analysis contained seventeen factors to be evaluated by the manager or supervisor (e.g., problem solving, initiative, productivity, interpersonal skills, and so on). Another section was devoted to strengths, areas needing improvement, and training needs. The final section, called the Work Planning and Progress Review Worksheet, is for recording major objectives, plans for action, achievement measures, and final results. Some of the new performance dimensions were partially represented in the seventeen performance factors on the old form, but many were not.

To ensure that the new dimensions would be taken seriously and woven into the company's performance culture, the form was rewritten. The dimensions became the centerpiece of the annual performance appraisal process. On the new form, employees are rated on each of the ten performance dimensions. The message to employees comes through loud and clear: "These dimensions, taken together, describe the things we value in our people. Aspiring to competence in each dimension will lead to success in this company."

Having blended the dimensions into the performance appraisal process, ATC turned to its hiring system, which is now being revamped. All managers and supervisors who conduct selection interviews are being trained in behavioral interviewing techniques that will allow them to probe for the presence of the desired performance dimensions. Once the new hiring system is up and running, the company will turn its attention to other human resource functions, assessing where the performance dimensions lead in the areas of succession planning, training, and reward systems.[4]

The Steelcase Company

The Steelcase Company, a highly competitive office-furnishings equipment manufacturer, concentrates its measurement externally with dealers and customers. Measurement efforts are derived from Steelcase's need for unity of strategy at each level of the distribution chain. Measures have been carefully selected to lead to a common view of the organization. The key areas that Steelcase measures are:

- Basic measures (e.g., financial, order fulfillment, economic value added, new products)
- Dealer loyalty (e.g., what do dealers think, how good are they and how well are they doing)
- Order fulfillment (e.g., orders fulfilled, orders managed, products made, and products delivered)
- End customer statistics (e.g., loyalty, happiness, and confidence)

After a measure is established, Steelcase assigns an owner to that measure—someone responsible for the measure. Specific goals are established for each measure based on history, but also incorporating a "stretch" goal. Steelcase uses green, red, and yellow as signals for control of specific measures. The green rule establishes expected performance. The yellow rule establishes at what point the measure would need closer scrutiny. The red rule establishes a point at which the measure is considered out of control and in need of corrective action.

For example, a baseline would be established for cost of goods sold. The green rule would establish that anything below that baseline is expected performance or better. The yellow rule would allow a tolerance of 5 percent above the baseline. If the measure moves to yellow, it would be watched and perhaps a root cause would be established, but no corrective action would be taken. The red rule establishes that immediate corrective action would need to be taken if cost of goods sold rose more than 5 percent above the baseline.

Steelcase displays specific targets and results in dedicated executive conference rooms. The "Big Board" in the conference room summarizes the details of the measures in grid format. The measurement description, owner, goal, and definitions of the green rule, yellow rule, and red rule are displayed on this grid for each of the measures as shown in Figure 2-1.

Each of the measurement categories (basic, dealer loyalty, order fulfillment, end customer) is displayed on a separate board. Each of these categories also contains two levels of more detailed measurement. For example, measures of dealer loyalty are broken down into dealer health, happiness, and confidence. Dealer health is then further broken into dealer efficiency/effectiveness and performance to plan. Similarly, order fulfillment is broken into four categories with another four to six subcategories under each.

Steelcase has taken a strategy dedicated to unity and loyalty in the distribution chain and translated it into a fully integrated measurement sys-

Figure 2-1. Process measurement rules for order fulfillment.

Measurement Description	Measurement OWNER	GOAL	Green Rule	Yellow Rule	Red Rule
Orders Fulfilled *M1* Orders scheduled in week customer requested Orders delivered complete and on time Orders delivered defect and damage free Cost of quality					
Orders Managed *M2* Total cost of errors Percent of orders acknowledged on time Days to acknowledge on regular orders Days to acknowledge on X12 orders Schedules achievable against factory quotas Sales services cost per line Specials acknowledged per customer request Days to acknowledge on special orders					
Products Made *M2* % of acceptable outgoing quality % of MUCs complete at 6 am % of MUCs complete at 6 pm Standard product lead times					
Products Delivered *M2* Shipped complete Damage free Dispatched					

Source: Steelcase Co.

tem. The company is able to generate a more complete understanding of loyalty issues by breaking it into multiple components and monitoring each component separately using a green–yellow–red ranking system to focus improvement efforts on areas that contribute directly to achieving overall corporate goals.

Xerox

Xerox Corporation is on a quest to define the optimum measurement system—one that links marketed products back to customer definitions and expectations of value. Xerox believes that this definition of value can be found in the myriad of buying decisions that occur daily. Peter Garcia, director of customer satisfaction and loyalty for Xerox, compares their system to more commonly publicized measurement systems, "They measure loyalty indirectly through asking the customer 'Would you buy again?' which we call attitudinal loyalty. We measure loyalty directly by understanding real buying decisions which we can then compare to our product offerings."

Xerox believes that multiple attributes affect a customer's buying decision. These include "purchase attributes," which are attributes the customer looks for at the time of sale, such as product features, price, and flexibility on terms and conditions. Xerox also believes that "past experience attributes" such as brand image, experiences with product reliability, and support services affect the buying decision. Xerox utilizes a double-blind survey of decision makers (the participants do not know who is sponsoring the survey, and Xerox does not know the identities of the participants) to "map out" the decision-making attributes. According to Garcia, with approximately 200 buying decisions they can determine why companies are buying and the relative weight of the attributes that contribute to the decision-making process (see Figure 2-2).

When Xerox assesses the buying decisions, they segment those decisions into one of ten buckets. First, the customers are segmented into one of three categories: replacement buyers, first-time buyers, and incremental buyers. Replacement buyers are those who are replacing an existing piece of office equipment—either Xerox or a competitor brand. First-time buyers have never purchased office equipment in Xerox's market. These would typically be small start-up firms. Incremental buyers are owners of office equipment who are purchasing more equipment—either for an office expansion or to get a new type of equipment for the office. The survey participants are asked to identify themselves as primarily Xerox customers or competitor customers—this expands the segmentation to five categories. At that point, the categories are further divided into the final ten categories based on whether they are loyal to their primary brand or switch to another (see Figure 2-3).

Xerox recognizes that the customer's experience with Xerox is affected by more than the product. The relationship continues after the sales during installation, training, invoicing, service, supply ordering, and so on. Xerox measures the entire life cycle, not just the end perception. Figure 2-4 shows how Xerox identifies key relationship contact points. There are three specifically identified survey points on this chart. Those customers who have not made purchases in the last three months cannot be asked about buying decisions, but can be surveyed on overall customer satisfaction with relation to the appropriate life cycle stage. Figure 2-5 outlines the interactions between customers and Xerox and the tools that can be used to monitor each stage as well as the appropriate feedback loops into the Xerox planning processes.

These customer value measurement techniques are ultimately translated into actions taken by Xerox to improve the quality of its products and services. They are used to prioritize investments in advertising, products, relationships, and so on. As customers are identified by SIC code, size of

Figure 2-2. Xerox's system for monitoring the continual interaction of customer attitudes and behaviors.

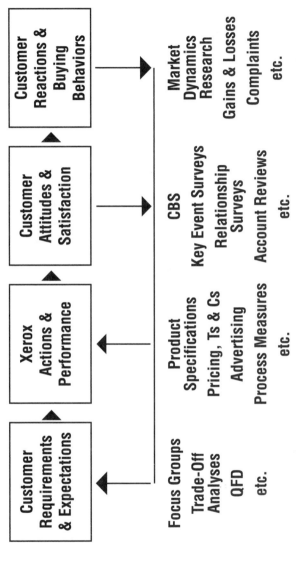

Customer Requirements & Expectations	Xerox Actions & Performance	Customer Attitudes & Satisfaction	Customer Reactions & Buying Behaviors
Focus Groups	Product Specifications	CBS	Market Dynamics Research
Trade-Off Analyses	Pricing, Ts & Cs	Key Event Surveys	Gains & Losses
QFD	Advertising	Relationship Surveys	Complaints
etc.	Process Measures	Account Reviews	etc.
	etc.	etc.	

Source: © 1998 Xerox Corporation.

Figure 2-3. Xerox's customer value assessment.

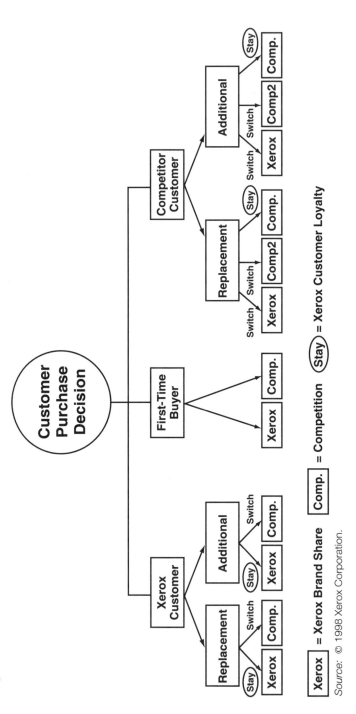

| Xerox | = Xerox Brand Share | Comp. | = Competition   (Stay) = Xerox Customer Loyalty

Source: © 1998 Xerox Corporation.

Figure 2-4. Key relationship contact points in Xerox's customer life cycle.

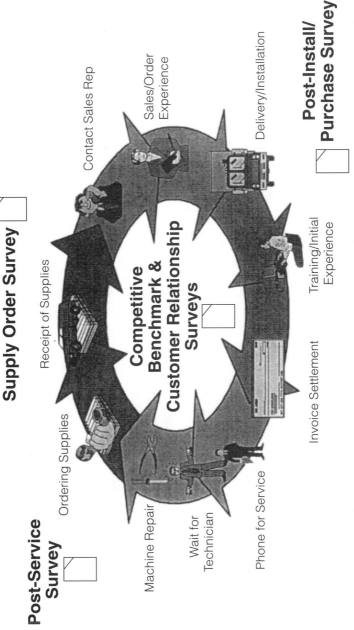

Supply Order Survey

Receipt of Supplies

Contact Sales Rep

Sales/Order Experience

Delivery/Installation

Post-Install/ Purchase Survey

Training/Initial Experience

Competitive Benchmark & Customer Relationship Surveys

Invoice Settlement

Ordering Supplies

Post-Service Survey

Machine Repair

Wait for Technician

Phone for Service

Source: © 1998 Xerox Corporation.

Figure 2-5. Xerox's chart of market dynamics (MD) and competitive benchmarking surveys (CBS).

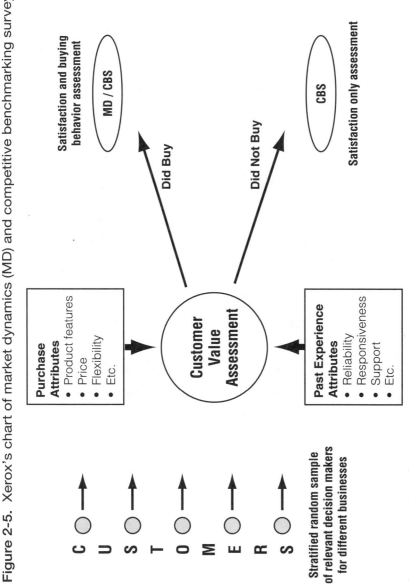

operation, and geographic area, Xerox can also analyze the profitability of their customers versus those purchasers who choose competitor products and determine the appropriate action for retention or new sale efforts.

Xerox identified customer perception and customer behavior as the most critical factors on their road to success. Therefore, Xerox uses the measurement process to directly monitor successes in the marketplace. This sends a message to employees that all improvements are to be focused on initiatives that will positively impact the customer.

ATC, Steelcase and Xerox are all operating in different competitive environments, but each chose a measurement strategy that pushes the corporation forward toward its high-level mission. ATC felt that its people were the competitive advantage, Steelcase its distribution chain, and Xerox its understanding of the end customer.

Performance Measurement Mission Statements

You must move quickly from understanding the overall corporate strategy to establishing a mission statement for the measurement team. Typically, the mission statement document should address the areas most important to the corporate performance measurement effort. It will outline the objectives of the measurement group—the reason for existence.

Over twenty companies participated in the Corporate Performance Measurement Benchmarking Study that serves as a basis for this book. (For a full list of participating companies, see the Acknowledgments.) Those who reported a document guiding the mission of their performance measurement effort were asked what areas that document addresses. This question was designed to determine why corporate measurement exists. Six categories thought to be important to measurement were provided as options (incentives, compensation, feedback to the organization, feedback to executives, outside measurement, benchmarking). We also allowed for free responses if other categories were addressed.

The six measures fall into three categories:

1. *Employee focused (incentives and compensation).* These goals specifically address individual or small group performance and are designed specifically to influence the behavior of employees.
2. *Learning focused (feedback to the organization and to executives).* These goals address ways in which the corporation can gain a greater understanding of its performance internally.

3. *Externally focused (outside measurement and benchmarking).* These goals specifically address comparisons of the company performance with the performance of other companies, whether inside or outside the industry.

As you can see from Figure 2-6, the two learning-focused objectives were the most commonly addressed in corporate performance measurement mission statements. "Feedback to executives" was closely followed by "feedback to the organization" in importance. The two externally focused goals—"outside measurement" and "benchmarking"—brought in 40 percent and 35 percent, respectively. These are closely related in that they also provide knowledge of the performance of the organization.

Knowledge will influence behavior by itself. Employees who understand that a company that performs well can provide long-term growth and stability for the employee will use the knowledge gained from a measurement program to continuously improve when possible. Also, the simple act of measuring a step in a process may inspire employees to improve because they know they are being watched.

Even so, pure knowledge is not a good reason to perform corporate measurement. Influencing behavior should always be at the top of the mission statement for a corporate measurement effort to have benefit to the company. Studies have found that, in addition to knowledge, direct

Figure 2-6. Performance measurement mission statements.

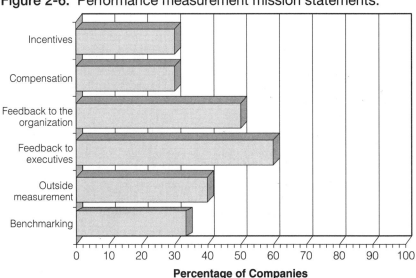

Percentage of Companies

ties to incentive and compensation plans are still believed the most effective way to influence employee behavior. It is quite interesting that the two employee-focused objectives are the least discussed in mission statements, at 30 percent apiece.

It seems that measurement groups are afraid to verbalize their true mission, which is to change behavior. Why is this? Perhaps they find it politically difficult. Most measurement groups are separate from the "real work" and may be viewed suspiciously by the rest of the company. It is much easier to be seen as the disseminators of knowledge than as the "spies" or "influencers."

Most companies will need to find a better way to express their ultimate goal of behavior modification leading to corporate improvement. It may not be appropriate to discuss specific techniques such as compensation packages, but the mission statement should include improving performance through employees, technology, and processes.

Since many companies are measuring *without* a mission statement, it is not clear at these companies what the ultimate objective of measures really is. In that case, what happens is that measurement tends to default to HR-driven objectives and loses the change orientation that most companies want out of their measurement process.

Establishing a Measurement Team

You have a strategy and a mission. Now all you need is a team. The resources dedicated to a measurement team say a lot about the understanding of measurement in the corporation.

A team can have dedicated members or virtual members or a combination of the two. A dedicated team provides stability to the measurement process and expertise in measurement techniques. Unfortunately, members often lose the perspective on the business processes that they had while they were an integral part of them. Virtual teams provide flexibility. You can bring in specific expertise when needed and send people back out when they are no longer needed. Virtual teams also provide process expertise that can help determine need for specific measures. Unfortunately, virtual teams often lack measurement expertise and end up redoing work that others had already done. They also are less effective in the organization due to a lack of stable leadership.

Most successful measurement programs keep a small, dedicated core team. This could be as few as one or two people who champion the measurement process. The remainder of the team is made up of virtual members who have other daily jobs.

Position of the Measurement Team

Placement of leadership for the corporate measurement process is key. Companies position measurement specialists in a variety of areas in the organization—from accounting to human resources. Measurement groups typically take on the mission and objectives of the groups within which they were placed.

Phillips Petroleum positioned the measurement leadership function within the human resources area. In this and other similar cases, the measures favored compensation and employee performance evaluation areas. Other companies located their specialist within accounting. The Prudential Insurance Company positioned an internal consulting group within the accounting organization to take on measurement tasks. While the group comes in with very strong accounting skills, its mandate includes a variety of corporate measurement functions such as marketing and operations that may or may not benefit by the group's placement in accounting. When considering organizational placement of the measurements function, be sure to take the measurements mission into consideration and look closely at the ease of interface with the areas to be measured.

Staffing the Measurement Team

Companies establishing new measurement programs will need either to hire outside individuals with measurement experience or train current company employees in measurement. The Corporate Performance Measurement Benchmarking Study found most companies looking to one of only a few areas internally for staffing the measurement group:

1. Accounting and finance is a popular area from which to hire measurement personnel. These people know numbers—where they are, how to get them, how to process them, and what they mean. The biggest drawback to bringing in accounting and finance personnel is that they often have limited operational expertise.

2. Human resources is a second primary area. With expanded roles in developing the organization, human resources professionals are constantly watching individual and group performance for the purpose of paying incentives and improving performance.

3. Operations people are good for the performance statistics related to delivering goods and services, but not always in the analytical roles as trained statisticians.

Of course, no category of person will provide a perfect solution. Hiring decisions should always be made on an individual basis, based on a combination of experience and expertise.

Many of the skills required for measurement efforts can also be filled by outside consultants. Outside consultants are used in a variety of roles, including:

- *Defining the measures.* The consultants bring ideas about the organization and types of measures.
- *Collecting data.* Consultants collect the data and provide the results and analysis.

Measurement Development Team

While you may have a limited core group of measurement personnel, you will most likely want to expand the team for the measurement development process. A more thorough understanding of the business and its individual processes is necessary for strong measurement development. There are multiple theories regarding who should be involved in measurement development. Many stress the involvement of those closest to the process, while others feel the more strategic view of members of the executive suites should be strongly represented. There is also a definite need for familiarity with statistics, accounting, organizational behavior, and team-building skills.

Measurement Development Skills

Each of the companies participating in the corporate performance measurement study was asked to describe the makeup of the group assisting in the development of measures to discover what, if any, positions were considered critical to the team makeup. Specifically, the participating companies were asked to indicate if their teams included one or more individuals from the following areas in their company:

- *Internal facilitator:* an individual trained in the art of facilitating group meetings and team decision making. Many companies keep employees on staff (typically as part of a human resources function) whose primary job function is to facilitate cross-functional groups.

- *Internal statistician:* an employee whose primary job function is to analyze and interpret statistics. Internal statisticians are often part of the measurements group itself, but they may also be found in a financial or manufacturing function.

■ *Internal coach:* a person who works side by side with the team to teach people how to gather measures.

■ *Internal accountant:* an employee whose job lies within the accounting department. Typically the measurement team will be soliciting the help of someone with a broad knowledge of the accounting system and financial information collected.

■ *Internal auditor:* an individual who is charged with ensuring that the company is being run properly, particularly from a financial perspective. The internal auditor is a watchdog, so typically will have a broad understanding of how the company works, the data that is collected, and potential problem areas.

■ *Process managers:* individuals responsible for the various business processes that are to be measured. For example, the director of manufacturing might be involved in determining manufacturing measures while the director of procurement recommends purchasing measures.

As you can see from Figure 2-7, the only two categories that stood out as being the most necessary for measurement developments were process management and internal accountants.

Every participating company included process management in the measures development process. Process management is key to generating the ideas for appropriate measures, determining the effect each measure

Figure 2-7. Measurement development team makeup.

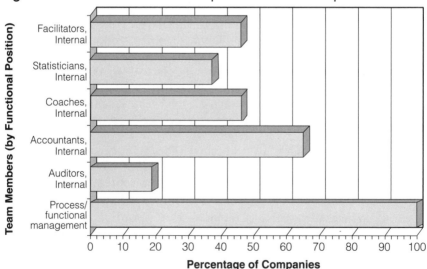

or incentive will have on behavior, and narrowing and focusing measures to the best possible list. Furthermore, immediate buy-in is gained when the individuals responsible for living up to the measures are involved in their development.

The majority of the companies surveyed also used internal accountants (64 percent). Those companies that did not use internal accountants made sure that at least one team member had a working knowledge of accounting and the accounting system. The primary reason for including internal accountants on the team appeared to be their knowledge of the accounting system. This system often became the basis for data collection and was therefore critical to the measurement effort.

The use of internal facilitators, internal statisticians, and internal coaches was present in approximately half the companies surveyed. There seemed to be very little fundamental difference between the companies that used internal facilitators or coaches and those that did not. The main difference we can point to is that the teams felt a need for internal facilitators or coaches most when they were not as familiar with the other team members or were not accustomed to working on a team. Those companies who had a strong team culture were less likely to need designated facilitators or coaches.

A slight majority did not use internal statisticians (60 percent). Most companies found an individual who had knowledge of statistics but was also considered a process owner to fill the role. Those companies that utilized internal statisticians only did so when others could not provide the required knowledge of statistics.

The vast majority of the companies surveyed do not use internal auditors (80 percent). It was revealed upon further examination that the internal auditor was not typically a source of measurement data. The auditor was familiar with what measures were currently being used and might have need for specific financial measures, but the auditor's contribution was typically duplicated by an internal accountant.

The evidence from the survey suggests that the inclusion of process management in the measures development process is key. It is essential to include process management in the development activity in order to ensure that the appropriate measures are being collected and to ensure buy-in from the very individuals who are being measured.

Other than that, the most important factor appears to be to get a proper mix of experience, skills, and knowledge. As was stated earlier, each of the functions in question was selected for a specific skill set that it would bring to the team. Most companies feel that, while it is important that the appropriate knowledge and skills are represented, it is not important to include designated facilitators, statisticians, coaches, accountants, and auditors if those skills or knowledge can be found in a person who can serve multiple roles. The best situation appears to be a process owner who also possesses some of the other necessary skills.

I want to say a word here about the role of *internal specialists*—those who are trained specifically in measurement and process improvement. Specialists also have the impact of moving the organization forward in ways that teams of process owners often cannot do for themselves. They organize the buy-in required in order to actually implement the changes identified through the measures process. Specialists can keep organizations from going "measurement crazy" and can guide them toward the ultimate goal of implementing change.

Specialists are employees of the corporation, not outsiders. These are the people most familiar with the day-to-day activities of the company and are best suited for socializing the measures and the findings. As a result, even if a company uses external improvement specialists, frequently it uses a series of internal specialists for moving projects forward.

Who are these people? Generally, the role is filled with analytically inclined professionals. They often are individuals on internal rotation or former external consultants. Specialists typically possess:

- An understanding of information system capabilities and limitations
- An understanding of the intricacies of accounting, including its precisions and imprecisions
- A people orientation
- An understanding of organizations, change processes, and behaviors

The positions in many companies occupied by such individuals are frequently seen as weak. The role of specialist is not generally viewed as adding directly to the products or services of the corporation. And in an attempt to further undermine the position, the position is usually not given the funding it requires, with management rotating people into and out of these positions. Successful measurement personnel see this area as a vocation and not a stepping-stone.

In company after company interviewed for this book, the success of the effort was based on the strength of the individual in the measurement position.

Individual Criteria

It is always a challenge to get the right blend of knowledge, skills, and personalities needed to create a successful team. Of course, a combination of factors play into the decision to put someone on a measurement team, but which of those factors are most significant?

Each participating company was asked to identify the type of criteria used to select individuals to develop measures. We asked the companies to indicate whether selection criteria fell under the categories of education, experience, aptitude, or a combination. We defined the selection criteria as follows:

- Education or training includes advanced degrees, majors, or technical training.
- Experience criteria might include experience with the specific process, broad corporate experience, or prior experience on measurements teams.
- Aptitude qualifications might include looking for someone with good math skills or people skills.

As you can see from Figure 2-8, selection was most commonly based on experience. This makes a fair amount of sense since experience is what gives an individual knowledge of the process and of the corporation. A majority of the companies also reported using education and aptitude as criteria, with no significant preference. Perhaps education was seen as an indicator of aptitude.

Figure 2-8. Criteria used to select individuals to develop measures.

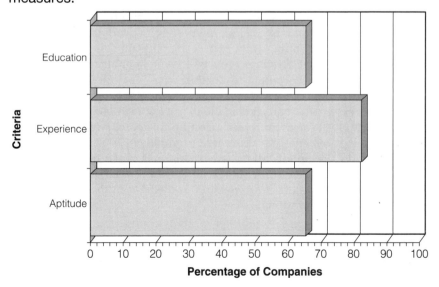

Some of the more common characteristics driving candidate selection within each category included:

- Financial background (e.g., M.B.A., C.P.A.)
- Quality background (e.g., statistical process control [SPC], monitoring)

Not surprisingly, most firms reported using multiple selection criteria. Using a greater number of criteria ensures that the best candidates will be selected for the team. Unfortunately, there are diminishing returns here as well. Don't make the selection process so cumbersome that you never get around to the work.

Experience seems to play an important role in the selection of individuals to develop measures. If your company does not currently consider experience when selecting a team, you probably should. It is the best way to be sure your team understands the process they are analyzing—from the perspective of the worker as well as from management's point of view. Of course, the study has shown clearly that a variety of criteria are important to be sure the best team members are selected.

Effect on Management Styles

While everyone in an organization is valuable, every well-managed organization is driven by the actions of the people at the top. While each department sees its own piece of the puzzle, executive management is the only role that can view business processes and obtain resources for them.

Every manager has his or her own style of leadership. Likewise, every corporation encourages its own leadership models. As you organize for measurement activities, you will want to analyze the pros and cons of your current corporate leadership style. The addition of a solid measurement program expands the range of leadership options. Not only does measurement aid managers in identifying critical processes and provide opportunities for them to set direction for teams through goal setting, but measurement can allow every employee to view his or her relationship to the organization as a whole and make better decisions accordingly. Measurement, in short, changes the leadership style and is widely believed to be the most essential ingredient in the success of today's complex organizations.

Empowered Leadership

Many managers have come to believe that the best management is the least management. Most companies believe that the greatest benefit will be realized when individuals feel they "own" the process and can make a difference. Management wants individuals with ownership who buy into decisions, not just more participants to the process. Since today's executive management does not have the knowledge of specific activities, employees need to be able to watch and communicate the effectiveness of their processes.

Managing by measuring is a style that requires management to set direction and demand results, but it does not control daily activities. Figure 2-9 shows the subtle differences between traditional and empowered leadership styles in which measurement becomes key in setting goals and evaluating performance.

Traditional managers set policies and procedures, controls, mandates, and budgets. These all specifically control employee activities. A leader of an empowered organization is more concerned with the end result than the means of achieving it. This leader tells the employees what they are to achieve (e.g., sets goals and strategies), who is to be involved in the effort (e.g., defines roles), but leaves the methods open-ended. Rather than relying on budgets for an assessment of success, the leader of empowered employees assesses performance through employee evaluations that are run as more of a dialog than a report card.

Traditional leadership is based on the assumption that only management has the ability to make high-impact decisions. Measurement is the underpinning of employee empowerment. A far-reaching measurements program gives employees the information they need to properly analyze tasks that they otherwise wouldn't be able to fully comprehend.

Open Book Management

One management style that has gotten a fair amount of attention recently and is made possible by solid measurement is open book management (OBM). It takes the concept of employee empowerment one step further by literally opening the financial records to the employees, allowing them to more fully comprehend the implications of their actions. The following is a short history and presentation of open book management that was excerpted from *Organizational Dynamics*.

Springfield ReManufacturing

When Jack Stack acquired Springfield ReManufacturing from International Harvester in 1983, it was on the brink of collapse. Crippled by a highly leveraged buyout, the company faced an 89:1 debt-to-equity ratio, a first-year operating loss of $60,488, and 119 employees who needed pay-

Figure 2-9. Traditional leadership versus empowered leadership.

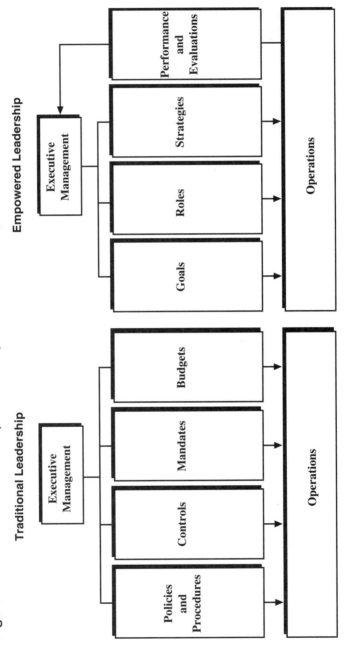

checks. All the signs indicated a rapid demise. But, within a few years, Stack had returned the business to profitability—a company with a healthy balance sheet and a promising future.

One key to Stack's successful turnaround of the Springfield, Missouri–based company stems from the way he reconceptualized the business. Instead of seeing the company's mission as reconditioning engines of worn-out bulldozers, tractors, and eighteen-wheelers, he saw it as educating workers in how business works. He persuaded employees to view running the business as a game they could learn to play and win.

Instead of viewing Springfield ReManufacturing employees as a liability, Stack chose to see them as assets. He shared the dismal operating results with the workforce, taught them to understand the financial statements, and offered them a share of the profits and an equity interest in the company if they would help him restore its vitality. In addition to educating employees in how business works, Stack initiated weekly meetings to review operating results in each department and how these results related to the firm's financial statements.

Slowly, employees began to realize how their performance influenced operations and began to take responsibility for those performance measures that would impact the income statement and balance sheet. Bit by bit, the numbers turned. By 1991, Springfield ReManufacturing had sales of over $70 million, a workforce of 650 people, and a stock price that had grown 18,200 percent in nine years. Employees holding stock worth a few dollars at the time of the acquisition found that their ownership stake was now worth over $35,000. News of this success spread to other companies, and Springfield ReManufacturing started holding on-site seminars to show other companies how to implement OBM. Currently, the company holds ten two-day Great Game of Business seminars each year to explain and demonstrate the Springfield ReManufacturing system. The seminars include practice exercises, simulations, and games designed to help other companies introduce OBM.

Stack is credited with formalizing and implementing the first fully developed example of open book management. This approach to managing is aptly named, in that it literally "opens the books" to employees and discloses a company's financial records, expenses, and sources of profit. By sharing detailed operating information and educating employees about how to use it, management provides its workers with the opportunity to contribute to the success of the enterprise. In return, companies practicing OBM give employees a stake in the business through profit-sharing plans or some form of stock ownership.

Principles of Open Book Management

While there is considerable variation in the ways that firms have implemented OBM, ten common principles underlie most of these applications.

1. *Turn the management of a business into a game that employees can win.* Recall that Jack Stack reconceptualized his business as a game rather than work. Managers and employees play on the same team. Each organization member is taught to understand how the game works and what their roles and responsibilities are in making the team win.

2. *Open the books and share financial and operating information with employees.* In most companies, owners and senior managers generally withhold detailed financial data and information about the operations of the firm. Managers and owners in open book companies view this line of reasoning as a fatal flaw in management. Only by knowing detailed financial data and operating results can employees begin to see how the company makes money.

3. *Teach employees to understand the company's financial statements.* In most companies, the majority of employees would gain little understanding of the firm's financial position if the financial statements were presented to them with no explanation. Both employees and managers need to be taught to understand and interpret the income statement, balance sheet, and cash flow statement, and this necessitates an investment of time and money.

4. *Show employees how their work influences financial results.* In most companies, employees have little understanding of the financial effects of their work. Early discussions may be quite modest and simple, such as breaking out the different expense categories on the income statement and showing how a particular department contributes to these expenses. Alternatively, discussions may show how excess inventory or delinquent receivables affect the balance sheet and the cash flow cycle.

5. *Link nonfinancial measures to financial results.* Most employees in operations do not influence financial results directly. They work with materials, information, or people. To evaluate their performance, companies use nonfinancial indicators such as on-time delivery, quantity of output, product quality, material usage, process measures, customer satisfaction, or customer service.

Open book companies set objectives jointly with employees in these areas and trace the financial impact of the nonfinancial objectives. For example, in most retail stores, banks, hotels, and other service businesses, there is a direct relationship between customers' satisfaction with service and the volume of sales revenue. As measures of service quality go up on customer surveys and comment cards, sales recorded in the cash register increase.

6. *Target priority areas and empower employees to make improvements.* After employees have gained an understanding of how their work

influences financial results, they will be in a position to analyze how they can improve the company's performance. Management then targets areas that have the biggest potential for financial improvement. By providing extensive information that is not normally disclosed, management shares a great deal of power and decision-making authority with employees. This is the best way to empower employees and earn their trust. Armed with needed information about the financial effects of their work, employees develop improved practices in the targeted areas.

Open book companies set demanding financial objectives in each area. Instead of senior management and the financial staff being in sole charge of financial results, employees take responsibility for specific figures on the income statement, balance sheet, or cash flow statement. The responsibility is shared by all divisions, departments, and levels of the company. To facilitate detailed analysis of different product lines and departments, tailored budget worksheets and other forms may be used before filling in the numbers on the financial statements. As financial performance improves in each targeted area, new priorities are added and employees turn their attention to investigating improved practices in these areas.

7. *Review results together and keep employees accountable.* Regular group performance review meetings, with representatives of all departments in attendance, are a common feature of all OBM systems. In small companies, all employees may participate. In larger organizations, appointed representatives attend, then report the figures for which they are responsible to their units. As the financial results are announced, the company accountant usually constructs an income statement on the spot.

8. *Post results and celebrate successes.* Most open book companies post performance results in a prominent place.

9. *Distribute bonus awards based on employee contributions to financial outcomes.* The icing on the cake for employees in open book companies is that they receive a share of the financial outcomes they helped to create. This is one of the keys to motivating employee performance.

The best systems allow employees to track the numbers that determine their bonuses. This takes the subjectivity out of the calculation and serves to motivate employees.

10. *Share the ownership of the company with employees.* A large number of open book companies have created employee stock ownership programs to encourage a greater commitment to the company.

Challenges of OBM

While the results in some firms practicing OBM have been quite spectacular, the challenges of implementing open book management can be considerable. Team values, frequent meetings, the posting of results, and the reward systems all increase the likelihood that OBM will be implemented in a supportive way. But will managers always rely on these principles, or will they take shortcuts? OBM can be most difficult to implement in the following circumstances:

- The business is large and established.
- Managers fear loss of control.
- Management doubts employee trustworthiness.
- Concerns about leaking confidential information to competitors are paramount.
- Excessive time and cost must be dedicated to employee education.
- Linking performance measures with financial statements is difficult.
- Weaknesses in conventional standard costing systems exist.
- An added burden is placed on accounting.
- Abuse of "management by the numbers" is a concern.[5]

Conclusion

Beginning a corporate measurement process is a big commitment. You need to start from the top—establishing corporate goals and letting those filter into measurement goals. Be aware, also, of the power of measures to change your corporation, including leadership styles. Be prepared to retrain and educate managers and employees in the objectives of your measurement program.

The measurement team should be strategically placed to achieve the objectives you have set for the program. Always remember to include team members—whether standing or virtual—from a variety of areas of the corporation and with a variety of needed skills. Measurement personnel need to form a highly functioning team to adequately perform the variety of tasks required of the measurement area.

3

Identifying Effective Measures

Introduction

Before there is a measurement program, someone must identify appropriate measures. Even after a measurement program is in place, top-performing companies continue to review measures and identify new ones to meet the needs of their environment as it changes. This section addresses the way organizations consider their needs to focus measurement activities.

There are two main components of a measurement system. Measures are performance characteristics that can be determined directly and numerically. Examples include processing time or number of on-time deliveries. Indicators are performance characteristics that are not typically measurable but which indicate "goodness" in a process. Indicators might include customer complaints or suggestions.

Guidelines for Measures and Indicators

The selection of good measures and indicators among most organizations is vital since they drive key decisions and actions. The following overall guidelines are used by organizations to develop effective measures and indicators:

- Understand stakeholders' needs for the measurement process and improvement in general.
- Link each measure to an overall improvement goal that is actionable.

- Include measures that address both operational issues and overall performance.
- Be sure you understand where the measurement data comes from and what influence other factors could have on the data.

Measures need to be formulated in a way that drives the critical needs of the corporation. Measures must also strive for a general level of acceptance among the participants. Measures should also be obtainable, at a fairly low cost, lead to action, and be repeatable from time period to time period. Finally, organizations need measures that they can use to compare themselves to others on the outside to see how they are doing. Excellent measures:

- Are simple and easy to understand
- Are meaningful to stakeholders and customers
- Are clearly defined
- Are economical to collect
- Are verifiable
- Are measurable
- Are repeatable
- Send a message consistent with corporate values, goals, and objectives
- Can demonstrate a trend
- Drive the right actions
- Accomplish the stated purpose

Once measures and indicators are selected, you will want to collect data on a trial basis for several cycles in order to compare the results to the criteria again. You will probably want to continue to compare to these criteria on a periodic basis, perhaps annually, to review the success of the measures.

If, for example, you were working on a process redesign of the payroll function, some of the measures and indicators you might want to include are:

Measures

- Cost per paycheck
- Payroll employees per thousand employees
- Information system cost per paycheck
- Percent of checks written manually
- Percent of checks with errors
- Percent of checks replaced
- Percent of checks returned (receiver not found)

Indicators

- Customer complaints
- Checks delivered late
- Questions about checks

Common Measurement Problems

Management consultant Rupert Booth, in his article in *Management Accounting* called "Accountants Do It by Proxy," has outlined five negative guidelines for a measurement program—what not to do. The most common measurement mistakes occur at the beginning of the process when:

1. Short-term measures predominate over long-term measures, leading to a willingness to sacrifice long-term development for immediate gain.
2. Financial proxies predominate over reality. The real corporate issues (e.g., product lead over rivals, delivery reliability, and levels of customer satisfaction) are ignored. In their place there is the language of earnings per share and return on capital.
3. Efficiency measures predominate over effectiveness measures, with the result that productivity takes precedence over the value of outputs, encouraging staff to become "busy fools."
4. Economy measures predominate over efficiency measures. Often not even the efficiency of conversion of input into output is calculated and performance measures simply record the amount of resource expended.
5. Functional measures predominate over customer-related measures. The measurement systems of a company typically concentrate on departmental performance rather than considering how activities in departments link together to satisfy a customer demand and add value to a customer.[6]

Structuring Measures Identification

Measures can be generated in a variety of ways. Our study found companies typically take one of the following steps in development of measures:

1. *They follow generally accepted brainstorming techniques.* This process focuses on one area, assembles a team, and then asks each participant on the team to contribute ideas of how measures are to be constructed to

meet the objectives of the organization. This technique can be an excellent means of getting ideas on the table, but does little for focusing the effort. Team processes for generating measures at best focus around "nice to have" virtues. Frequently, they lead to too many measures that either cannot be obtained or, if obtained, cannot lead to meaningful change within the organization. If the process is not better focused, teams can spend so much time developing detailed measures that they become "worn out," and measurement gets dropped by the organization.

2. *Organizations may look to outsiders to define an acceptable set of measures based on a set of standard "industry" or "process" measures.* While this can be helpful in assuring that measures will be relatively easily comparable to those of other corporations, this kind of measurement generation leads to a series of nonspecific measures that again fail some of the tests of depth of understanding and relevance. Companies find quickly that there are no standard measures that apply to their specific situation. Measures are highly relevant only in a situational context. Measures are also heavily impacted by the nature of the needs of the organization that charters their development.

3. *Some companies use a structured process for defining general areas of measurement, with the understanding that no single measure fits all situations.* Measures are then formulated to fit into these categories using multiple techniques for idea generation and the narrowing of measurement. Chapter 4 goes into greater detail regarding the multiple tools that can be used in this stage.

Process Analysis

At the heart of any measurement system is the concept of process analysis. Process analysis allows you to view your corporation as a series of inputs and outputs. Recently, companies have focused on defining the processes that drive their organizations rather than focusing on skills-based corporate departments. The business must be understood as a series of processes in order to fully appreciate the impact specific statistics or measures have.

For example, in the past the purchasing department was the group that bought all the materials that the company needed. Process-oriented management has redefined procurement as part of a supply chain. The supply chain not only includes purchasing activities, but also the activities prior to the purchase—the chain of suppliers that impact the process. In this example, measurement activities would focus not only on direct procurement activities (e.g., purchase orders per purchasing agent), but also on the relationship with the supplier and their supplier. This allows measures such as supplier quality to come to the forefront.

Once business processes are more fully understood, you will be able to formulate measures that more closely align with critical points in the process—those points that have the greatest effect on process performance. Process analysis is more fully discussed in Chapter 4.

Processes Used to Identify and Limit Potential Measures

Each company that participated in the Corporate Performance Measurement Benchmarking Study was asked to discuss what specific methodologies they used to identify and limit potential measures. Answers were solicited to five specific processes:

- *Public lists of measures.* These include any lists of measures that are used by other companies, whether found through business journal articles or associations you might belong to.
- *Consultants.* Consultants often recommend specific measures based on their previous experiences in the area, combined with your specific need.
- *Auditor recommendations.* Auditors, both internal and external, typically make formal recommendations in conjunction with their reports that could prove useful in the measurement process. Informal auditor insights are also worth soliciting.
- *Recommendations from process management.* Process management is most familiar with the needs and may have good ideas for how to fill them.
- *Brainstorming.* This is a well-known technique for idea generation. Brainstorming would most typically be used in a team setting that may include some of the individuals (e.g., consultants, auditors) named above.

There are two important activities mentioned in this question. The first is the identification of potential measures. It can be difficult for a measurement group to generate all appropriate measures from scratch. Brainstorming is one of the most common techniques used when one is starting from ground zero.

It would seem that the efficiency of the measurement identification process could be significantly improved and the amount of time and research needed to determine appropriate measures decreased by using information that is readily available such as:

- Publicly available lists of measures
- Consultant recommendations
- Auditor recommendations
- Process management recommendations

The second facet of the question is the limiting of measures collected. No company can afford the time and effort to measure everything it might find useful someday. It is up to the measurement group to discern the most important measures from the list of possible measures.

It would seem that using publicly available lists of measures and consultant recommendations in the measurement focusing phase would help a company to select measures that had been tested before. This would increase the likelihood that the company is selecting quality measures, as well as increase the chances of finding other companies who collect similar measures with whom to benchmark.

Process managers' recommendations should again carry significant weight in the limitation of measures because of their familiarity with the process to be measured.

Because auditor recommendations are likely to carry a somewhat limited perspective, we did not expect them to play a significant role limiting potential measures. Likewise, brainstorming is a technique that applies specifically toward idea generation and is not likely to be applied to measurement limitation.

As you can see from Figure 3-1, the one source every company used

Figure 3-1. Processes used to identify and limit potential measures.

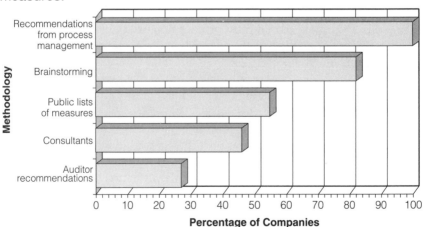

for identification and limitation of potential measures was process manager recommendations. This makes sense as stated before because of the wealth of knowledge these individuals are able to impart based on their experience. A vast majority of the participants also used a brainstorming technique. This technique allowed them to capture ideas from process owners and other team members.

Approximately half of the more than twenty companies surveyed used either publicly available lists or consultant recommendations (or both). It is surprising that so few used what appears on the surface to be a logical source of information.

Upon further conversations, it seems that the majority of those companies that did not use public lists of measures did not find lists available that met their needs (e.g., they were attempting to measure a new industry-specific process). Others felt that publicly available lists of measures were too limiting or did not produce the appropriate behavior.

Public measures also had a high degree of inapplicability, since measures frequently fit just one business situation, not all.

Most companies that did use lists were more likely to use them for idea generation than for the limitation of their list of measures. Most of the culling down of measures was performed by an analysis group that would examine the need for collection of a given measure.

Those companies that did not use consultants felt that the cost outweighed the potential benefit. Companies were most likely to use consultants to start up a measurement program but typically intended to carry out the ongoing operations themselves.

Only one-fifth of the participating companies used auditor recommendations for identification and limitation purposes. Auditor recommendations are not a highly valued resource for the measurement effort. This is most likely due to the fact that auditor recommendations present a very limited view of measurement—that of the financial side of the house—and may lack a perspective that typically encompasses manufacturing, marketing, or other needs.

Our research shows that the most successful companies use a variety of resources to identify and limit potential measures. We see no reason why all of the aforementioned resources cannot be used in tandem.

There is no question that you should tap the resources you have available to you in process management. Furthermore, brainstorming appears to be a very successful technique for the initial phases.

Public lists can give you a great advantage, but we would not recommend using them exclusively. They are excellent in the idea-generation stage, but may need to be modified or tailored to specific situations.

Consultants are not necessary for a solid measurement process. Some consultants have developed specific measurement tools that may be of use to the corporation, and most will have more experience than your employees in the field of measurement. Even so, a carefully blended team can function well without paid consultants. Our recommendation is to analyze your situation carefully to determine the cost-benefit of using a consultant. The times when it is most likely that a consultant will add benefit include start-up of a measurement program and a period of rapid growth when you can't spare many team members to dedicate to the program.

While auditor recommendations do not provide a complete perspective on a company's measurement needs, they do typically provide some insight into what should be measured. One would think, therefore, that it would not be unreasonable to include auditor recommendations in the initial idea-generation process for corporate measures. Most companies are not, however, missing out on a significant resource by limiting their use of auditor recommendations.

Focusing Lists of Measures

The issue of focusing lists of measures is critical. Often, brainstorming or nominal group technique can generate long lists of measures. It is very important to narrow down those measures into a smaller group of measures. Otherwise, corporations can get overwhelmed by collecting too much low-impact data. A key criterion that is used in focusing measures is finding a balanced family of measures that cover a variety of key issues (e.g., productivity, quality, customer satisfaction, cycle time, and control). Many corporations find it useful to include both process measures (e.g., key measures at various points in work processes) and end-results measures. Also, corporations have found that it is important to consider criticality of measures versus ease of data collection. For example, if two possible measures cover the same issue, but data collection is much easier for the second measure, then it may make sense to use the second measure.

Each participating company was also asked what methodology it used to focus lists of measures. Answers were solicited to three specific approaches:

- *Team prioritization.* Corporations often use a team of key individuals to prioritize measures.
- *Process/functional management prioritization.* Process and functional management is most familiar with key leverage factors within the

corporation and may have good ideas for how to prioritize measures.

- *Consultants.* Consultants often can prioritize measures based on their previous experiences in the area, combined with the corporation's input.

As you can see from Figure 3-2, two sources that were used heavily for focusing lists of measures were team prioritization and process/functional management prioritization. Over 60 percent of corporations used team prioritization and over 70 percent used process/functional management prioritization. Surprisingly, less than 10 percent used consultants. Our research shows that the most successful companies use internal resources to focus their list of measures. There is no question that you should tap internal resources to focus your list of measures. This means that your corporation will take better ownership of the measures and will therefore be more likely to use measurement data to improve work processes. In addition, by involving key individuals within your corporation, measures will be better aligned with your corporation's key business issues.

Generally, consultants may not be necessary for prioritizing a list of measures. Consultants may not understand your work processes or the key issues in your corporation as well as your employees. Perhaps consul-

Figure 3-2. Focusing lists of measures.

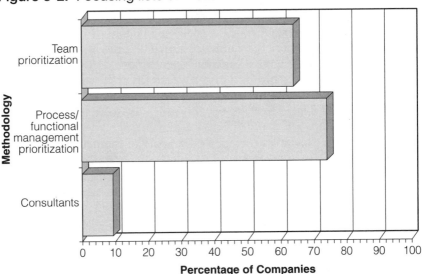

tants could be of help when team members or management have limited time. One would also have to weigh the costs and benefits of using consultants. However, most corporations appear to be able to focus a list of measures without consultant input.

Normalizing Data

When measures are collected, companies need to state findings in a manner that makes individual company data comparable to other organizations. Data can be distorted by a number of factors.

For example, differences in economic situations among organizations in different parts of the country reflect local economic differences and will lead to distortions in overall costs. For example, if one organization is located in New York, New York, and another in Houston, Texas, then wages paid in both cities will reflect local conditions.

In order to adjust the two sets of figures, there are several sources of data that can be used. Federally published data shows the differences in aggregate cost of living in different parts of the country. In certain cases, the data can be made more specific by using tables that relate to specific occupations. These tables should be reviewed in order to make sure that they adequately represent the positions that are being studied.

Some companies also use public surveys such as comparisons of the wage rate differential using a recruiting firm's public survey. When using a generalized survey it will be helpful to understand the size and composition of the sample. Surveys that are skewed to represent only those who responded or are of limited size are often not helpful.

In addition to normalizing for economic factors, companies should be careful not to include special events such as fires, floods, and other disasters in statistics. In one recent study, an explosion in a facility caused all normal activity to be directed toward clean-up. If the true performance statistic looked at the employee productivity, it would also reflect all the unusual activity related to clean-up. It is necessary to adjust the raw data for such special events.

Companies must also consider the impact of regulatory differences on the amount of work that has to be done. This is especially important when analyzing regulated industries such as utilities and telecommunications. In accounting, these differences can impact the number, type, and time it takes to record certain types of transactions.

Keep in mind that local custom can drive, among other things, the number of holidays in an area. Although the impact may be small, in some cases this may cause a difference in the number of days worked or the length of the typical business day.

Other adjustments include benefits differences, nonmonetary compensation, company-paid transportation, profit-sharing plans, and day care.

It can be useful to look at data in both normalized and "raw" forms. Doing this ensures that the reviewer is aware of the purpose and scope of normalization efforts.

Testing Measures

Companies have historically tested measures based on the premise that came out of academia that all theories needed to be tested. Companies used to apply that same stringent rule to business situations. Long, contemplative tests were performed to determine measurement quality.

Today, companies are quicker to introduce their measures. Companies are willing to take the risk that the measures that they are developing may not be perfect now, but that measures can be continually refined over time. This real-world testing is more common and has grown in acceptance among most companies. In fact, all measures will change with time, and each measure is likely to have a beginning, a life cycle, and a death.

At inception, measures may be formulated to meet specific needs. For example, a company faced with late deliveries may begin by focusing on the number of untimely deliveries. After learning that this only gives a little information, they may begin to segment late deliveries by delivery channel. They may also recognize that geography plays an important role in defining measures. Finally, when the lateness disappears over time, the organization may begin to focus on other areas in its measurement activities. This real-world testing shortens the measurement cycle time while allowing for improvement of measures over time. A formal testing program is probably not required.

Developing Measures Used for Appraisal

Frequently companies administer measurement programs out of their human resources organization. The HR department becomes the data collector for a variety of human resources needs. This process frequently is not tied to real process improvement, but instead is tied to pay. Developing measures for a compensation system involves different stakeholders than a process improvement system. Furthermore, the measures cannot be changed as frequently because of the potential effect on employee morale. The following are four examples of corporations that recently developed or modified a performance appraisal system.

Alliant Health System

When Alliant Health System began developing a total-performance management approach, they included employees in the conversation regarding performance criteria. A team including managers, directors, and employees conducted research on strengths and areas for improvement regarding the current Alliant appraisal system. Behavioral event interviews (or BEIs) were conducted with top management to identify criteria to be used in developing performance appraisals that were seen as relevant to work done at Alliant.

Alliant intends to include these competencies in all aspects of managing performance. Fifteen senior managers in the company were first to be appraised based on competencies with plans to expand this appraisal approach out to all employees. Managers and employees have received training on setting expectations, defining jobs through the competencies, and defining behavioral expectations in jobs. The next step is to train employees on selecting employees using competencies, and coaching employees regarding the competencies.[7]

Allstate Insurance Company

This case study was originally published in Training & Development.

Allstate Insurance Company developed a set of task and skill profiles. The company consolidated several processing centers around the nation into three data management centers. Task and skill profiles were used to assess skills of the employees in these locations. The goal was to match existing skills with the skills needed in the new environment. Learning agreements were developed to bring skills up to required levels. This process resulted in closure of hundreds of skill gaps and helped every employee in the three centers to transition to new roles with minimal impact on the company's productivity. This success led to implementation of a skills management system and an employee training and skills database. This effort covers all 60,000 Allstate employees and agency staff. Employees take courses based on learning agreements to close skill gaps. The approach integrates task and skill profiles for full-scale performance management. Allstate believes that this process has been improving employees' understanding of their jobs, lowering training expense by using targeted training, improving employee satisfaction with training, and improving customer-focus.[8]

Caretenders

Caretenders, a home health-services company, formed a committee to develop a criteria-based performance appraisal system. Criteria are based on the employee's job description and are measurable. Measurable criteria decrease rater bias and improve employee understanding of expectations. Management and clinical staff have been using the new system with implementation among support and clerical staff to follow.[9]

Texas Instruments

This case study was originally published in Training & Development.

Texas Instruments has a set of job-role profiles. The information technology group at Texas Instruments has developed "job-role profiles and an integrated skills-management system in order to ensure rapid response to changing business demands and to facilitate a reorganization from a hierarchical organization to a team-based one." Texas Instruments' goal was to identify current job requirements, to project future needs, and to provide training focused on skill gaps. Forty-three job functions were identified. Also, seven to eight critical skill requirements were identified for each function. These included skills in communication and teamwork, as well as job-specific technical skills. Jobs and skills were compiled in one source and were distributed to all employees.

The approach focuses on business and personal needs in developing education approaches. The job and skill profiles are used in "self-assessments, career development, skill inventories, project assignments, and curriculum development."

Skill requirements for each job are tied to The Education Center's courses. An employee knows which course to take if there is a deficiency. A computer database is used to track training needs.[10]

Notice that the following factors appear to be critical to human resources–based measurement as portrayed in the preceding four cases:

- The involvement of employees in determining the factors to measure (Alliant BEIs, Caretenders)
- How programs are slowly rolled out, beginning with executives and cascading down (Alliant, Caretenders)

- Use of assessments to improve employee performance (Allstate, Texas Instruments)
- How factors are carefully defined for employees (Alliant BEIs, Allstate task and skill profiles, Caretenders criteria, Texas Instruments job-role profiles)

Developing Measurement for Process Improvement

Performance measures are measurable characteristics of products, services, processes, and operations the company uses to track and improve performance. The measures or indicators should be selected to best represent the factors that lead to improved customer, operational, and financial performance. Measures should have the impact of identifying key change areas. Those that are weak get the most attention through the use of internal improvement processes.

While the measurements area may be based in human resources or financial services, measurement for performance improvement requires coordination with process managers who can best define what needs to be changed. Many companies find that measurement programs begin or take on a new life when a reengineering project is in the works.

The two cases that follow demonstrate two very different approaches to measurement in the reengineering process. Caterpillar began with an overall view of restructuring that necessitated measurement to function properly. Sisters of Charity began with an understanding that the current process wasn't working and discovered the need for measures along the way. Pay close attention to the variety of measurement tools that are used in these cases including cross-functional focus groups, flowcharting, customer focus groups, process measurement, outside industry data, informal benchmarking, and employee performance measurement.

Caterpillar Measurement Implementation

To remain competitive, companies need to institute a balanced set of financial and nonfinancial performance measures that relate directly to the organization's mission, objectives, strategies, and critical success factors such as customer delivery, quality, flexibility, productivity, and financial performance. Without them, companies won't have an accurate picture of how they are performing, in which areas they are achieving success, and in which areas they need to make changes.

At Caterpillar's Wheel Loaders and Excavators Division (WLED) in Aurora, Illinois, significant revisions have been made in both organizational structure and performance measures. The revisions came about largely because Caterpillar changed its overall corporate structure from a "functional bureaucratic" organization to a "profit center" organization and instituted performance measures appropriate to the new structure. Since then, the division has achieved outstanding success and continuous improvement. During the process, participants discovered some performance measurement principles that other companies can apply, regardless of size.

The Road to Change

Until 1990, Caterpillar's organizational structure focused on functional areas such as engineering, manufacturing, and accounting. The idea was that if each functional area achieved its goals and objectives, the customer would be happy and the corporation prosperous.

Then in mid-1990, Caterpillar initiated the restructuring of its functional organization into one composed of thirteen profit center divisions and four service center divisions. Product groups within the profit center divisions focus on serving the needs of the customers associated with a product line. Product group managers have direct control over engineering, manufacturing, and marketing. Accounting is a separate organizational unit that provides financial services to the product groups.

One goal of the reorganization and new performance measurement system was to increase responsiveness, flexibility, and customer focus. As a result, Caterpillar created mini-businesses within the company that concentrate on each customer's product needs. This decentralized approach allows each division to focus on product design, manufacturing, pricing, and parts and service for each customer.

For example, under the previous structure, a customer who wanted to buy a hydraulic excavator would contact a dealer who would work with the massive Caterpillar organization. Today the same customer still would contact a Caterpillar dealer, whose role is unchanged, but the customer's needs would be addressed by the Hydraulic Excavator Product Group within the WLED.

Another goal of the reorganization and new performance measurement system was to drive authority, responsibility, and decision making downward in the organization—empowering employees and holding them accountable for results. By so doing, Caterpillar believed it would develop more broadly based businesspeople throughout the organization and allow them to make better use of their experience and innovativeness within their areas of expertise.

Measures at WLED

Before 1990, the Wheel Loaders and Excavators Division was considered a cost center whose purpose was to reduce the cost of designing and manufacturing products. It monitored departmental costs and the costs of all parts and products closely. But revenue, profit, financial ratios, and nonfinancial performance measures were not implemented at the division level. Instead, they were monitored at the corporate level. The ratio of direct labor hours/machine hours was used to measure efficiency in the factory. Because the WLED had no direct linkage to the customer or to the bottom line of the company's income statement, the coordination of business decisions was not as effective as it could have been.

Developing New Performance Measures

In January 1990, Caterpillar Chairman of the Board Don Fites and Vice Chairman Jim Wogsland selected a team composed of high-level corporate managers and divisional financial personnel to oversee the development of new performance measures for all divisions. This ad hoc team solicited input from Caterpillar worldwide and visited companies such as AT&T, Texas Instruments, and IBM. They used this simplified approach to benchmarking because they wanted to pursue an aggressive schedule for developing the performance measures. Based on development time available, your company's approach to benchmarking may differ.

The ad hoc team decided that the new performance measures must relate to the corporate mission, the new organizational structure, the desire to push authority and responsibility downward in the organization, and critical success factors. They also were to be an integrated set of financial and nonfinancial measures that emphasized both long-term and short-term results.

After the ad hoc team developed the measurement concepts for the overall performance measurement system, a business measurements team was formed in corporate accounting to recommend specific performance measures and facilitate implementation. This team coordinated the efforts of numerous cross-functional teams in the division and worked closely with the accounting firm of Price Waterhouse & Co., which was engaged to help pull the data together to make the system operational. The business measurements team strove to ensure that all users understood and supported the behavioral implications of the new performance measures before they were implemented. In fact, each user attended a two-day training session for that purpose.

In the fall of 1990, the business measurements team developed and implemented financial performance measures used to assess divisional performance. This time frame would allow budgeting in the "new mode" for 1991. All Caterpillar divisions were directed to use these performance measures.

Next, a team composed of WLED Controller Jim Cromer, product managers, and accountants developed financial performance measures for each product group and major component group as well as all nonfinancial performance measures to be used at the WLED. These measures were developed and implemented by the end of 1992. Refining of the performance measurement system continued through the end of 1994.

The business measurements team has since been disbanded, but the ad hoc team still meets quarterly or as often as needed to discuss various measurement issues. Revisions of top-tier measurements must be approved by the ad hoc team, but the individual divisions continue to monitor and refine performance measures to meet their needs.

■ *Financial measures.* In the WLED's current organization, the division and each of four product groups are profit centers. Profit also is determined for major component groups such as machine structures, machine attachments, and parts, even though they aren't designated as formal profit centers. Obviously, to determine profit, revenues and costs must be identified for each segment.

The revenue for individual products and components is based on the price stated in the price list to the dealers. Market-based transfer prices are used to determine income for internal transfers because they provide an objective, arm's-length measure of revenue and cost. These market-based transfer prices are a key element in the development of the other financial measures currently in use.

To determine costs as accurately as possible for each product and major component, Caterpillar allocates indirect costs to each of the segments using the cause-and-effect criterion to the greatest extent possible. It avoids arbitrary allocations of indirect costs to these segments because they can distort profit.

The benefit of determining profit by major component groups as well as by product groups within divisions is to push accountability to lower levels in the company and to create constructive conflict among intraorganizational units. This approach aligns well with the strategy in place for "cost ownership" at the WLED, which is a team concept where representatives from all functional areas (e.g., purchasing, engineering, accounting, manufacturing, marketing) work together to minimize costs for each component and product. This level of profit analysis helps to identify areas of the business that are having difficulty and that require special efforts to improve profitability.

The profit for the division, product groups, and major component groups is used in the financial ratios of return on assets and return on sales. Other financial measures used include cash flow, inventory and fixed-asset levels, and warranty expense.

- *Nonfinancial measures.* Because a successful performance measurement system should include a balanced set of measures, the WLED employs several nonfinancial measures in addition to the financial measures for each profit segment. Measures of customer and employee satisfaction, delivery performance, process improvement, and conformance to plan are used for the division and for each product and major component group.

The predominant factory performance measure is the efficiency ratio of direct labor hours/machine hours, which was in use before the reorganization. Although efficiency ratios are computed for each profit segment at the WLED, the division is de-emphasizing this performance measure because it may reward behavior that builds unnecessarily high levels of inventory just to meet a manufacturing plan, regardless of whether the plan still reflects customer demand.

Factory personnel have said that new nonfinancial factory performance measures congruent with current strategies, critical success factors, and processes are needed. Examples include measures of material and parts delivery time, throughput time, due-date performance, quality, machine flexibility, and inventory levels. A team now is in place to make these performance measures operational. The division also is attempting to relate these nonfinancial factory performance measures to specific product groups and major component groups.

A major benefit of nonfinancial measures is that they usually can be reported on a more timely basis than financial measures. As a consequence, if a nonfinancial measure indicates poor performance, action often can be taken before adverse financial consequences occur.

In general, improved performance related to nonfinancial measures ultimately should translate into improved financial performance. Yet the linkage between improvement in operating nonfinancial performance measures and financial performance is tenuous. For example, what effect does improvement of on-time delivery performance or higher levels of employee satisfaction have on income?

- *Service department measures.* In addition to the division, product groups, and major component groups, the WLED has three service departments that are not profit centers. The service departments are business resources (accounting and information services), human resources, and technology resources. They exist to serve all product groups and major component teams.

The primary evaluation of service department performance is the comparison of actual spending versus budgeted spending, and user satisfaction is the most important nonfinancial performance measure employed in the evaluation.

Gearing Up for the Future

Managers and other employees at the WLED say that the new financial and nonfinancial performance measures in place at the division, product group, and major component group levels have been significant drivers in changing the culture to one of accountability. An unprecedented level of culture change has occurred as authority, responsibility, and decision making have been pushed down to lower levels. Employees, regardless of their functional areas, are making better business decisions because each profit center is evaluated by a balanced set of performance measures. If a profit center is not performing according to expectations, the personnel in that profit center are prepared to take the necessary corrective actions.

All employees at the WLED receive incentive compensation based on corporate and division profit. But the division, product group, and major component groups must make sure that short-term profitability is not enhanced to the detriment of long-term corporate profitability. For example, have annual R&D, employee training, or equipment maintenance costs been reduced to increase this year's segment profit with a possible adverse effect on succeeding years' profitability? At Caterpillar, this problem is addressed by division and product group long-term profit forecasts, which are approved and monitored by corporate headquarters. Also, the 150 new products introduced over the past few years are enhancing long-term profitability.

Because of the potential short-term focus on performance measures such as profitability and return on assets, the greatest change in the future will be to emphasize the development and use of more nonfinancial performance measures. These measures will relate to a new plateau of performance being sought through process breakthroughs (not just process improvement), improved assembly throughput, and the integration of better work values into the WLED's culture. They also will focus on developing human resources to the greatest extent possible and measuring how effectively managers are using these resources in a climate of continuous change. Measuring whether change initiatives have attained their goals can be the difference between achieving successful change or change that does not cause improved results.[11]

Sisters of Charity Health Care System

The Sisters of Charity Health Care System is a values-based, Catholic health-care system headquartered in Houston, Texas. The system includes fourteen acute-care hospitals, four long-term care facilities, a system of seven long-term acute-care hospitals, primary care clinics, physician networks, and a variety of health care entities in Texas, Louisiana, Arkansas, Utah, and Ireland.

Texas Louisiana Recovery Association (TLRA) was formed as an in-house collection agency for the Sisters of Charity twenty-six years ago, and today operates as a function of the System Office. Although TLRA provides services to other entities both inside and outside of the SCH system, the focus of this case study will be on services provided to the Sisters of Charity acute-care hospitals that make up the largest part of its business. The company currently manages $190 million in accounts receivable per year, with a rolling average of over 250,000 active accounts at any one time. TLRA now provides many different types of accounts receivable follow-up for its customer base, and the combination of services provided to each facility is customized to meet that hospital's needs. Today it is viewed by its patron hospitals as more of an extension of the business offices.

Impetus for Change

The nature of TLRA's business has changed dramatically during the last decade as changes in the delivery of health-care services occurred. One major change is that the volume of patient accounts TLRA services for the SCH system has increased substantially, with smaller average balances being collected on each patient account. Additionally, as the result of a benchmarking effort at Sisters of Charity several years ago, the hospitals are sending patient accounts to TLRA sooner for collection—oftentimes soon after the patient's bill becomes payable. Because of these and other changes to the environment in which the company operates, TLRA began to provide a much broader spectrum of services to its client hospitals. Suzanne Marchand, manager at TLRA, sums it up by saying, "With all of the changes in health care, the measurement tools we used to gauge whether or not our system was successful changed. Starting about ten years ago, these changes started affecting our business."

Another major change in TLRA's environment that acted as an impetus for business process reengineering was the companywide conversion from a mainframe computer system to independent networked systems at the hospitals. Before the system conversion, the communication link between TLRA and the individual hospitals was not as direct, but rather it went through the mainframe staff (I/S) at corporate headquarters (see Figure 3-3).

The introduction of the new computer network shifted the communication structure so that TLRA had much more interaction at various levels including facilitating more of the data exchange (see Figure 3-4).

The introduction of automated dialing systems used to accomplish repetitive tasks also significantly impacted the work processes in place at TLRA. While this added technology enabled significant cost reductions, it also made it even more apparent that company resources were not being allocated appropriately and that work processes needed to be scrutinized. Clearly, the processes used to run the business began to change dramatically on several fronts; the company realized that it had weathered these changes but the changes required action. Marchand describes the situation SCH found itself in as follows: "Every time we brought on some new project, we had to spend more time thinking about how to plug it into an operation that didn't lend itself well to that. Staying with the same arrangement just didn't make sense."

Figure 3-3. Former work flow diagram.

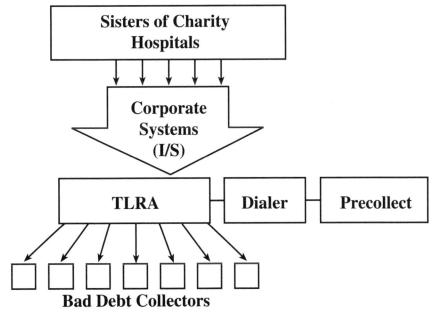

Figure 3-4. Supplier/customer new work flow diagram.

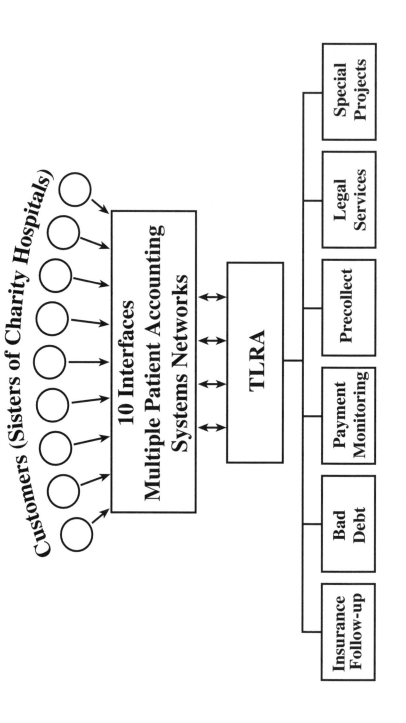

Investigating the Current State and Identifying Opportunities for Change

Phase one of the reengineering process began and centered around the basic goal of reconfiguring the structure and relationships of individuals.

Top management agreed at the outset that the focus should be on quality and maximizing customer satisfaction throughout the process. With this in mind, a team was formed to begin the process. The redesign team was composed of individuals both from inside and outside TLRA. A project team from Arthur Anderson assisted the TLRA redesign team. From within the company, team members included the following personnel performing the following functions within the group:

- Manager/TLRA: Project Leader
- Supervisor/Collections: Unit Leader
- Supervisor/Precollect: Unit Leader
- Supervisor/Systems: Unit Leader

Top management at the company felt it was important for representatives from both active accounts receivable and bad-debt accounts receivable to participate actively in the team function. The organizational hierarchy was traditional in structure at the start of business process reengineering (see Figure 3-5). However, Marchand stresses that, "We really wanted to re-think the whole picture at TLRA and to define the organization in terms of its processes rather than its functions/positions."

Redesign team members began the process by gathering information from a number of sources. Cross-functional focus groups were organized with employees and were moderated by the Collections supervisors. During these sessions, employees from different functions within the company spent time mapping each work process in minute detail using flowcharting. Brainstorming sessions with these employees were used to obtain suggestions on how work processes currently in place could be improved.

Representatives from all of the Sisters of Charity acute-care hospitals participated in a daylong feedback session. Participants were asked to specify which aspects of TLRA's services they liked and disliked. Suggestions for improvement were elicited as well. A list of suggestions was created and spin-off ad hoc groups were formed within TLRA to investigate specific issues raised by customers at this session.

Redesign team members from the outside consulting firm were assigned to determine the ways in which new accounts entered the system, the length of time required to collect accounts, the degree to which human intervention was used in the collection process, and how automation of specific tasks within the system was impacting the collection process.

Figure 3-5. Old TLRA organizational structure.

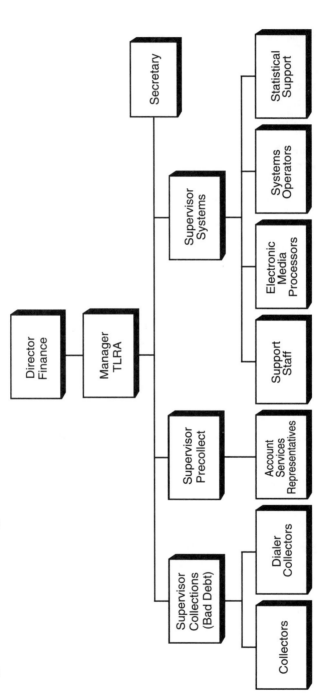

The National Health Care Collectors Association (NHCA) provided benchmarking data to the redesign team. TLRA has participated in NHCA survey studies sponsored by this organization in the past, and the data provided was examined by the team to identify the operational processes that work well in the industry. The redesign team leader, Suzanne Marchand, also met with similar organizations on an informal level to discuss their processes and procedures, and to examine "best practices" that exist in the industry.

Restructuring TLRA

Using the data collected, the redesign team focused on how it wanted the structure of TLRA to look when it completed phase one of the reengineering process. Of primary importance to the team was to structure the organization so that the focus was on customer satisfaction. The fact that groups of geographically integrated care delivery networks had recently been formed in the Sisters of Charity system acted as a guideline for change.

The new company structure that evolved enables all functions related to each region to reside within that unit of operation at TLRA. The core concept used as a basis for this design was that the customers served in each region would serve as common ground for the units. Each regional unit supported its own team that managed accounts on a geographic basis. A central systems support team served as the common denominator for the teams. A management team that included team leaders from each region provided the overall strategic guidance for the team (see Figure 3-6). Team members determined early on that people within the organization did not have a clear understanding of the core process as a whole, but understood only the part of the process they performed. Consensus was reached among team members that having an understanding of how each function fit into the core process would benefit all employees and the reengineering efforts being undertaken.

Additional time and effort was expended by the redesign team to examine and map the core process performed by TLRA. The core process involved a combination of automated and human intervention to accounts to produce some resolution of that account. The process was defined in terms of data inputs and potential outputs (see Figure 3-7).

The redesign team discovered the process itself involved numerous loops. TLRA would receive data from its client hospitals, but could run a single account through various subprocesses before reaching a resolution (see Figure 3-8). Additionally, it was determined that there was little consistency in the way tasks were performed within each function. Suzanne

Figure 3-6. New TLRA organizational system vision.

Multiskill Cross-Functional Service to Health-Care Entities

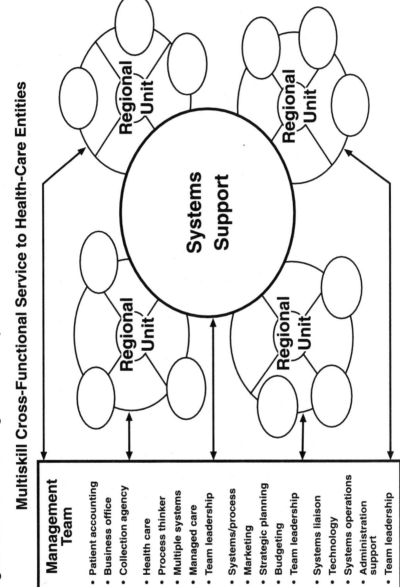

Figure 3-7. TLRA core process.

Input	Process	Output
• Self-pay • Third party	• Account analysis • Phone calls • Letters • Documentation • Hospital contact	• Worker compensation • Payments • Cash • Terms • Write off ("uncollectable") • Disputes • Bankruptcies • Deceased • Skips • Litigation • Settlements • Adjustment

Figure 3-8. TLRA subprocesses.

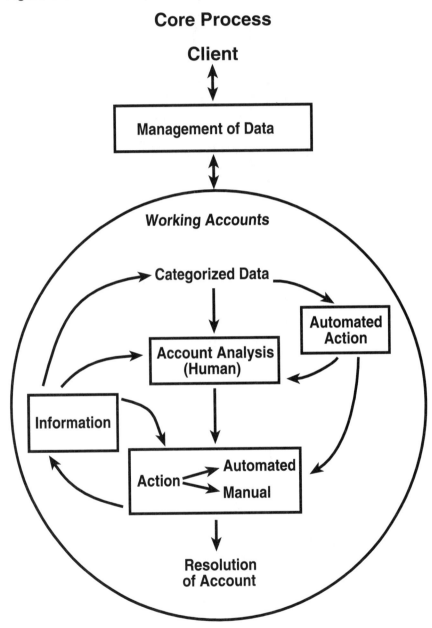

Core Process

Marchand observes that, "Standardization is particularly important in an automated system that causes accounts to fall into or out of a loop. This work process required consistency." Thus, educational efforts and standardization of tasks became areas of focus for the team.

The internal structure of each regional unit was developed and mapped. The function of each team member and the team's relationship with the customer and TLRA management was defined (see Figure 3-9).

After the redesign team reached consensus on how to reconfigure the basic company structure, it was determined that two additional changes needed to be made. First, all employee positions were eliminated and everyone was required to apply for positions in the new company structure. Skill requirements for jobs created by the new structure were analyzed by the redesign team and a matrix was created using ten key criteria (see Figure 3-10).

Second, new office space was prepared to better meet the needs of TLRA. Before business process reengineering began, the office space occupied by the company was cramped and segmented. Marchand reports that "There were a lot of walls—both visible and invisible—separating people who needed to work together. This made the flow of information more difficult. Basically, we tried to get rid of the walls that separated our employees." Modular units were installed and more open spaces were provided. Employees within the same work unit (i.e., Southeast region) were grouped together.

At the conclusion of phase one, the redesign team worked to develop and implement a compensation plan that fit the new corporate structure. The objectives of the performance-based compensation plan were developed.

The plan's design has been reassessed at intervals and employees are solicited for feedback about how the plan is working and how it can be improved.

Rollout

According to Suzanne Marchand, "TLRA's redesign team was concerned about trying to implement something so radical. In essence, we changed almost everything about our business and everything our employees did. The changes were dramatic." After careful consideration, the redesign team decided that because of the nature and size of TLRA's business, the phase one portion of the business reengineering process would be implemented all at once. The physical movement of employees into new office space and into new jobs happened in one step.

Constant communication with employees throughout the process was

Figure 3-9. Team profiles and regional unit functions.

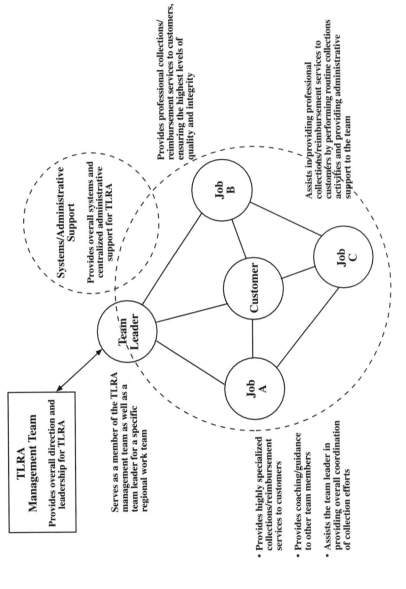

TLRA Management Team

Provides overall direction and leadership for TLRA

Serves as a member of the TLRA management team as well as a team leader for a specific regional work team

Systems/Administrative Support

Provides overall systems and centralized administrative support for TLRA

Team Leader

Job A

Customer

Job B

Job C

Provides professional collections/reimbursement services to customers, ensuring the highest levels of quality and integrity

Assists in/providing professional collections/reimbursement services to customers by performing routine collections activities and providing administrative support to the team

- Provides highly specialized collections/reimbursement services to customers

- Provides coaching/guidance to other team members

- Assists the team leader in providing overall coordination of collection efforts

Figure 3-10. Relative degree of knowledge, skills, and abilities by job.

	Knowledge of		Interpersonal Communication Skills	Written Communication Skills	Analysis Information	Problem/ Issue Resolution	Project Team Activities	Adaptability/ Flexibility	Decision Making
	System	Collections/ Reimbursement	Patient Financial Counseling							
Job A	●	●	●	●	●	●	●	●	●	●
Job B	◐	◐	◐	●	◐	◐	●	◐	●	◐
Job C	○	○	○	◐	◐	◐	◐	◐	◐	◐

Degree of knowledge, skills, and/or Abilities

● Advanced   ◐ Solid   ○ Basic

instrumental to the success of both the development and implementation phases. Weekly (and sometimes daily) meetings were held to keep personnel informed every step of the way and to involve them in the data-gathering and decision-making processes. The process for change is seen as evolving at TLRA—with the driving force being the desire to do the job accurately, quickly, well, and in a way that best supports the needs of their customers.

Results of Phase One

The redesign team also worked to clearly identify specific processes in need of improvement. In order to gain consensus as a group on which matters TLRA should address first, the group developed an extensive list of potential processes to be targeted for improvement. The group then produced a grid listing potential areas for improvement and assigned each issue a rating on five criteria:

- Scope of problem (small/medium/large)
- Ease of change (difficult/easy)
- Potential savings (large/medium/small)
- Cost of change (large/medium/small)
- Fit with goals/vision (indirect/direct)

Based on these ratings, the team prioritized issues into those to be targeted immediately and others to be "put on a back burner" to be addressed later.

The following are examples of issues the redesign team targeted:

- A new account classification structure has been developed and put into place that appropriately categorizes patient accounts and allows work groups easier file access.

- A new process has been developed to handle small balance accounts. Patient accounts of this size comprise fully 80 percent of TLRA's self-pay business, and the redesign team determined that improvements made to the way these accounts were handled would significantly impact the company.

- A more detailed account classification process has been developed and protocols have been created to determine when human intervention is appropriate and when efforts to collect on these accounts should cease.

- A complex process has been developed and implemented to automate bank deposits on patient accounts and to update posting information back to the SCH hospitals. Automation of this process has significantly reduced the worker-hours required to accomplish these tasks and has increased the interest earned on deposited funds because of rapid payment posting.

Phase Two of the Process

Phase two of business process reengineering at TLRA then began. During this phase of the process, which is ongoing, the redesign team plans to develop and implement customer satisfaction measurements in order to quantify customer satisfaction and pinpoint performance gaps. Plans are for results of these investigative efforts to be trended over time and tied to employee compensation packages in the future.

Teams have been formed within the work units and these teams have been given responsibility for scheduling, accountability issues, and work assignments—a marked deviation from the old structure where supervisors made all of these decisions. The new corporate structure lends itself easily to employee involvement in issues that affect them, thus promoting buy-in. Standard CQI (Continuous Quality Improvement) team guidelines and methods have worked well for these groups.

The perspective at TLRA is that the company is constantly evolving into something better, and because of business process reengineering, employees feel they are better prepared to face challenges that lie ahead. Suzanne Marchand concludes that, "Even for employees who stayed on, the changeover has been difficult and new ways of thinking have taken time to permeate the company. It has taken time for the employees to feel proficient and competent in what they do. We continue to look at the processes that make our business run better, but we are also concentrating on making our employees feel like they are truly owners of the business. We are now concentrating on making the human element better, while continuing to refine work processes and improve team skills."[12]

Both Caterpillar and Sisters of Charity are reengineering success stories precisely because of their use of measures. Caterpillar structured its entire reengineering effort around the institutionalization of a measurement program. Because size was less of a hindrance to Sisters of Charity, it paid closer attention to process practices. Even so, SCH used measures extensively to identify performance gaps for the improvement effort. Note that both companies made extensive use of process management, used multiple measures to create a balanced picture of the organization, linked measures to behavioral goals, trained employees in the new system, and continued with measurement after the improvement effort.

While Caterpillar did not retain its measurement team, the ad hoc team continued to meet quarterly to refine the measurement system.

Gaining Organizational Acceptance

Measurement programs can have a huge impact on an organization. Human resources–based measurement very personally affects each and every employee. Performance improvement measurement changes the structure of the organization and the roles of individuals within the organization. Needless to say, a new measurement program faces a highly politically charged atmosphere.

Organizational acceptance is one of the toughest roadblocks to effective measurement. In our earlier discussion we described the characteristics of effective measurement staff as having a thorough understanding of organizational dynamics. This really means that they can implement measures in a highly political environment.

No measure is perfect. The only way to measure a process is through a balance of measures. It is therefore quite easy to criticize the imperfections in measures, the adequacy of measurement programs, and the "hidden" agendas behind measurement. Measurement personnel must have an understanding of both the benefits and inadequacies of measurement. They must also be able to communicate to all stakeholders why the benefits outweigh the inadequacies. Many individuals have the technical skills necessary to be measurement professionals, but they are discouraged by the political maneuvering. To be a success, you must learn to weather the battles.

Whirlpool

This case study originally appeared in Across the Board.

When Whirlpool Corp. created its so-called top sheet in December 1991, people bought into the four value-creating objectives pretty easily, according to Harry S. Burritt, corporate director of planning and development. But many protested loudly that certain measures weren't appropriate to their organization.

The company replaced 60 percent of the measures—but not the strategic objectives—when it updated the top sheet last year. Says Burritt: "Without the permanence of the value-creating objectives, the whole measurement system would have fallen under its own weight."[13]

Conclusion

The development of measures and indicators is often the biggest step toward a strong measurement program. Measures must be economical to collect, understandable to employees, and actionable. They must also be broad in scope—embracing the needs of all stakeholders. Remember, though, a measurement system evolves. While you must lay the groundwork now, measures and indicators can and will be revised on a regular basis in response to unexpected consequences of the measures or simply changes in the environment.

4

Measurement Tools and Techniques

Introduction

Every measurement group will need to use a variety of tools and techniques throughout the measurement process. Some of these tools have received a great deal of attention in the press over the past few years. Others are old stand-bys that many may already be familiar with. The intent of this chapter is to present examples of a handful of tools that can aid in measurement identification, analysis, and application.

Measurement Application

Measurements must be linked to business strategy and be meaningful within the context of the business as a whole. There has been lengthy debate in the press over the last few years regarding the proper way to value a business and predict its overall health. The debate initially appeared in the context of investors, but is also being applied internally to business units and overall performance ratings. After all, the CEO and internal analysts are attempting to answer the same question as investors: How is the business performing?

What follows are discussions of some of the most popular evaluation techniques and predictive methods. Four evaluation techniques—economic value added, activity-based costing/management, process value analysis, and balanced scorecard—are described in depth. Eight cases are used to demonstrate how balanced scorecard and other measurement analysis tools are applied in real life.

Economic Value Added (EVA)

The following material originally appeared in *Business Credit:*

> Many of the traditional corporate performance measures have
> been found to poorly correlate, or even conflict, with manage-
> ment's primary objective of maximizing the market value of a
> firm's stock. Now, there are several new measures in the fi-
> nancial world that attempt to align the behaviors of an organi-
> zation with its stockholders' interests. One measure that has
> received a great deal of notice and acceptance is economic
> value added, developed by Joel M. Stern and G. Bennett Stew-
> art III of Stern Stewart & Co.
>
> Implementation of one of these measures, such as EVA,
> can fundamentally change the behavior of an entire organiza-
> tion. The new measure focuses the behavior of individuals
> throughout all parts of the organization in a way that is better
> aligned with creating stockholder wealth. Because perfor-
> mance compensation incentives are based on the new mea-
> sure, employees and stockholders mutually benefit.
>
> The financial function is uniquely qualified to take a lead-
> ership role in communicating an understanding of the new
> measure. Our challenge is to gain a deep understanding of the
> underlying principles of the measure and to communicate
> them in a meaningful way to all parts of the organization.
> There can be pitfalls in translating the theory to practice, but
> we have the opportunity to provide the appropriate counsel.[14]

What Is EVA?

Economic value added simply balances a company's profitability
against the capital it employs to generate this profitability. If a company's
earnings, after tax, exceed the cost of the capital employed in the business, EVA is positive. Market studies have indicated that a company that
continually generates an increasingly positive EVA will be rewarded by a
higher stock price. In the book *Quest for Value,* Stern Stewart & Co. provides substantial statistical evidence that supports this relationship. Of
course, if a company's long-term prospects are impaired, due to market
conditions, litigation, management change, or some other reason, then its
stock price will not necessarily increase.

A definition of EVA is net operating profit after taxes (NOPAT), less
an internal charge for the capital employed in the business (i.e., opportu-

nity cost of capital). To illustrate the intuitive nature of EVA, a company with $1 million of net operating profit after tax may not have necessarily performed well. It depends upon how much capital the company uses to generate the profit. If this were General Electric, the result would be abysmal. If this business were run from a telephone in a small office, the EVA would be extraordinary.

When computing EVA, there are adjustments to both NOPAT and capital employed to reduce what could be considered noneconomic accounting and financing conventions on the income statement and on the balance sheet. (See Figure 4-1.)

When a company's net operating profit after tax exceeds its capital-employed charge, its EVA is positive and value has been created. If the result equals zero, the firm's management merely met the expected returns of debt and equity holders.

Why Is EVA So Popular?

EVA is a powerful tool for several reasons: It aligns employee behavior with stockholder value generation, separates employee incentive compensation from the traditional performance measurement that compares actual to budgeted results, and is relatively easy to communicate and understand.

Like EVA, corporate governance has become a widely discussed topic over the past several years. There are numerous situations where man-

Figure 4-1. Calculation of economic value added (EVA).

1. Net operating profit after taxes (NOPAT)
2. Adjust for noneconomic accounting and finance conventions
   - Last in, first out (LIFO)
   - Bad debt
   - Deferred taxes
   - Inventory obsolescence
   - Warranty
   - Interest expense after taxes
3. Less opportunity cost of capital
   (weighted average cost of capital × capital employed)
4. = EVA

Notes:
1. Operating leases are a form of debt and should be capitalized.
2. Noneconomic adjustments are equity equivalents.
3. Weighted average cost of capital are the expected returns of debt and equity holders weighted proportionately. It will vary by firm.

agement's obligation to act on behalf of shareholders is in conflict with its own best interests. Growth, either internally generated or through acquisition, is typically in the best interests of management because compensation is often based upon such factors as sales volume, size of department, and size of budget. Yet, only growth that provides increasingly positive EVA contributes to shareholder value.

When EVA becomes the basis for management incentive compensation, management's decision making is aligned with shareholder value creation. Management is more highly focused on growth that generates a positive EVA. There is also the added benefit of decoupling the budgeting process from incentive compensation. Most practitioners have participated in budgeting processes where the best negotiators end up with the most achievable budgets and therefore the highest incentive payouts. Not only is there a fairness issue, there is also the issue of providing incentive compensation for results that do not necessarily create shareholder value. Using budgets as a basis for incentive compensation institutionalizes payment for mediocre performance.

Incentive compensation under EVA is formula driven and is automatically adjusted annually for the current year's performance, as well as for a performance improvement factor. The budget process becomes one of maximizing EVA through increasing profitability and balance sheet management.

A further benefit of EVA is that is can be boiled down into a message that all parts of the organization can understand and apply to their daily activities. Simply said, the message is to increase overall profitability while reducing the capital tied up in the business.

The EVA Message

EVA properly motivates the financial organization. Problems on the balance sheet must be dealt with sooner rather than later. Why carry an impaired asset (e.g., excess or obsolete inventory or problem receivables) month-after-month, with the associated capital-employed charge, only to write it off at some later date? It makes sense to avoid the cost of capital charge and gain the tax benefit sooner. The longer such a decision is deferred, the lower the net present value of the tax benefit of the ultimate write-off.

Publicly traded firms are under intense pressure to meet Wall Street's quarterly earnings projections. This often results in pushing manufacturing to rush orders to completion in order to "make the quarter." Higher operating expenses attributable to quarter-end shipments result in lower NOPAT. In addition, the capital-employed charge is higher because inventory is converted to receivables, which includes the gross margin on the product. EVA discourages this behavior and encourages more even production and shipments throughout a quarter.

From a strategic perspective, management will direct resources to grow the parts of the company that can generate positive EVA results. Those parts of the business that are not contributing a positive EVA get closer scrutiny and may become candidates for divestiture.

The message of EVA is equally clear for other parts of the organization and can be readily translated to the various functions within the organization. The message to the sales organization is that extended payment terms result in higher receivables, and consignment inventory results in higher inventory. Balance the incremental sales against the higher capital-employed charge. For industries that require long production times, the message is that progress billings and advance payments can have a huge EVA benefit. Work on the customer's money.

This is not today's news, but there is now an economic incentive to do the right thing for the organization and its shareholders. To the marketing organization, the message is that products provided on trial to key customers have an EVA cost. The asset, once used, will likely need to be written down, and it will sit on the balance sheet, incurring the monthly capital-employed charge. To the manufacturing and materials organization, the message is to invest in productive machine tools rather than in brick and mortar to reduce cycle times, improve throughput, and reduce inventory levels. EVA increases if capital investments return more than the cost of capital. Those investments that return less than the cost of capital should be rejected.

Create a Foolproof System and Only a Fool Will Use It

While EVA is a powerful measure, it does not eliminate the need for thought. The developers of the technique, Stern Stewart & Co., make it clear in their writings that not all companies will calculate EVA in precisely the same way, so it must be customized for the company involved. Industries also differ, and some of the adjustments recommended may not apply or may be considered immaterial. This means that once EVA is defined for a company to exclude designated immaterial adjustments, one must reexamine the calculation to determine if what had been immaterial yesterday has not become material today.

The Short and the Long Term

The EVA focus within an organization may result in decisions that improve short-term EVA results and hurt long-term EVA results. It may be as simple as deferring maintenance on machine tools this year, thereby incurring a much larger expense at a later date. Or on a larger scale, it may be opting to not make investments (e.g., acquisitions, machine tools) that have short-term negative EVA outcomes but positive long-term EVA outcomes.

The EVA incentive plan, if used, takes precautions to address this risk. The EVA incentive plan sets a limit on the amount of bonus paid in a year and banks the balance for future year payouts. If subsequent year EVA results are too low, the banked bonus can be lost.

There is risk that decisions will be made that only maximize short-term EVA when management believes that the EVA incentive plan may be replaced by a different plan. Also, members of management may be contemplating a career change such as retirement, transfer, or changing employment. Finally, there is simply human nature. Get the maximum bonus this year and fix next year as necessary. These factors may be the cause for decisions that are skewed to improve EVA over the short term.

EVA can bring great value to a company by focusing the entire organization on activities that produce results valued by shareholders. With a well-grounded understanding of EVA, the financial organization is uniquely capable of providing counsel that will ensure successful implementation of this new measure.

Shell Oil

This case study originally appeared in Fortune.

No company is more devoted to the number-crunching school than Shell. In the early 1990s, oil prices were falling and Shell's earnings were dismal to nonexistent. The creation of the Shell Business Model, as it is called, "was part of the company's larger, overall transformation," says Philip J. Carroll, Shell's president and CEO.

Shell divided itself into four operating companies: Exploration & Production, Oil Products, Chemicals, and Services. Each of these businesses received its own internal board of directors and its own bottom and top lines. The results of the operating companies were consolidated into a single overall balance sheet. The reorganization looked good on paper, but something was missing. Carroll needed a way to get his people more focused on the business. Shell's employees viewed themselves as working primarily for a technology concern. And while they excelled at drilling deep water wells from vessels and floating platforms anchored in the choppy Gulf of Mexico, they did not excel at watching the corporate wallet. As a result, Carroll decided to give "people working in the company a better way to understand economics," as he puts it. In other words, he wanted a way to change behavior.

The Shell Business Model was the answer. "Historically at Shell, managers would talk about how to build something like a chemical plant or a platform better, faster, or cheaper," says Thomas M. Botts, Shell's treasurer and general manager. That conversation still takes place, but now it is in the context of running the business profitably. "We're no longer focused just on how to build something," says Botts, "but on how it can create value. The intent is to have all 21,000 people know what drives value for the stockholder."

Shell's model uses a simple four-square matrix. The top left quadrant of the matrix contains a measurement for revenue growth. The top right-hand box of the four-square matrix is where Shell's model keeps track of what it calls its "intrinsic business value," which indicates the overall market value of the company—what it would be worth if it were put up for sale. In the bottom right quadrant is a number similar to economic value added, or EVA, that tells Shell's managers whether they're earning more than their cost of capital. Finally, in the bottom left quadrant, there are measures for return on investment.

"[The model] is not a program that lets me sit at a computer and figure out what the East Chicago revenue is going to be," says Carroll. "Rather, it influences the way I can discuss and evaluate the changing business strategies of the business units. We think of it as a financial beacon that supports decision making in a very rigorous way," he says.

So how does it work in practice? When Shell evaluated its shallow-water drilling business in the Gulf of Mexico, using the model, it discovered a whole host of economic drivers affecting that business's success. "One of the major things we determined was that the time between the discovery of oil and gas and when it came on production was an average of four years," Carroll says. Until the model, Shell did not recognize the effect those long lead times had on profitability, since the company historically focused on maximizing return on investment and not so much on revenue growth. As a result, it undervalued the contribution of revenue growth to the company's bottom line.

After putting the model in place, Shell's managers learned that there was a causal link between revenue growth and shareholder value. As a result they have made shorter cycle times one of their objectives.[15]

Activity-Based Costing/Management (ABC/ABM)

ABC/ABM advocates linking real activities to the drivers of cost. For example, an automobile manufacturer links the manufacturing costs such as direct labor, cost of equipment, facility maintenance, and power. The result is a "true" cost of a car. The proponents of ABC/ABM believe that companies can "know" their true profitability and make business decisions on that basis.

While this knowledge can be extremely useful, it does have its limitations. The primary problem with ABC arises when capacity consumption is a driver of cost allocation. Telecommunication companies and airlines are particularly susceptible to this problem.

When an airline is flying a full airplane, the allocation of costs makes sense. You can, as in manufacturing, allocate costs to the end cost object, the customer. When the company is flying at less than full, then what is the cost of flying a customer? That cost then becomes a subject of great debate. How much cost does it really take to provide the service to the last passenger on a plane?

Not everyone is a fan of ABM. Richard Schonberger wrote "ABM, however, is redundant. Process management works well enough on its own; no need to bless every improvement in dollar signs, as ABM would do. To illustrate the point, one company found, via activity-based cost analysis, that 'the cost per purchase order was abnormally high. Investigation disclosed that more than fifteen separate forms were required for each purchase. No process improvement team, however, needs a cost study to prove that fifteen separate purchase documents is waste. (ABC is highly valued, however, in helping to reveal when certain product lines are not paying their way or when pricing is out of whack with real costs.)"[16]

Process Value Analysis (PVA)

The following material originally appeared in *Management Accounting– London:*

> Traditional management reporting systems have generally considered where cost was incurred (the cost center), what the cost was (the type of resource), when it occurred (the period), and who was responsible (the manager of the responsibility center). Activity-based management (ABM) methods then helped identify why cost was incurred by examining the cost-drivers of activities. The cost-drivers then indicated performance measures that would provide incentives to tackle the underlying causes of cost. Unfortunately, the final part of the picture—how to improve—has not always been present. This shortcoming has been most evident in some benchmarking ex-

ercises. The hapless manager has been presented with "world class benchmarks" for the "key performance indicators" of the "core processes" that determine the "critical success factors" of the organization, yet is given no indication of how to improve his woeful performance. Even the most gung-ho "just do it" manager needs to be told how.

This question cannot be answered by measurement alone. Instead it requires an understanding of how the activities link together into processes, how those processes should operate, and how they fail. This analysis is generally called process value analysis.

The components of PVA are familiar. The centerpiece is a process map. A map showing the activities and their interrelations is drawn for each process. There are many drawing conventions, but whichever is used, it is useful to annotate the map with descriptions of how the process breaks down. Improvements can then be discussed. Apart from eliminating failure, these might include: eliminating duplicated activities; avoiding generating unnecessary information; avoiding unnecessary decision points; combining process flows; separating process flows; avoiding unnecessary movement; synchronizing activities. The graphical representation assists in discussion on how to make these improvements.

Naturally the quest for improvement should have a clear direction. The direction, of course, is to improve those performance measures that the earlier work (using balanced scorecards or cost-drivers) had identified as meriting a place in the corporate measurement framework. Typical measures might be lead time for new product introduction or flexibility on short-term changes to manufacturing schedules.

After a PVA exercise, the manager therefore is equipped with a tool that shows why a measure is the value it is and how that value can be changed. The theory is straightforward enough, but the real challenge is to identify where the process is failing and how to improve it. Not surprisingly, a structured approach to this task is preferable to trusting to serendipity.

One simple and effective way is to combine the PVA with the first two interviews of an activity-analysis program. The purpose of the first interview is usually to define the activities. This occasion can also be used to collect details of the symptoms of process failure (i.e., the general whinings about things being late or done wrong). Process maps are then drawn, using activities in the standard library, and the causes of the under-lying process failure are identified and possible process improvements identified. Then, during the second interview, which is usually used to trace costs to activities, the proposed solutions and improvements are fed back and discussed. This simple procedure produces relatively quickly a set of process maps, activity costs, and performance improvement concepts.[17]

Balanced Scorecard

The following material originally appeared in *Fortune:*

A corporate scorecard is a sophisticated business model that helps a company understand what's really driving its success. It acts a bit like the control panel on a spaceship—the business equivalent of a flight speedometer, odometer, and temperature gauge all rolled into one. It keeps track of many things, including financial progress and softer measurements—everything from customer satisfaction to return on investment—that need to be managed to reach the final destination: profitable growth. For example, a scorecard might graph customer service (is it improving or deteriorating?) and at the same time tally product defects (are they rising or falling and where?).

Even more important, scorecard software, which is usually distributed throughout a company's computer network, lets managers across the entire organization be certain they are talking about the same thing when they get together. If, say, customer satisfaction is dropping, the folks from sales, manufacturing, and R&D will all be reading the same score, and thus will be able to tackle the problem from common ground. It is little wonder, then, that according to a recent study by the Institute of Management Accountants, 64 percent of U.S. companies are experimenting with some sort of new performance measurement system.

But not all is so simple these days in the land of scorecards. A controversy is raging between two schools of thought. One school of thought, led by companies such as Motorola and Analog Devices, a high-flying semiconductor maker, believes that a scorecard should be balanced. Analog, for instance, not only keeps close watch on financial performance numbers like gross profit margins on new products, but also measures the softer processes—such as the time it takes to get a new product to market and employee satisfaction.

But there's another school of thought, led by companies like Fortis, a financial services giant, and Shell Oil, that says that the balanced scorecard confuses the issue, that a company should have a sophisticated way to measure itself but that those measurements should be purely financial. Here, managers use hard measurements like revenue growth and return on investment to guide the business.

"This is the big philosophical discussion right now," says John K. Shank, a professor of accounting at Dartmouth's Tuck School. Shank favors the more holistic balanced-scorecard approach: "At great companies like Motorola, they don't talk profits, they talk key drivers," he says with uncommon intensity. "How are you managing your manufacturing yield rates? Your cycle times?" If you manage those, the balanced-scorecard fans argue, the bottom line results will come. "But managing by the financials," says Shank, "won't necessarily get you better financial results, because the financials only tell you where you were—they're history. They don't tell you where you're going. And they certainly don't tell you anything about your potential."

Advocates of the hard-number approach strongly disagree. "It can be very difficult to make decisions with a balanced scorecard," says Larry Selden, a professor of finance at Columbia University's graduate school of business administration. "How do you know the cost of gaining or losing a customer, for example? How do you know the lifetime value of a customer?" Those in Selden's camp—call them the number crunchers—believe you first have to measure how much value each activity contributes to (or destroys for) the company as a whole. "If I don't measure it, I don't understand it," says Selden. "Maybe you can use the balanced scorecard after you've done the financial analysis, but you have to begin with the financial measurements to decide what's on the scorecard."

So which approach is right: Shell's or Analog's? Says Mike Uretsky, a professor at New York University: "The value of these devices is in the assumptions you build into them." Different companies at different times have different needs and aims. For example, if you're a media company that's just merged, you wouldn't build a strictly financial model that focuses, say, on productivity. Output per employee isn't a driver for that business. (Just because you're merging doesn't mean you will need fewer people to shoot a TV program.)

"So it all depends," says Uretsky, "upon what the company is wrestling with." Indeed, the real value of any model is that it forces you to reexamine your assumptions about what in your business really drives performance. It forces you to focus and become much more explicit about what matters to the customer and ultimately what matters to the most important person of all—the shareholder.[18]

Analog Devices

This case study originally appeared in Fortune.

While Shell has done well with its purely financial approach, companies like Analog Devices believe that the numbers alone don't tell the whole story. The company's mainstay products are computer chips for use primarily in communications, military, aviation, and cellular phone applications.

"In the mid-1980s we were not doing well. We simply needed to become more competitive," says Arthur M. Schneiderman, the MIT-trained engineer who developed the world's first balanced-scorecard model for Analog when he worked for it back then. "So we surveyed our customers and did benchmarking studies and found that they cared about things like delivery time and improved quality." Analog then built a model that would help its managers track and thus better manage such things. "Overall, there were about fifteen nonfinancial measures that we identified as critical to the company's performance," Schneiderman says. These were things like the rate of on-time deliveries, product development cycle times, number of new products, and so on. Analog managers can now get a history of how Analog is doing and where it is going overall. They can check on defect rates plant by plant and see how each plant's quality is improving.

But Analog's model isn't just about the soft stuff. It links measurements like on-time deliveries to certain financial indicators. For example, the model now measures the percentage of sales due to new product introductions and gross margins on new products. Shell, by contrast, puts greater emphasis on more traditional, corporatewide indicators like revenues and return on investment. Once a quarter, Analog's twelve senior managers get together for a full day to discuss, among other things, results from their scorecards. "The managers," says Goodloe Suttler, the company's corporate vice president for marketing, quality, and planning, "are then asked to explain in front of the group any variances in their results and what they are going to do about them." One manager, for instance, once had a problem with what Analog calls its "new product ratios." This is a scorecard item that helps managers judge how effectively the company is spending its R&D dollars. The balanced scorecard showed that one division was lagging in new product development. Under the old system this wouldn't have been noticed because all the conventional short-term financials looked just dandy—because it was too early for the R&D slump to show up in the numbers.

So what does focusing on the soft stuff do for the bottom line? Analog's revenues doubled to $1.2 billion [in 1996], from $538 million in 1991. Operating profits have increased steadily, from a dismal 3 percent of sales in 1991 to a more respectable 19 percent [in 1996]. In April 1993, Analog's stock was selling for some $7 a share. Currently it is trading at about four times that price, hovering in the $28 range. Not bad for a company that manages itself with a model that is almost entirely devoid of traditional financial measurements.[19]

Mobil AM&R

This case study originally appeared in Across the Board.

The promise of improved alignment attracted Mobil American Marketing and Refining (AM&R) executive VP Bob McCool to the balanced scorecard in early 1994.

"When I went out to our refineries and asked people what our strategic themes were, many of them didn't have a clue," McCool admits. "Our corporate planning staff was coming up with great game plans, but people in the field just did their own thing. The strategy wasn't cascading down."

Under the old system, measurement wasn't a communication device; it was a control mechanism, and a poor one at that, he says. Reports coming up from the field provided exhaustive detail on financial results— margins at the regional level, for example. But what McCool really wanted were lead indicators on how each business was contributing to strategic objectives.

So when AM&R finished its divisional scorecard in August 1994, Mc-Cool turned to his strategic business unit (SBU) heads and said: Now it's your turn. Develop a set of strategic objectives and measures that represent the direction of your business. Here's a copy of the division's scorecard, but don't worry about making yours a carbon copy.

Greg Berry, the AM&R division's manager of business performance analysis, explains: "We knew we'd need consistency among scorecards to achieve alignment. But we wanted the SBUs to feel they owned theirs. McCool saw the scorecard as an opportunity to give strategy development back to the business units."

The tactic worked. When all seventeen SBU scorecards were complete, in February 1995, most ended up remarkably consistent with the division's—despite the diversity of their businesses, which range from pipeline operations to retail gasoline chains. Berry's group began meeting one-on-one with each business unit to work out any wrinkles. "A number of people told me, 'This feels really good. I finally understand how what I'm doing fits into what the division is trying to do,'" says Berry.

Today, scorecards are embedded in the management process at AM&R. When SBU heads meet with the division's executive leadership team, they are encouraged to bring just one piece of paper: their scorecard.

"It's the basis of every conversation," says McCool. "When I go out in the field and talk with a guy running a coker on the midnight shift at one of our refineries, he can tell me what he's doing to impact the scorecard."[20]

Pitney Bowes

This case study originally appeared in Across the Board.

Even when top management is sold on the idea of tracking nonfinancials, settling on a workable set of measures is no picnic. Pitney Bowes's U.S. Mailing Systems, headquartered in Stamford, Connecticut, started with a list of no fewer than 500 "key" measures on its first pass. According to Mark Green, the division's director of business analysis, "We had to come up with a separate set of measures just to rank the measures."

The final group of seven measures became the basis for a business information system, online since October 1993. It's used by executives across the division, including sales, divisional controllers, marketing, president's staff, human resources, and finance.

Any collection of nonfinancial measures will be the product of compromises, Green says. "The information that's most strategic—how customers view you versus competitors, for example—is nearly impossible to gather. And information that's readily available—your cost of processing an invoice, for example—doesn't tend to be highly strategic."[21]

Metro Bank

This case study originally appeared in Kaplan and Norton, From the Balanced Scorecard.

Metro Bank was the retail banking division of a major money center bank. It had 30 percent market share of the region's core deposit accounts; however, with deregulation, increased competition, and a lower interest rate environment, income from these retail accounts could no longer be sustained. A strategic review revealed excessive reliance on these accounts and a cost structure that could no longer profitably serve 80 percent of the bank's retail customers. Metro embarked upon a two-pronged strategy to deal with these two problems:

- *Revenue growth strategy.* This strategy reduces the volatility of earnings by broadening the sources of revenue with additional products for current customers.
- *Productivity strategy.* This strategy improves operating efficiency by shifting nonprofitable customers to more cost-effective channels of distribution (e.g., electronic banking instead of personal banking).

In the process of developing a balanced scorecard at Metro Bank, these two strategies were translated into objectives and measures in the four perspectives. Particular emphasis was placed on understanding and describing the cause and effect relationships on which the strategy was based. For the revenue growth strategy, the financial objectives were clear: broaden the revenue mix. Strategically, this meant that Metro would focus on its current customer base, identify the customers who would be likely candidates for a broader range of services, and then sell an expanded set of financial products and services to these targeted customers.

When customer objectives were analyzed, however, Metro's executives determined that its targeted customers did not view the bank, or their banker, as the logical source for a broader array of products such as mutual funds, credit cards, and financial advice. The executives concluded that if the bank's new strategy was to be successful, they must shift customers' perception of the bank from that of a transactions processor of checks and deposits to a financial adviser.

Having identified the financial objective—to broaden revenue mix— and the new customer value proposition dictated by the financial objective—to increase targeted customers confidence in Metro Bank's financial advice—the scorecard design process then focused on the internal activities that had to be mastered for the strategy to succeed. Three cross-business processes were identified: 1) understand customers, 2) develop new products and services, and 3) cross-sell multiple products and services. Each of these business processes would have to be redesigned to reflect the demands of the new strategy.

The selling process, for example, had historically been dominated by institutional advertising of the bank's services. Good advertising plus good location brought the customers to the banks. The branch personnel were reactive, helping customers to open accounts and to provide ongoing service. The bank did not have a selling culture. In fact, one study indicated that only 10 percent of a salesperson's time was spent with customers. A major reengineering program was initiated to redefine the sales process. The goal of the process was to create a relationship-selling approach where the salesperson became more of a financial advisor. Two measures of this process were included on the balanced scorecard. The *cross-sell ratio*—which is the average number of products sold to a household—measured selling effectiveness. This "lag indicator" would tell whether or not the new process was working. The second measure, *hours spent with customers,* was included to send a signal to salespersons throughout the organization of the new culture required by the strategy. A relationship-based sales approach could not work unless face-to-face time with customers increased. Hours spent with customers therefore was a "lead indicator" for the success of this piece of the strategy.

The internal objectives led naturally to a final set of factors to implement the revenue growth strategy. The learning and growth component of the scorecard identified the need for salespersons to undergo a major role change. This role change would require a broader set of skills (e.g., a financial counselor with broad knowledge of the product line), improved access to information (e.g., integrated customer files), and realignment of the incentive systems to encourage the new behavior. The lead indicators focused on the major changes that had to be orchestrated in the workforce:

- The upgrading of the skill base and qualified people, or the *strategic job coverage ratio*
- The access to information technology tools and data, or the *strategic information availability ratio*
- The realignment of individual goals and incentives to reflect the new priorities, or *personal goal alignment*[22]

The "lag indicators" included a productivity measure, average sales per salesperson, as well as the attitudes of the workforce as measured by an employee satisfaction survey.

National Insurance Company

This case study originally appeared in Kaplan and Norton, From the Balanced Scorecard.

National Insurance was a major property and casualty insurance firm that had been plagued by unsatisfactory results for the past decade. A new management team was brought in to turn the situation around. The strategy was to move the company away from its "generalist" approach—providing a full range of services to the full market—and move toward becoming a "specialist company that would focus on more narrowly defined niches." The new senior executive team identified several key success factors for its new specialist strategy:

- Become better at understanding and targeting desired market segments.
- Better select, educate, and motivate agents to pursue these segments.
- Improve the underwriting process as the focal point for executing this strategy.
- Better integrate information about claims into the underwriting process to improve market selectivity.

The executives selected the balanced scorecard as the primary tool for the new management team to use to lead the turnaround. They selected the scorecard because they believed it would help clarify the meaning of the new strategy to the organization and provide early feedback that the ship was turning. In the first step, the executives defined the strategic objectives for the new specialist strategy. They selected measures to make each objective operational by gaining agreement on the answer to a simple question, "How would we know if National Insurance achieved this objective?" The answers to this question yielded the set of "core outcome measures." The core outcome measures were also referred to as *strategic outcome measures* because they described the outcomes that the executives wished to achieve from each part of their new strategy.

The scorecard would not be meaningful if industry-specific measures did not appear, but these measures, by themselves, would be inadequate to signal the factors that would lead to superior performance within the industry. Besides having only industry-generic measures at this point in the scorecard development process, however, an additional problem became obvious. Every one of the outcome measures was a lagging indicator; the reported results for any of the measures reflected decisions and actions taken much earlier. For example, if new underwriting criteria were enacted, the results would not be reflected in the claims frequency for at least a year; the impact on the loss ratio would occur with an even longer delay.

The strategic outcome measures presented a "balanced" view of the strategy, reflecting customer, internal process, and learning and growth measures in addition to the traditional financial ones. But a scorecard consisting only of lagging indicators did not satisfy management's goal of providing early indicators of success. Nor did it help management to focus the entire organization on the drivers of future success: what people should be doing day-by-day to enable successful outcomes to be produced in the future. While the issue of balancing lagging outcome measures with leading performance driver measures occurs for all organizations, the extremely long lags between actions today and outcomes in the future were more pronounced in the property and casualty insurance company than in any other we have encountered.

National Insurance executives went through a second design iteration to determine the actions that people should be taking in the short-term to achieve the desired long-term outcomes. For each strategic outcome measure, they identified a complementary performance driver. In most cases, the performance drivers described how a business process was intended to change. For example, the strategic outcome measures for the underwriting process were:

- Loss ratio
- Claims frequency
- Claims severity

Improving performance of these measures required a significant improvement in the quality of the underwriting process itself. The executives developed criteria for what they considered to be "good underwriting." The criteria defined the actions desired when underwriting a new opportunity. The executives introduced a new business process to audit, periodically, a cross-section of policies for each underwriter; this auditing process could then be used to assess whether the policies issued by the underwriter were in conformance with these criteria. The audit would produce a measure, the Underwriting Quality Audit Score, which would show the percentage of new policies written that met the standards of the new underwriting process.

The theory behind this process is that the Underwriting Quality Audit Score would be the leading indicator (the performance driver) of the outcomes (e.g., loss ratio, claims frequency, and claims severity) that would be revealed much later. In addition to the underwriting quality audit process, similar programs were developed for outcome objectives related to agency management, new business development, and claims management. New metrics, representing performance drivers for these outcomes, were constructed to communicate and monitor near-term performance.

The National Insurance case again illustrates how the process of building a balanced scorecard creates change and results. Development of the performance-driver metrics forced executives to think through the way that work should be done in the future, and to introduce entirely new business processes the underwriting quality audit, the claims quality audit, and specific programs to enhance staff skills and expand information technology to employees. In addition to providing measures for the scorecard, the criteria developed by the executives for the underwriting quality and claims quality audits helped to develop improved underwriting and claims processes that could be communicated to the workforce. The underwriting and claims quality audit scores were not off-the-shelf measures. The executives developed unique, customized measures to reflect the new underwriting and claims processes they wished to see implemented at National Insurance.[23]

Henry Ford Health System

This case study originally appeared in Trustee.

Five years ago, board members at Detroit's Henry Ford Health System decided that the financial report they routinely received—two pages, including a balance sheet and operating statement—wasn't enough. They wanted to round out their knowledge of the system with information on measures such as patient and physician satisfaction and market share.

The idea came from the quality committee, says Vinod Sahney, Ph.D., senior vice president of planning and strategic development. Committee members asked him to help them develop a quality report with ten to fifteen nonfinancial indicators.

Sahney was happy to oblige. Just afterward, however, he stumbled upon an even better idea for monitoring the system's performance across multiple dimensions. An article in the *Harvard Business Review* advocated the use of a balanced scorecard. This measures organizational performance using "operational measures that are the drivers of future financial performance" (e.g., patient satisfaction and market share, to name just a few, that a typical health system might use) in addition to traditional financial measures. Such a scorecard, the authors insisted, would give top managers "a fast but comprehensive view" of the business.

That sounded like the right idea to trustees at Henry Ford. So they asked their executives to come up with a balanced scorecard for the system. That scorecard measures the system's progress in four main areas: growth, customer satisfaction, system integration, and being a low-cost provider. Three or four indicators are used to paint a picture of performance in each of these areas. "If you have too many indicators, people don't pay attention to them," says Sahney. "At the board level, we don't want more than fifteen."

Today, that balanced scorecard is the centerpiece of Henry Ford's strategic planning process. The board and management set the scores that the system will strive to achieve—for example, a $50 million bottom line in 1997—and managers make sure that their own efforts and the efforts of those under them are aligned with these goals. It can't just be lip service, either; executives' evaluations and bonuses are tied to achieving the performance targets set by the scorecard.

Despite its multiple levels of influence, the actual scorecard that the board sees is a simple diagram that fits easily on one sheet of paper, with room to spare. The circular diagram (which, in the lingo of continuous quality improvement, is known as a spider diagram) shows the extent to which the system is meeting its target goals for each of the measures listed.[24]

Allstate Insurance Company

The balanced scorecard does not work alone. Allstate Insurance Company uses a hybrid of popular performance measures, including balanced scorecard, EVA, customer satisfaction measurement, benchmarking, and others. This case study originally appeared in Best's Review.

Allstate's process, also known as the balanced scorecard, develops goals and strategies at the corporate and business unit levels, then allocates resources to reach those objectives. The Northbrook, Illinois–based company focuses on four areas: shareholders, customers, business processes, and employees. For example, Allstate improved operating income by tweaking a process in its claims department.

Allstate monitors shareholder value creation to see if its cash flow exceeds the cost of capital.

"We tailor these concepts to Allstate and develop what we think makes sense for us," Lauren Hall, assistant vice president of finance and planning, says. "The concepts are what's important, and I think corporations at times get in trouble when they carte blanche take those concepts and drop them into their organization. You need to understand the culture of your organization, understand the concept and then interpret that concept into your organization."

Insurers are loath to depend on just one performance measure. They say it's important to rely on a variety of benchmarks—financial and non-financial. "What are the business economics that cause growth and profitability?" Allstate's Hall says. "It's customer satisfaction, it's growing your customer base, it's having processes that enable you to satisfy those customers and be efficient, and it's having employees with skills and capabilities to have those 'best in class' processes. All those things fit together. If you start focusing only on profitability, at times you really don't have a handle on the drivers of profitability."[25]

Conclusion

Each company will blend measurement tools as best fits its needs. This chapter has summarized a variety of tools that you will find useful in different areas of your measurement program—including identification and focusing, analysis, and application. Don't just stick to one tool that you find most useful in each stage. Try many different tools in varying situations and see which helps most. Companies like Metro Bank, which combines process value analysis with a scorecard, or Allstate, which combines EVA with a scorecard, have the opportunity to view a situation from a variety of angles that not every company is able to use to its advantage.

5

Measuring and Reporting Internal Performance

Introduction

A common measurement problem is the need to identify performance for different divisions of a corporation. Different divisions can represent either similar operations or different operations.

In the event of similar operations, the companies that participated in the research for this book reported that most of the time they maintained performance measures at the divisional level. The most common roll-up was at the geographic level if the products were similar. If products were dissimilar, the measures program generally did not segregate performance and instead followed product-related divisions separately.

Divisionalizing Performance

Since divisionalized data sets up a good comparison tool among companies, measurement groups use the data to compare performance and practices among groups. Historically, it has been common for companies to have a "best division" status or benchmark for performance. The measures processes we are now seeing look beyond the traditionally competitive nature of divisions to improve the companies on an overall basis.

Companies such as Intel use the performance statistics at each plant as an opportunity to leverage improvement opportunities with each other and thereby improve the overall performance of the organization. In this way the overall health and growth of the organization is emphasized over the performance of specific plants or divisions.

In the event of different operations, frequently financial measures still play an important role. Since the product margins and markets differ for different groups, straight measures need to be tailored back to the situations that led to the performance. In the Intel example, the current technology processors typically have the greatest margins, while the older products have correspondingly lower margins. This puts the production of an 80386 processor behind the Pentium in what it can achieve. Intel knows this and sets up specific margins for each product along with a specific set of expectations.

Unfortunately, there is often mistrust in corporations between divisional offices and corporate headquarters. While headquarters may establish measurement policies, it is up to the division to self-report statistics. Thus, it is important that the divisions are involved in setting measures initially. They need to understand why specific measures are important at the corporate level, and headquarters needs to understand which measures are specifically relevant at the operational level.

Charters for Performance Measurement

A charter for performance measurement is simply a document that outlines the mission and provides further details on measurement goals and responsibilities. While it is helpful to have a charter in order to gain organizational buy-in, it is not a necessary step. Where it becomes more necessary is in companies that will have measurement in multiple locations or multiple business units.

Participants in the Corporate Performance Measurement Benchmarking Study were asked if business units had charters for performance measurement and, if so, whether they were separate, tied to a corporate document, or a combination.

Separate performance measurement charters occur when the corporation requires little more than that measurement be performed. It is left up to the individual business units to determine how to carry out the measurement.

Performance measurement charters tied to a corporate document occur when headquarters outlines the mission, goals, and even individual measures for business units.

Of course, some charters can have elements of both. We left the answer open so that companies could respond "yes" to both questions. It is possible to have a business unit measurement charter that is tied to a corporate document but still be a separate charter. For example, corporate might outline the mission while the business units are left to the details of the individual goals.

The question becomes one of degree of acceptable autonomy for business units. Some corporations take an extremely centralized approach while others take a more decentralized approach. The Motorola case (see Chapter 9) is an example of a centralized mandate requiring decentralized solutions. We hypothesized that most companies would take a similar stance on centralization to the one they take in most other operations.

Reasons for separate charters might include the need for added flexibility to address significant differences in the business environments. Reasons to be tied to a corporate document include the attainment of efficiencies in the measurement process. Additionally, it is often helpful to have business units collecting the same measurements for comparison purposes.

As you can see from Figure 5-1, a significant majority of the companies reported business unit measurement charters tied to a corporate document. Even so, close to half of the companies also considered their business unit performance measurement charters to be "separate."

Upon further discussions, we found specific policies and procedures mandated by a corporate group. Typically corporate groups are driving the process.

Even so, you cannot force a decentralized corporation to be centralized in one aspect or vice versa without pain. A corporation that is suc-

Figure 5-1. Charters for performance measurement.

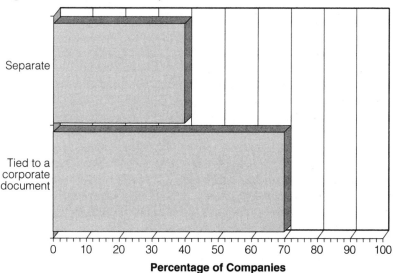

Percentage of Companies

cessful with a decentralized structure should have separate charters for business units; one that is highly centralized should keep measurement charters tied to a corporate document.

Assuming, though, that your corporation is somewhat middle of the road, you should probably look at the following questions:

- What measures are so critical to corporate performance that all business units should collect them (i.e., you should probably mandate them corporately)?
- Do the business units typically have customers in common (if so, customer satisfaction goals should be similar)?
- Do employees transfer easily/frequently between business units (if so, employee incentives should be similar)?

The answers to these questions will give you a guideline for where measurement should be linked. Otherwise, it can be helpful to leave your business units flexibility while providing them opportunities to learn from other business units whenever possible.

Formalizing Measures

Once measures are defined, they must be formalized and routinized. While measures have a fluid life cycle, as previously discussed, they must be formal at a given point in time for communication and collections purposes.

Many companies find a need to keep centralized control of what measures are in use. They find that, given the opportunity, many individual departments or managers will overmeasure. Focusing on a handful of strategic measures is much more important than a sea of detailed measures. Also, corporations find a need to maintain consistency within divisions that might otherwise form a separate measurement program.

All measures must be carefully defined. Think of all the ways that a retailer could calculate inventory turns, for example. On one hand, the turn rate can represent the entire inventory sold in the last year related to the sales of the retailer. One may wish to treat specific types of inventory differently. For example, active inventory, inventory by department, obsolete inventory, or inventory on consignment may be expected to have significant differences in turn rates.

The same goes for revenues. Does one count all revenues, or just some part of the revenues? These seemingly minor distortions make almost all measures incomparable. A standards organization oversees the development of measures so that they conform to the needs of the organization.

Policies for Recording Critical Performance Measures and Actual Performance

We asked each participating company if it had a specific policy that directed how critical performance measures and the actual performance to them were to be recorded.

Critical performance measures are those measures that contribute directly to the success or failure of a corporation. Typically a company will narrow down the multiple measures to three or four key measures that chart the overall success of the corporation.

A policy might address definitions, specific extraordinary items to exclude, frequency of data collection, an appropriate distribution list, and confidentiality.

The intent of the question was to explore whether specific policies regarding critical performance measures and the recording of actual measures were important to a successful measurement program.

As you can see from Figure 5-2, a majority of the participating companies had such a policy. From further research we found that typical policies outlined a variety of topics:

- Definition of measures
- Sources of measures (internal and external)
- Reporting frequency
- Relationships with outside firms to compare data

Figure 5-2. Policies that direct the recording of critical performance measures and actual performance.

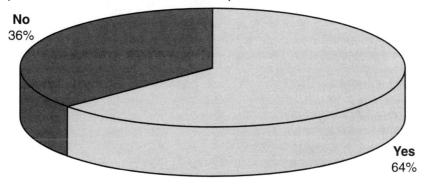

No
36%

Yes
64%

Those companies that did not have policies addressing critical performance measures felt they could do so based on measures developed by the field. They let the field define their own measures. For instance, Chevron allows all its business units the ability to set detailed measures in addition to the corporate measures.

While it appears to be important to have a good understanding of the measures that are being taken and which ones more closely define success for the corporation, a written policy regarding these critical performance measures does not seem to be critical to the measurement process. In fact, the written policy may be somewhat limiting.

Identifying Similarity in Divisions

When divisions are similar, it makes more sense for measurement to be centralized. That way, divisional performance can be more easily compared. As in the Intel example, though, it is possible for divisions to be compared on some aspects while not on others. Divisional characteristics that you will want to probe for similarities include physical characteristics (e.g., size, dollar revenues, capital employed, geographics, cost of labor), market characteristics (e.g., margins, competitors, innovations, ability to change, market agility, product life cycle), and distribution characteristics (e.g., channels, physical characteristics, costs to distribute). Figure 5-3 shows this graphically. Keep in mind, divisional similarities and differences usually cannot be normalized (that is, you just can't add 10 percent to get from one division's scores to another).

Physical characteristics are those that define the firm itself. These may change substantially in the long run but are generally static, or slow to change, in the short run. Physical characteristics include:

- *Size.* Company size can be measured by the number of employees. This factor represents the "bench strength" of the company in taking on large and complicated tasks. For example, an engineering company can be just one or two people. When competing against a firm in the thousands, the size and complexity of projects becomes an issue. Big companies can do things that small companies cannot.

- *Dollar revenues.* Since the ability to achieve scale advantage is important to competition, the total dollar revenues of the companies are important. The common administrative costs for large companies are amortized over a larger number of projects and become a smaller part of the larger companies.

Figure 5-3. Divisional characteristics.

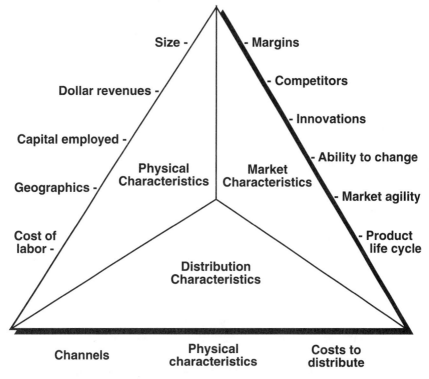

- *Capital employed.* Certain industries (e.g., chemical manufacturing) require the large expenditure of capital for the purpose of building plants and purchasing equipment to conduct their business. Other service businesses do not have the same capital requirement.

- *Geographics.* A firm's geographics greatly influence its cost structure and logistics requirements. Costs (e.g., labor, taxes, real estate) will vary by location, but so will infrastructure. In order to keep cycle time low, one must often locate near suppliers and customers.

- *Cost of labor.* Certain industries have a higher cost of labor in order to conduct their efforts. For example, the accounting profession requires the use of licensed CPAs to conduct its business. This is substantially more expensive than using nonlicensed bookkeepers.

Market characteristics vary greatly by product and may be either static or quick to change, depending on the industry. For example, new competitors enter high tech industries daily while the steel industry has a relatively stable set of competitors. Market characteristics include:

- *Margins.* Margins are a key differentiator of businesses. They determine the nature of what the market is willing to price a product compared with what it costs to produce a product. Margins for some similar products are substantially different. The automobile industry is the best example of the differences. The midsize family car is a commodity, carrying a minimal markup and arguably providing most of the profit on sale of aftermarket parts. On the other end of the spectrum is the sport/utility vehicle. This segment has high margins and is priced at a premium.

- *Competitors.* Competitors influence industry pricing. A few industries exist without natural competitors. Some of these industries are natural monopolies because they make small products for which the markets are so thin that there are only one or two producers (an example is the cellophane market).

- *Innovations.* Innovation also drives divisional similarities. Certain industries, like the personal computer industry, have a high degree of innovation, while other industries, like the silicone industry, can have the same product for fifty years.

- *Ability to change.* Specifically, this is the ability of a company to change from one product to another. Frequently, companies are locked into producing just one product and find it difficult to innovate past the basic products.

- *Market agility.* Market agility is the speed at which innovation is introduced, from the time a new idea is generated to the time that it is introduced to the end customers.

- *Product life cycle.* There are inherent changes in product profitability due to the age of the product. Products typically move from "hot" high-margin products to commodity-like products. Keep in mind that the length of the life cycle (or shape of the life-cycle curve) may differ by product. It is also possible to renew an old product (e.g., the repopularizing of Winnie the Pooh and other Disney characters).

Distribution characteristics describe the way products are provided to the end customers. These can include:

- *The costs to distribute.* Here we can compare the costs of shipping solids versus liquids, heavy versus light goods, bulky versus non-bulky goods, and so on.
- *Product physical characteristics.* These characteristics also play a role in differentiating products. Caustic products may have a different handling due to environmental concerns. The ability of products to be damaged also plays a role in the characteristics of distribution.

■ *Channels of distribution.* Some products are sold directly to the end customer through either direct sales or telephone. Others go through multiple levels of distributors.

Reporting Internal Measurement

Once measures are formalized and integrated into the business units, a company must have an effective method of reporting information companywide. A measurement program means nothing unless it is also able to modify behavior. To do that, every employee must understand the measures, their individual role in improvement, and that improvement potential is real. Reports can be as simple as a Microsoft Excel spreadsheet or as complex as an interactive system accessible by managers from their PCs.

There are a variety of ways the measurement group can report back to the process owners. The breakdown on methods from the group we surveyed follows:

■ Conducted readout sessions (37.5 percent)
■ Attended employee meetings (87.5 percent)
■ Reported in newsletters (87.5 percent)
■ Issued special reports (75 percent)
■ Sent on-line mass e-mail (62.5 percent)

Notice that all the companies used multiple methods. Periodic data reviews provide a structured mechanism for reporting data to relevant units within the corporation or corporatewide. Face-to-face presentation/ discussion sessions with key groups of stakeholders can build commitment to the process and can lead to more action resulting from the data. Like any other communication effort, repetition is key to creating a lasting message. Also, it is important to target the audience specifically. Executives may find e-mail most convenient while factory workers want to hear about it in employee meetings. The following example is excerpted from the *Small Business News-Akron*.

Babcock & Wilcox's Nuclear Equipment Division provides a good example of how to motivate the process owners as your messengers. More than anyone else, process owners have the credibility to create enthusiasm for measurement. The history of union-management relations at Babcock & Wilcox's Nuclear Equipment Division is typical of old-line manufacturers. So when B&W's union-management steering committee formed a team to reduce the amount of money spent on sand in the foundry, the initial results were predictable. At the first meeting of the shop managers, technicians, and union production workers chosen for the project, all seven sat in a room waiting for someone else to speak up. A year later, however, they were making detailed group presentations to audiences as large as 1,500 about the technical improvements they recommended. These recommendations helped the foundry's waste better meet Environmental Protection Agency (EPA) standards, reduced the risk of accidents caused by molten-steel runouts, and saved the company $600,000 by reengineering the movement of sand throughout the production process.[26]

What follows is a series of case studies that highlights how different companies report measurements. Notice that the main goal is always to present a complex picture in the simplest way possible.

Nucor Corporation (Nucor Steel Division)

At Nucor, simplicity in presentation makes measurement quite relevant and meaningful. In order to keep costs low, standard presentation formats are used. Throughout its annual report, Nucor Steel uses only one format for presenting all of its data, the horizontal bar chart. This has been a characteristic of its reports for many years. Figure 5-4 shows the common format used by Nucor to present its financial and operational data.

Figure 5-4. Standard bar chart format for presenting operational data.

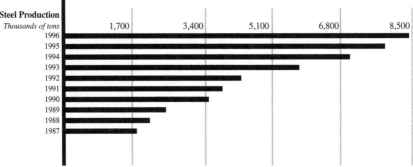

Source: Nucor Corporation.

Suburban Hospital

This case study originally appeared in Trustee.

Mark Rothman remembers the days when his board went over a twelve-page finance report at every meeting. "It was boring for everybody," laughs Rothman, who as former finance committee chairman for Suburban Hospital of Rockville, Maryland, had the dubious honor of presenting a summary of the hospital's balance sheet, profit and loss statement, and detailed information on utilization, revenue sources, and cash flow.

To make matters worse, trustees frequently got bogged down in the report's unnecessary details. For example, someone might ask why computerized tomography (CT) scan volume was down in July, and the board would then spend anywhere from five to twenty minutes discussing it. "The level of detail presented distracted people away from global issues," notes CEO Brian Grissler.

Those kinds of discussions don't take place anymore. Shortly after Grissler became chief executive, he and the trustees sat down and changed their approach to keeping trustees informed. And now, says Grissler, "It takes five minutes to give the board a quick picture of what's going on in the institution."

That picture emerges from a few key reports, all of which are short and easy to read. Trustees now get a one-page, dashboard-style version of the twelve-page finance report (which is no longer reviewed during board meetings), along with one-page summaries of the other committee reports (which previously added up to another inch or more of paper). The hospital's progress on each of its strategic initiatives is briefly reviewed in Grissler's report to the board, which is distributed in advance. Quarterly, he also adds benchmarking information that shows trustees "in a quick, visual way" how the hospital compares on a dozen or so key variables with local competitors, other comparable hospitals statewide and nationally, and other A+ and A-1 rated hospitals.

How has this new package of information affected the board's ability to contribute to the hospital's success? "It's enhanced it," says Grissler. "It's allowed them to spend their time and energy on policy and strategic issues, and that's where their value is for the hospital; it's not in determining whether the table saw in the capital budget is better than the table saw they can buy at Home Depot for less money. But when I came here, there was that level of discussion."

Chairman Robert Snider agrees. "We were a good board, but now we're a better board. Going over too many details was wasting too much time." Now his trustees have more time to devote to the important issues, such as converting their organization from a hospital to a system. They're also able to have half-hour educational sessions at the start of each meeting and still finish up in two hours tops. Before, board meetings often ran as long as three hours. And even though they now receive less paper, Snider believes trustees are now getting a more sophisticated picture of how their hospital is doing.

Which all goes to show that when it comes to data, less is often more. "Overwhelming paper can prevent board members from asking the tough questions," observes Grissler. "Very few board members will read two inches of paper. It's a lot of confusing mumbo jumbo and unconnected dots. It's top management's job to connect the dots for trustees; to interpret it, not just lay it out."[27]

BC Rail

This case study originally appeared in CMA *magazine.*

During the early 1990s, BC Rail had developed business unit scorecards containing financial and productivity information. The scorecards summarized the measures available from existing information systems; little emphasis was placed on establishing new measures. The scorecards were incorporated only into the monthly corporate financial statement package. Although business managers initially viewed them as useful tools for consolidating information, the scorecards never came to be considered integral to the management process. Why not?

A major flaw was the lack of a direct link between the performance scorecards and corporate goals. Although BC Rail had completed a strategic plan in 1990–1991, the company had failed to recognize the significance of the plan to the development of performance metrics. When it updated its strategic plan [in 1996], the company needed to rethink how it used and communicated its metrics. Most important, the performance measures had to become a direct outcome of the strategic plan.

As it worked through this process, the company established consensus on each component necessary to achieve its strategies and goals. Strong CEO leadership created an environment that encouraged innovation and creative thinking throughout the planning process.

The performance measures established while developing the strategic plan must be implemented throughout the company in order to align areas that might have had competing objectives. If an area integral to strong customer service is encouraged to cut costs, the company must carefully balance that area's emphases on service delivery (to maintain market share) and cost management (to maintain or reduce pricing). A useful tool in aligning apparently conflicting departmental objectives is technology such as client-server software for reviewing and analyzing performance against plan. This technology allows the company to distribute information to many people, both rapidly and cost-effectively.

Given their expertise in using technology to collect, summarize, and distribute information, it made sense for BC Rail's financial managers to take on the task of seeking out and selecting particular software products to help them manage and report on performance measures. Their challenge: In broadening BC Rail's reporting to include key metrics across widely varying disciplines, how can the company assemble and distribute text and graphical information in a cost-effective, timely way while reducing the workload of the financial reporting staff? In essence, how to do more with less?

The company had considered several products that would allow it to move from its traditional paper-based financial reporting system toward an electronic system, but it had balked at the stiff entry costs of most executive information systems software. Now, less expensive products had become available, including the package that BC Rail eventually purchased: PB Views from Panorama Business Views. Like today's intranets, this software allows users to scroll through electronic information (text and graphics) and zero in on pertinent information.

The resulting product—a relatively small PB Views information system, properly interfaced with the corporate and divisional systems—allows the company to share the performance measure results, as well as provide focus and alignment with key corporate and department targets. BC Rail (or any organization) can also use such software as a reference source to link performance measures directly with action plans for improvement. And because these action plans are linked to individual managers' annual performance reviews, the company can provide financial incentives in a pay-for-performance compensation plan.

Like a management briefing book, a good performance measurement system provides current reporting and analysis across many key business indicators. By using an organizational hierarchy of measures—in which each measure gets a percentage weighting within the family tree of departmental or area measures—divisional and corporate management can assess their own performance. Not all metrics are equally critical. Establishing a relative weighting enables the company to focus on the key metrics across the balance scorecard. The color-coding feature of PC-networked software allows the company to quickly determine which measures or groups of measures are below target and need to be addressed. Color-coded briefing book tabs permit this ready reference to performance. Using a PC-driven projector, managers can view a wall-sized reference panel to facilitate discussion on key drivers of improved performance.[28]

Sun Microsystems: Data Visualization

This case study originally appeared in Industry Week.

Sun Microsystems has adopted a data visualization technique that allows it to be flexible yet extremely detailed in the presentation of findings.

"The task at Sun was not to develop the awareness for quality or to create the data, but to use data visualization to integrate and graphically present the quality tracking metrics that were already being collected by our global operations," says James Lynch, Sun's director of corporate quality. (The firm consists of five operating companies spread across more than thirty countries.)

"Our mission was to develop and implement a scalable tool that could present a macro view of information to executive users and more detailed information to Sun's 15,000 employees in North and South America, the Pacific Rim, and Europe."

First visualized in the early 1990s by Scott McNealy, Sun's chairman and CEO, the system incorporates refinements he acquires through regularly scheduled idea exchanges with other CEOs—including Fred Smith of Federal Express, Gary Tooker at Motorola, and Paul Allaire of Xerox.

Sun based its quality information system on data visualization software from SAS Institute Inc., of Cary, North Carolina. Designed to run on its Solaris operating system and distributed on the Sun Wide Area Network, Sun's system distributes corporate quality information to all its global locations. Lynch says data visualization speeds and simplifies comprehension, which is an important issue, considering that 15,000 Sun employees routinely access the system.

One of the most important features allows viewers to drill down into the information hierarchy for data on the consolidated customer dissatisfiers and geographic or product-specific information. The index also includes analysis capabilities such as goals versus actuals, key drivers, control charts, and costs of seventeen of the thirty-two customer dissatisfiers that the company has identified. The data visualization software also has the capability to relate what those seventeen dissatisfiers are costing Sun financially, on a per-share basis.

Now in the second year of operation, the system has documented a reduction in the overall number of customer dissatisfiers, despite substantial growth in volume of shipments and installed user base, says Lynch. "In some cases, we had growth as high as 20 percent, but we were still able to reduce the absolute number of dissatisfiers."

He says there are plans to amplify data visualization capabilities by integrating the SAS software with Sun's Java technology. Still under development, that could add such capabilities as real-time calculations and animation to the data visualization capabilities of the system.

Lynch believes the success and the visibility of the system is influencing other management reporting activities at Sun. "It is motivating people to rethink how they're managing key metrics in their organization to accomplish the results that they've targeted." For example, the company's financial managers are considering the data visualization approach for financial reporting systems, involving key indexes (such as inventory turns) in closing the books.[29]

Not every company needs to have a system as complex as the one used by Sun Microsystems. While Sun's system allows each division to view the statistics and comparisons most pertinent to its operation, it is an expensive undertaking. Many other forms of presenting simplified information work well in less complex circumstances. The most important qualities to remember in internal reporting are simplicity and clarity. If the manager's do not grasp the relevance of the measurement (as the BC Rail managers didn't) or get too bogged down in details (as the board at Suburban Hospital did), the effort of measurement is wasted.

Establishing Performance Standards

Internal comparisons are important, but ultimately companies are confronted with the need to come up with a set of performance standards or objectives. Many executives are challenged to set goals for measures they don't fully understand. For this reason, it is often necessary to incorporate measures brought in from outside sources—for example, industry studies and environment statistics—and report them alongside internal measures.

Chevron

While most companies see measurement at the micro-level, Chevron looks at measurement as a global strategy. The question "How is the company doing?" is constantly displayed at the corporate and business unit levels.

Chevron looks at eight key performance measures to gauge progress towards achieving their vision of being "Better than the Best" of their competitors. Chevron uses its Corporate Vision Metrics to communicate to

employees the key drivers that will enable them to achieve the vision and
current performance within these drivers.

Figure 5-5 is a model of Chevron's Vision Metrics. Components of
Chevron's vision are shown in the bubbles and the associated metrics are
identified under each component. This model clearly shows the *cause-
and-effect* relationships between vision components. Chevron's primary
objective of superior stockholder return is the result of superior performance in the other Vision Metric components. The Vision Metrics are updated quarterly, displayed at all Chevron facilities, and are also available
to employees via Chevron's Intranet.

The Vision Metrics provide Chevron's employees with a snapshot of
the corporation's overall performance. The metrics also provide business
units and operating locations a framework for communicating their local
performance measures. Often, business units will display their performance metrics beside the Vision Metrics, allowing people in the field to
see how their performance makes a difference to the corporation as a
whole.

Following are descriptions of the metrics used to track Chevron's vision of becoming "Better than The Best." Where possible, Vision Metrics
not only report current Chevron performance, but also report relevant
trends and comparisons with meaningful peer competitors or internal targets.

Safety Metric

Providing a safe work environment is fundamental to business at Chevron.
Chevron uses the OSHA (Occupational Safety and Health Administration)

Figure 5-5. Chevron's Vision Metrics.

Source: Chevron.

index to calculate its safety performance. By using the OSHA reporting methodology, Chevron can compare safety performance to that of its peer competitors. See Figure 5-6 for an example of how safety metrics are reported.

Employee Commitment Index Metric

Employee commitment is an expression of attitudes toward an individual's organization, one's job, and one's behavior on the job. Chevron conducts a periodic Worldwide Employee Survey (WES) to gather information on employee commitment and satisfaction. The information collected from the WES is used at the corporate, business unit, and departmental levels to bring about positive change at Chevron. See Figure 5-7 for an example of how employee commitment index metrics are reported.

Customer Satisfaction Metric

Customer satisfaction is an indicator of the degree to which customers prefer Chevron's products and services over its competitors. As Chevron

Figure 5-6. Chevron's safety report.

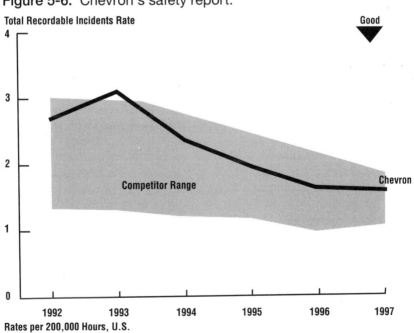

Source: Chevron.

Figure 5-7. Chevron's employee commitment index report.

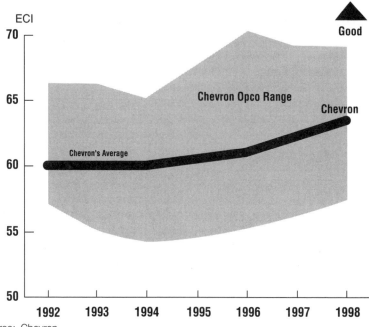

Source: Chevron.

offers a variety of products and services worldwide, the customer satisfaction metric highlights a different operating company's performance each quarter. See Figure 5-8 for an example of how customer satisfaction metrics are reported.

Public Favorability Index

Chevron strives to be viewed favorably, as compared to its competitors. How the public perceives a company can influence the degree to which it is welcome in the community. Public perception is influenced by many things including environmental record, financial performance, advertising, employee attitudes outside of work, and customer satisfaction. Through random telephone interviews with both customers and noncustomers, Chevron tracks public favorability with Chevron, its peer competitors, and the oil industry in general. See Figure 5-9 for an example of how public favorability indexes are reported.

Total Shareholder Return Metric

Total shareholder return (TSR) is a key financial measure which defines Chevron's "Better than The Best" vision. Chevron measures its TSR per-

Figure 5-8. Chevron's customer satisfaction report.

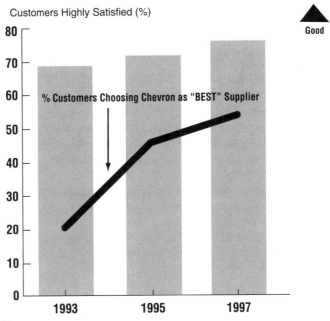

Source: Chevron.

formance relative to peer competitors and the S&P 500. See Figure 5-10 for an example of how total shareholder return metrics are reported.

Operating Expense Metric

Operating expense per barrel is a measure of overall corporate efficiency, which is a primary driver of profitability. By measuring unit operating expense, Chevron can realize improvements either by lowering absolute costs or by gaining economies of scale through higher volumes. Being an efficient, low-cost provider of products and services is vital to competing in the commodity-driven industry in which Chevron competes. See Figure 5-11 for an example of how operating expense metrics are reported.

Return on Capital Employed Metric

Return on capital employed (ROCE, the ratio of operating earnings to average capital employed) is a capital effectiveness measure. Earning a respectable return on invested capital is a critical driver of profitability in the capital-intensive petrochemical industry. See Figure 5-12 for an example of how return on capital employed metrics are reported.

Figure 5-9. Chevron's public favorability index report.

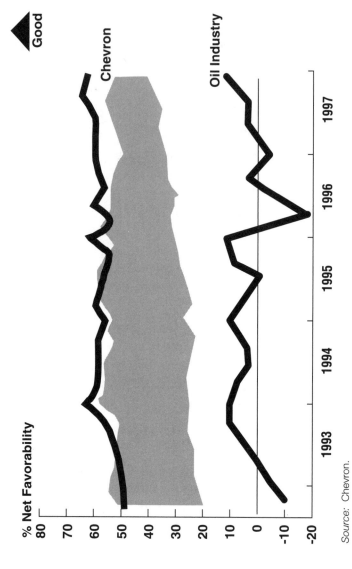

Source: Chevron.

Figure 5-10. Chevron's total stockholder return report.

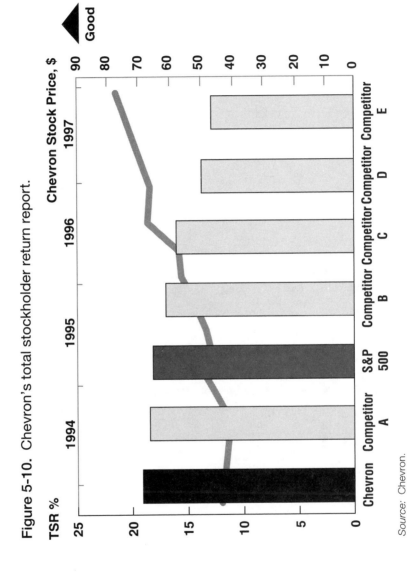

Source: Chevron.

Figure 5-11. Chevron's operating expenses report.

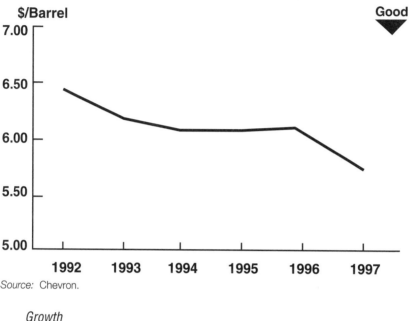

Source: Chevron.

Growth

Growing the business is a strategic imperative for Chevron. Earnings growth is an important driver of profitability. Volume growth is also tracked to eliminate commodity price effects that heavily influence the earnings metric. See Figure 5-13 for an example of how growth metrics are reported.

Conclusion

While everyone recognizes that internal measurement is important, it can present a very difficult task for those companies that are divisionalized or that have multiple locations. There must be some degree of control centrally so that similar measures can be analyzed and compared across locations. Yet, measures must be established that are both meaningful to the individual divisions and to the corporation as a whole. Most companies have found that a mix of central and local measures is the most effective route.

Once corporatewide measurement is established, the issue of meaning crops up again when reporting those measures back to the divisions. BC Rail found the scorecard it reported back to managers was not being

Figure 5-12. Chevron's annualized return on capital employed.

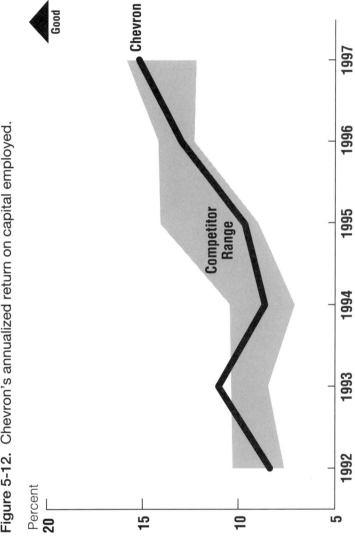

Source: Chevron.

Figure 5-13. Chevron's growth report.

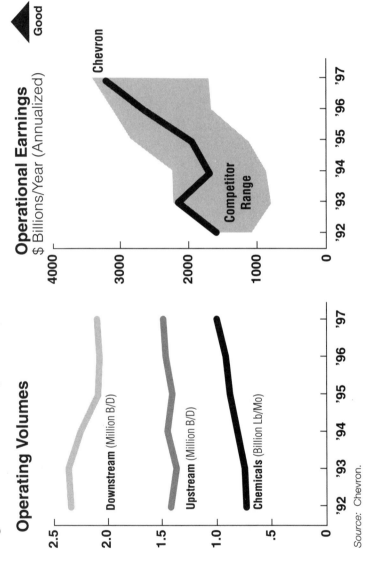

Source: Chevron.

used because it wasn't linked to operational objectives. Sun Microsystems has implemented a sophisticated technology solution to this problem. Through data visualization, its employees can get needed high-level information or query the system for more detailed background information.

Every company, though, will need to go beyond internal measurement to establish appropriate goals and to monitor the environment. The next two chapters deal with specific types of external measurement—customer satisfaction measurement and benchmarking.

6

Customer Satisfaction Measurement

Introduction

An analysis of gaps between customer expectations and corporate performance is key to monitoring corporate performance. Companies today are relying on customers to drive corporate products and services because, ultimately, it is the customer who decides whether process outcomes are acceptable or not. Customers can also be a source of competitive information (e.g., customers may be asked to rate products on a questionnaire).

A study of the winners of the Wisconsin Manufacturer of the Year (MOTY) award in *Corporate Report Wisconsin* pointed to the benefits of getting employees involved, but also involving customers in the improvement process.

> Winners consistently pointed to three areas—"customer focus, market niche targeting, and employee focus—as the key factors for developing a sustainable competitive advantage. Use of a structured approach for getting customer feedback was considered to be critical. Smaller companies tended to use a telemarketing approach, while larger companies tended to use surveys. The companies that used surveys most effectively were the ones that created measures of customer satisfaction and based action plans on the results, and/or the companies that directed their feedback to formal corrective action efforts. Company personnel at these companies participate in visits to customers. Among the most common measurements of customer satisfaction were "on-time performance, complete order

shipments, and improvement in survey results year-to-year." Typical feedback mechanisms in the short-term included monthly mail-out surveys and surveys that were sent with orders. A distinguishing feature of successful innovation and product development programs was immersion with the customer. A number of successful companies also included customers in the strategic planning process.

In addition, each of the thirteen successful companies identified market niche targeting as a key success factor. Market niching, in this context, refers to segmenting your customer base into distinct markets; identifying one or more groups of value buyers in each market; and tailoring your product/service package to each unique buyer group. Often, sales bonuses, incentives, and measures to monitor performance supported the niching strategy. A strong employee involvement focus was the third success factor.

Factors contributing to a successful employee involvement effort were the establishment of strong trust and communication, provision of training, and implementation of empowerment for employees. Communication regarding the company's financial results, the goals of management, and objectives for improvement were seen as vital. It was also seen as critical to obtain employee feedback. Training was also important to success of employee involvement. Incentive plans were seen as an enhancement to employee involvement efforts.

Customer satisfaction measurement (CSM), then, provides that necessary link between the outside world and the products and services of each organization.[30]

Importance of the Customer

Customers are:

- The users or buyers of your product and/or service
- Internal (corporate) or external (end customer)
- Definers of quality who can complain if expectations are not met

External customers are those individuals and businesses we typically consider customers—those who buy or use your end product or service. Many people don't think about their *internal* customers. These customers are employees within the corporation who use another group's services to perform their jobs. Examples might include a corporate planning group that uses high-level trend analysis or a director of manufacturing that needs to monitor the performance of specific equipment.

In all processes, customers will similarly fall into the internal and external classifications. While products and services like financing and information systems serve internal customers, billing, accounts receivable, credit, customer service, accounts payable, and others clearly service external customers.

Clearly, external increases in loyalty lead to higher price premiums. Customers are willing to pay more for exceptional service. This service can come from any customer interaction point. One's opinion of various long-distance telephone services, for example, is affected not only by the quality of the call, but by experiences with billing errors or other interfaces with the company. Realize, too, every company has a service aspect whether they are traditionally thought of as a manufacturing environment or not.

When a company earns a reputation for quality in service, it can charge higher prices. This increase in both the customer base and the revenue dollars increases the overall stability of the organization. It no longer has to fight for customers based on price and has a known loyal customer base.

When business operations are stabilized, the company can afford to make changes that will reduce operating costs. For example, there may be fewer dramatic changes in marketing plans. Much less effort is put toward maintaining a steady marketing plan than constantly revising one. Of course, one shouldn't take this to mean that there is no creativity left in the company; stabilizing and routinizing operations allows a company to cut daily costs.

The flip side of the coin is growth. If the company has a loyal customer base and is not fighting for survival, it can leverage that base or those profits into new growth opportunities. The company could investigate new products or services, thereby strengthening the relationship with the customer once again. And the cycle repeats itself. There is no real beginning or end to this cycle.

Figure 6-1 shows the chaining of customer needs and how the needs relate to the ultimate cycle of profitability for the organization. Since it is a cycle, there is no end to the process.

In many magazines, experts have been quoted as saying that companies can boost profits by almost 100 percent by retaining just 5 percent more of their customers. This factor, more than all others, points at the value of the process.

Figure 6-1. Customer-needs-to-profitability cycle.

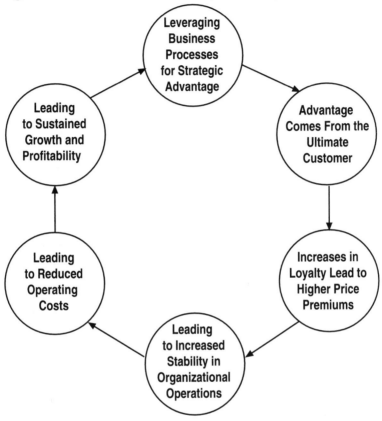

What Is Customer Satisfaction Measurement?

Frequently companies develop their own misconceptions that begin to act as surrogates for real customer needs. These become an integral part of the belief structure and actually get in the way of real improvement. It is nearly impossible to convince a group that believes that it is "perfect" that improvement is possible.

In an article in *Marketing News,* Entergy Corporation, a major utility holding company, reviewed its philosophies relative to customer satisfaction. Its viewpoints represent a philosophy that can keep an organization focused on true customer satisfaction:

- Customers don't know how the business works.
- You are not in touch if your customers think that they get "poor" answers to their "logical" questions.

- Customers believe you need to be more sensitive to the impact of your actions on their business.
- Prompt service is the single most important concern to the customer.
- Remain open to new reasons behind what you think causes customer concerns.[31]

Customer satisfaction measurement is a series of processes that gather real information about what past, current, and future customers perceive about a product. CSM examines gaps relative to expectations and competitive products, then turns the results into actionable findings to close the gaps. Gaps in performance are typically characterized as "dissatisfaction" with the product or service:

> Usually customers begin to experience dissatisfaction when they feel they are no longer getting superior relative value from their current supplier. Thus, customer satisfaction becomes a leading indicator for predicting revenue growth in relation to total market growth or market share.[32]

Some sources of dissatisfaction include performance gaps related to:

- Taking customers for granted (i.e., not attempting to fully understand customer needs and concerns)
- Price (e.g., customers feel that they are overpaying for services)
- Quality (e.g., too many errors)
- Delivery times (e.g., products or services that take too long to prepare)
- "Gaps" in expectations (e.g., overselling the benefits of the product, then finding the final product does not meet expectations)

When performance gaps are identified, customer needs can be fulfilled and dissatisfaction avoided. It is only when we can identify where the gaps exist that we develop measures for improving performance and customer satisfaction. Leading-edge management sees these gaps as an opportunity to improve performance.

Organization of CSM

Depending on the size and complexity of your customer base, CSM can be a relatively simple task tracked by your sales force or a highly complex task with its own organization. CSM is also a popular program to out-source because it may take extensive labor to conduct a survey, yet the work only occurs a few times per year, not consistently.

Should You Outsource?

Most corporations surveyed in the Corporate Performance Measurement Benchmarking Study are administering their customer satisfaction program in-house. Eighty percent of corporations are administering the program in-house, while only 20 percent of corporations are outsourcing the management activity. However, a larger component of participants used outside service bureaus for actual surveying activities.

You might consider the use of consultants in the design and development of customer satisfaction measurement tools, particularly if you do not have that type of expertise in-house. Also, if you have lengthy assessment tools or believe that customers would be concerned about anonymity issues, outsourcing data collection might be helpful. If you do administer customer satisfaction assessments in-house, be sure that you have the staff capability and systems support available to do this work. Geographically dispersed and/or small decentralized business units may not always have the resources to administer these kinds of assessments themselves. In these instances, a corporate group or outsourcing may be an option.

Who Should Be Responsible for Customer Satisfaction Measurement?

The location of the process owners of customer satisfaction measurement within the organization is an important issue. If measurement is appropriately located in the organization, then the organization will have a better understanding of the measurement issues and will therefore use the data more effectively in implementing action plans to improve customer satisfaction. If measurement is located in a less appropriate organizational unit, then there is a danger that customer satisfaction could become an academic exercise, with little practical benefit for the corporation.

We asked each participating company to explain who is responsible internally for customer satisfaction measurement. Answers were solicited regarding three specific groups:

- *Corporate measures group.* Organizations often use a group at the corporate level to focus on measurement issues, including customer satisfaction measurement.

- *Customer satisfaction group.* Many corporations have a group that is focused on customer satisfaction, including measurement issues.
- *Business unit.* Since customers often relate to the products or services of a particular business unit, the business unit can be a logical organization to support customer satisfaction measurement.

As you can see from Figure 6-2, most corporations locate the customer satisfaction measurement effort in a group that is dedicated to customer satisfaction. Some corporations deploy customer satisfaction measurement within business units, while fewer measure customer satisfaction in a corporate measures group. Over 60 percent of corporations located customer satisfaction measurement in a customer satisfaction group, over 40 percent deploy this function at the business unit level, and over 20 percent conducted customer satisfaction measurement from a corporate measures group.

Our research shows that the most successful companies house customer satisfaction measurement within a customer satisfaction group or at the business unit level. It is recommended that you consider housing customer satisfaction measurement in one of these areas. A customer satisfaction measurement group can develop internal expertise in CSM issues across your corporation and provide helpful assistance regarding data-gathering strategies, survey administration, data interpretation, and

Figure 6-2. Customer satisfaction measurement responsibility.

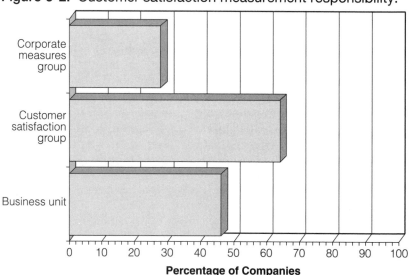

Percentage of Companies

implementation of key findings. For the same reasons, business units can also be viable process owners for customer satisfaction data because business units are very close to the needs of their customers.

While corporate measurement groups can sometimes house customer satisfaction measurement efforts, there is sometimes a concern that these groups are not as close to the voice of the customer. The corporate measurement group may be worth considering as a home for customer satisfaction measurement when the customer satisfaction group does not have technical expertise in measurement. Also, the corporate measurement group can be an effective owner of customer satisfaction measurement when business units are small or geographically dispersed. In these situations, there may be economies of scale in locating customer satisfaction measurement in the corporate measurement function. In addition, for a corporate measurement function to do an effective job in this area, there is a need for periodic, face-to-face feedback sessions in key business units. However, most corporations appear to be able to effectively measure customer satisfaction within the customer satisfaction group or their business units.

Designing the Survey Instrument

Types of Surveys

To be meaningful, CSM data collection should focus on one of the primary levels of improvement:

- Product development (i.e., how products and services are structured)
- Operational processes (i.e., how the task is carried out)
- Customer delivery (i.e., satisfaction processes at work at the point of delivery of product or service to the customers)
- Post-delivery (i.e., follow-up processes with the customers to gauge satisfaction after delivery)

The area you are targeting for improvement will most likely dictate the type of survey instrument you use. For example, feedback on current products can be obtained through written surveys, telephone interviews, focus groups, roundtables, or complaint monitoring. A key advantage of the written survey is the relatively low cost of administration and data analysis. An advantage of the telephone survey is that one can do more probing of improvement opportunities, to ensure that data is actionable.

If you want opinions of potential new products, though, it would be best to use focus groups or roundtables. Figure 6-3 outlines several types of CSM tools that can be used and the times when they are most effectively used.

Survey Length

In today's environment of information overload, it is important to keep the survey concise while continuing to focus on critical, actionable issues. A shorter survey will generally improve the response rate. Also, some levels of higher-level managers within the corporation may be unwilling to complete a survey. Therefore, for these individuals, one may need to conduct a brief interview as a substitute for conducting a survey.

Identifying Factors Important to the Customer

In order to initially develop meaningful questions, sometimes it is helpful to conduct structured, open-ended interviews with key internal customers to determine what issues should even be included in the survey. Often, this kind of interview can be helpful in choosing wording for questions that match the customers' frame of reference. These kinds of interviews can result in a deeper understanding of key issues and can build relationships with key customers.

Additionally, you will want to track importance levels over time.

Figure 6-3. Customer satisfaction measurement tools.

Tool	What It Is	When Used
Written surveys	A series of questions about a company, product, or service that determines satisfaction perceptions	Varies; some companies use them monthly, some annually
Telephone interviews	A telephone-based interview to get perception information	Same as surveys
Focus groups	Issue-oriented gatherings among product or service users for the purpose of identifying changes to existing products (e.g., software)	Usually done in conjunction with user meetings
Roundtables	Discussions with customers and noncustomers to obtain satisfaction information and to redesign future products	When redefining the products and services of a company
Complaint monitoring	Systematic method of categorizing and monitoring complaints	Continually
Internal service negotiations	Agreement between customers and service providers about services and service levels	Internally within companies or when a traditional customer relationship does not exist

Customer satisfaction has two components. The first is the satisfaction rating itself (i.e., excellent, good, fair, poor). The second dimension is the importance rating by the customer. The weight that a customer places on a factor is important so that the company knows how to properly respond to scores. For example, a customer may be asked about satisfaction in two mutually exclusive areas—cost and speed of delivery. A customer may show dissatisfaction with the cost and satisfaction with the speed, but without further analysis, you don't know whether to decrease the speed to lower the cost. It all depends on the value the customer places on speed versus cost.

There are three ways that importance is derived:

■ *Priority ranking.* Usually this involves asking the customer a set of questions designed to determine the importance of key product attributes. For example: "On a scale of one to five, rank the importance of the timeliness of your product delivery."

■ *Attribute ranking.* Usually this forces the customer to make a trade-off decision on two clearly independent product characteristics. For example: "What is more important, a timely product delivery or a shipment without error?"

■ *Statistical analysis.* This involves testing the relative impact of changes to your products and services over time. Usually this is accomplished using multiple regression analysis. Many believe this method shows the most accurate picture of importance ratings because it is based on real behavior as opposed to how the customer believes he or she would act. Unfortunately, it can only be performed when adequate historical data is available. In many cases, sufficient detail in historical data is impossible to get. In other cases, sufficient sample sizes may not be available. Without sufficient sample size, there could be inadequate statistical power to use regression-based techniques, and the results could be misleading or invalid. Help from a consultant or internal professional with a strong statistics background could be helpful in identifying appropriate sample sizes. This is also an important issue if regression-based techniques are used with segments of the respondent population.

Scoreable Survey Instruments

Designing a scoreable survey involves the creation of clear questions posed to a customer to obtain perceptual feedback about the characteristics of your product or service. A few examples of scoring methods include:

- *True and false.* True/false questions work well when the answer is binary (i.e., "Would you buy from us again?").
- *Rating scale.* Generally, a rating scale is used in most surveys to obtain numeric information based on keywords. Usually companies using this form of question assign attributes such as "excellent," or a numeric value such as "10." Variations can then be plotted.

Since some of the comments customers provide in a survey do not fit into a convenient matrix, it will also be necessary to plan for recording and interpreting verbatim responses from customers. Comments can provide a means for validating numeric data. Also, with well-constructed open-ended questions, the comments can often be a source of rich, actionable data that can be used to develop and implement action plans to improve measurement processes and to meet internal customer needs.

Trending

In addition to single reference points, customer satisfaction measurement is useful in developing trend information over time. The first survey administration is analogous to a snapshot. Multiple administrations of the survey are more like a "motion picture," because one can see trends in improvement or decline or specific issues. Also, structured open-ended comments can identify changing needs and issues over time. For example, timeliness may have been a key concern in the first survey administration. If the service provider improved timeliness, it may no longer be seen as a key performance gap by the second administration. Another issue—for example, user-friendliness of the report format—may not have been seen as critical in the first administration, but may be a more critical performance gap in the second administration, because customer needs have changed. Over time, it may be important to add new numeric or comment items to reflect changing concerns of customers. In general, it is also important to keep many items consistent so that trend data can be examined.

Since trends in perception impact the ultimate relationship between internal suppliers and internal customers, knowledge of the complex perceptions of products or services will allow one to respond to the needs of internal customers. Perceptions also need to be compared to trends to spot unusual situations.

Test Surveys

For surveys to be useful, companies often pilot the surveys on a limited scale before relying on the survey in large-scale administration. Testing is usually done using a limited number of customers. Key ambiguities are recorded and the survey instrument is modified. The objective of testing is to assess the adequacy of question and rating scale formation. Testing may also help to reduce the number of questions, thereby improving response rate and survey focus. Consultants can sometimes be helpful in this phase, because it is important to have a clearly worded survey that is focused properly.

Administration of the Survey

Administering the survey can be a particular challenge if you do not administer surveys frequently. Usually it is a high human-capital endeavor. Someone needs to make the phone calls, enter data, collect responses, and so on. Many companies that administer large but infrequent surveys find it more economical to outsource this operation to a company that specializes in surveys.

It is important to have a brief, clear, compelling reason for individuals to complete the survey. Often, this can be done in a clearly written cover letter. If surveys have been administered in the past, then the cover letter can describe how survey results have been used to develop and implement action plans based on customer needs. If possible, the cover letter should state a commitment to act on some of the findings from the survey. The commitment to act on the data is a key factor in encouraging customers to participate in the survey effort and in encouraging customers to share honest feedback. In addition, care should be taken in deciding who should sign the cover letter. While every letter should not necessarily come from the CEO, the cover letter should be signed by someone who has strong credibility among the population being surveyed. In addition, if there are periodic face-to-face meetings between the measurement groups and their customers, a key representative from the measurement group can conduct a brief presentation/discussion session with the customers to explain the purpose and value of the survey.

Sampling

Unless a company has relatively few customers, it is probably impractical to call everyone on the list. It is probably not a good idea to use a specific characteristic to limit the calls either, if one wants a broad picture of the customer base. (Of course, it may be to the company's advantage to get a picture of just a particular segment in certain cases.) Generally, you want a fairly small random sample of customers.

Companies first determine how accurate they need the data to be.

Many companies are happy with a 95 percent confidence level. There are statistical methods of determining the appropriate sample size based on confidence level desired, size of population, and variance within that population. Figure 6-4 provides guidelines for balancing sample size against accuracy requirements.

Data Collection

Of course, collecting data does very little good without the ability to interpret and report that data. You will want to plan in advance for data collection tools. Typically, some sort of information system will need to be established so that the data is in a central location and is easily accessible for analysis. A customer satisfaction information system is an automated (or manual) system that:

- Collects customer satisfaction perceptions and information in a structured manner
- Stores the results of CSM activities
- Assists in processing the information
- Segments and stratifies key issues
- Identifies actionable change
- Links to the organization in order to quickly change processes

A customer database that details interactions with customers can be very helpful. Customer information enters the corporation all the time—for example, through orders, CSM data, and service complaints. Figure 6-5 depicts various sources of information that can be used to build that database.

Typically, customer databases contain basic sales information about customers and customer groups, such as account number, purchase history, and history of sales contacts. It should also include basic company information for corporate customers that may be helpful in segmentation, such as revenues, employees, and cash flow. Finally, the databases sometimes contain all points of customer contact, such as complaints, requests for information, and mailings. Figure 6-6 portrays typical categories for a customer database.

The most difficult information to relay effectively is customer comments. These comments are extremely important to process improvement efforts but are not easily aggregated. Some data analysis tools (such as affinity diagrams) can be helpful in succinctly reporting this information.

Figure 6-4. Basic statistical sampling.

Problem:	Customer population is very large, but the resources to survey are relatively small.
Objective:	To survey enough to build a sufficient confidence in the findings to promote internal action
Complicating factors:	Asking the wrong group of people about their perceptions, even if selected randomly
Risk:	Improper identification of satisfaction needs and the required corrective action
Potential options:	1. Segment the population into major and minor customers (and potential customers). Select samples from a small population.
	2. Survey a large enough number of customers using:
	a. Systematic
	b. Random
	c. Customized criteria (target groups)
What you need to decide:	1. What percent of the variation am I likely to tolerate? (error estimation)
	2. What percent of the time am I going to be wrong? (outside that error estimates)

Note: Most corporations use a rule of thumb of 300 to 400 in their random samples.

Figure 6-5. Sources of information for the customer database.

Use of Customer Information

Segmenting and Targeting the Market

When considering customer needs, it is not sufficient to know what customers require in the aggregate. Customers vary in their desires and willingness to pay.

Segmenting the customer base does three things:

- It allows a company to determine the specific requirements for groups of customers that would be misleading in the aggregate.
- It reveals segment-specific improvement opportunities.
- It can limit the financial commitment by surveying profitable groups.

The first point is key to developing a new process. Aggregate customer satisfaction data can be misleading if customers are polarized on a specific issue. For example, customer survey data may show moderate satisfaction with your bill format. How do you increase satisfaction? Ag-

Figure 6-6. Typical customer database information.

Basic:	Sales information:
Account number (or prospect number)	Last sales call
	Salesperson
Name	Salesperson history
Address	
City	**Complaint history:**
State	Nature of complaint(s)
Zip	Resolution of complaint
Telephone number	Cost to settle complaint
Fax number	Number of complaints
	Desirability of continued relationship
Purchase history:	
Noncustomer (prospect)	**Financial information:**
First purchase	Profit/loss
Last purchase	Assets
No purchase since	Cash flow
Patterns of purchase	Going concern
What purchased	
Purchase volume	**Other:**
	Customer information request
Company information:	Dispute
Revenues	Letters and correspondence
Employees	Mass mailings
Locations	Target mailings
SIC codes	Responses to mailings

gregate data may show no clear direction, but segmented data may show your elderly customers would much prefer a larger-type format—even if it requires extra pages in the bill. Younger customers, on the other hand, may find a one-page bill easier to deal with, even if it means smaller type. The measurement group must identify these differences so that you can build the capability into your process to satisfy both groups of customers.

If you don't look at customer segments, you may also miss the full importance of a reported problem. For example, surveys might show that less than 2 percent of your customers desire alternate billing formats that your organization is not set up to handle. Do you change for 2 percent of your customers? If you segment the statistics by size of account, the answer can look very different. What if all of your top-twenty accounts wanted the alternate billing formats? Suddenly the problem looks more serious. Figure 6-7 depicts typical customer segmentation categories for consumer marketing.

Figure 6-7. Consumer segmentation example.

Primary:
Age
Sex
Marital status
Education level
Income level
Income potential
Special certification/licenses

Family/Ethnic:
Nationality
Family size
Family stage (no children, infants,
    adolescents, high school,
    college, married)

Religion:
Religious preference
Degree of involvement

Life Stage:
Infant
Adolescent
High school
College (or no college)
First job
Middle career
Late career
Retired

Preferences:
Lease vs. buy
New vs. used
Service expectations
Store vs. mail order

Community:
Neighborhood age
Home size
Car model
Typical construction

Geography:
Temperature
Humidity
Terrain
Vegetation

Health:
Health status
Insurance coverage
Weight
Height
Physical characteristics (baldness,
    etc.)
Prior history

Employment:
Relationship with employers
    (employee/contractor)
Inside/outside
Travel/nontravel
Supervisory/nonsupervisory

Competition:
Available competitors
Market type
Price sensitivity

Even your internal customers can have vastly different needs. Marketing may be pressuring the measurement group for real-time product sales reports while human resources can wait but needs a higher degree of accuracy for compensation. In an ideal process, one would produce up-to-the-minute, 100 percent accurate reports. However, that can be extremely expensive. Perhaps the marketing group is willing to sacrifice some accuracy for its purposes.

Segmenting customers can also allow the company to save on marketing research. Companies want to strategically choose to look at only those customers that have the most impact on the bottom line. For example, you may wish to look only at purchasers of specific high-margin products.

Value Management

Dr. Bradley T. Gale, author of *Managing Customer Value*, describes a second step beyond ascertaining pure customer satisfaction. Gale recommends looking at what value you are providing to customers from their point of view and letting that information drive business strategy.

According to Gale:

> The customer value approach focuses on how people choose among competing suppliers (attraction, retention, and customer and market-share gains). This approach leads companies to search for the answers to three customer value questions:
>
> - What are the key buying factors that customers value when they choose among our business and our toughest competitors?
> - How do customers rate our performance versus competitors on each key buying factor?
> - What is the percentage importance of each of these components in customer value?
>
> The results are pinpointed marketing strategies that win, and win big. Recent empirical research shows that a business's customer value position, relative to competitors, has a dramatic impact on its market-share gain and profitability.[33]

Customer Value Analysis

Companies are spending a great deal of time and effort measuring the value to the company of their customer base. "Pizza Hut, Inc., Dallas, is one company that has actually quantified the value of a loyal customer. According to its calculations, each Pizza Hut patron who returns to the restaurant on a regular basis is worth $7,500 to the company over his or her lifetime. Armed with data like this, Pizza Hut's CEO, Allan S. Huston, has developed a passionate commitment to customer satisfaction. . . . Huston hopes to spread his concerns for customer service throughout the organization by tying restaurant managers' pay to customer loyalty levels."[34]

Customers fall into one of three categories:

- High-value customers (i.e., purchasers in high volume of high-margin products)
- Low-value customers (i.e., purchasers of low-margin products)
- Negative-value customers (i.e., those who buy products in a manner or pattern that the company actually loses money on them)

Companies realize that it may not be of strategic value to cater to each customer's desires. Increasing the complexity of your process in order to meet differing requirements can be costly. You also risk becoming a "jack of all trades and master of none."

Customer value analysis allows companies to determine which customers are most important to their success and target improvement efforts to meeting their specific needs. Through the use of a matrix, you can calculate the value of retaining customers (or customer segments) over their lifetime. You will need to calculate the net present value (NPV) of the sales to that segment less the net present value of the cost of sales to the segment over the lifetime of a product to determine the value for the segment. When considering adding a specific attribute to a product, you will need to estimate the expected market share with and without the attribute. The incremental market share obtained by adding the attribute is multiplied by the estimated segment value to obtain the value of the attribute in each market. Sample calculations are laid out in a grid in Figure 6-8. The total profit value to the company for adding the attribute is in the lower right-hand corner of the grid.

This same analysis can be performed in a slightly modified format for internal customers. Although many companies cannot put a dollar value on internal customers, they can determine which are more important to satisfy, since it is impossible to satisfy everyone. The first step is to define the customers, the products, and the services. How do customers use the product and services? Do any customers depend on that information? Once you know what the process is, you can determine how vital each piece is—both to the customer and to the company as a whole. For

Figure 6-8. Sample calculation for a customer value analysis.

Attribute #1

	Customer Value			Importance		
	Net Present Value (NPV) Segment Sales (lifetime)	NPV Cost of Sales (lifetime)	Estimated Segment Value	Estimated Market Share Without Attribute	Estimated Market Share With Attribute	Estimated Value of Attribute
Segment A	5M	3M	2M	30%	60%	.6M
Segment B	10M	9M	1M	40%	45%	.05M
Segment C	1M	.2M	.8M	5%	60%	.44M
Total	16M	12.2M	3.8M	-	-	1.09M

example, if marketing is asking for daily sales reports, the first question to ask is, how do they use those reports? The timeliness of a report that is used to make quick decisions about advertising media may have a higher impact on the corporation than that of a report that is used for employee evaluations. Prioritize the value of services to each organization that uses the information. There may be a better way for marketing to get the information it needs than to go through financial systems, but it's how marketing has always done it. Again, the final goal is to find a process with attributes that maximize value to the corporation as a whole. Again, Figure 6-9 shows a sample grid.

Reporting Findings

Survey feedback can be presented in a variety of ways, including online, printed feedback reports, video, articles in company newsletters, voice mail, and one-on-one meetings with key customers. One of the most effective methods for presenting survey feedback is in face-to-face group meetings. In this setting, results can be presented and then discussed by the participants. Often, with a well-facilitated discussion, this kind of meeting can be an effective precursor to planning and implementing ac-

Figure 6-9. Sample calculation for customer value analysis (internal customer).

Attribute #1B

	Value to Company	Attribute Importance (to Process)	Value of Attribute (to Company)
Process A	.9	.2	.18
Process B	.05	.7	.035
Process C	.5	.6	.3

Total   .515

tions to respond to key findings from the survey data. In addition, the discussion at this type of meeting can validate and refine the understanding of key issues in the data.

Metropolitan Property and Casualty

This case study originally appeared in Personnel Journal.

Metropolitan Property and Casualty (Met P&C) is a prime example of a firm that integrated internal customer satisfaction measurement into a re-engineering measurement program. This led to further external customer satisfaction measurement and eventually a process redesign.

Initially, employees from the marketing and customer service departments reviewed the company's computerized system of delivering new and old insurance policies. In such a highly competitive and closely regulated business, the difference between success and failure is often the quality of service and the speed in which transactions are conducted. Because the goal was initially viewed as a technological function, the role of human resources didn't emerge until later—only after the relationship between customer service and employee satisfaction was acknowledged as symbiotic.

Customers, for example, expect outstanding service, and employees want recognition and compensation that relates to the achievement of customer service goals. Customers want to deal with knowledgeable decision-making servers; employees want to be in charge of their careers and informed. Employees also want to be led, inspired, recognized, and empowered, not simply managed and watched. Hence, HR has become a change agent in Met P&C's reengineering effort—ensuring that managers and employees are properly informed, trained, and compensated to meet the demands of its growing clientele.

This is how the actual reengineering effort at Met P&C, which provides insurance products to more than 2 million customers, has unfolded:

About a year after the systems-delivery review, several of the managers attended a training session in Boston. Inspired by business consultant Michael Hammer, co-author of *Reengineering the Corporation: A Manifest for Business Revolution,* Met P&C's President and CEO Dan Cavanagh called for a formal reengineering team. It was composed of members with computer systems and customer service management experience and backgrounds (believed to be useful in the analysis of the company's business flow).

The team reported to the vice president of automated technology, who is a member of the company's senior management team. Included in the senior body are the vice presidents of human resources, underwriting legal services and public relations, financial planning, claims, sales, marketing, and compliance. The effort was viewed primarily as an internal services department project—excluding human resources and marketing—focusing solely on equipment technology and workflow processes.

But the briefing sessions conducted by the team with members of the company's senior management eventually revealed two missing elements. The recommendations for change lacked the voices of the customers and the attitudes of the employees about Met P&C's customer service. This vital input of the product users and employee deliverers had to be included in the company's reengineering effort if real progress was to ensue. Senior management then communicated its total commitment to a movement from talk to action to gain multisource feedback on the company.

The charge of seeking customer feedback and employee criticism of the company's service was given to John Rutecki, vice president of marketing, and Bob Stonaker, vice president of human resources. Also called to action was a steering committee comprising HR, division vice presidents, marketing personnel, and external consultants. Add to this an ambitious set of deadlines, a limited budget, and no experience in gathering this type of information and you've got the makings of great, short-lived corporate fiction. Fortunately, they stayed on track.

By two years into the effort, human resources was working side by side with the marketing and customer-service areas. As they began to create and conduct the employee survey, [Barbara Kaplan, an outside customer researcher] worked with the marketing department to coordinate the customer focus groups. Rutecki went to work on product, pricing, advertising and strategic positioning views from every angle. Stonaker sought current operational information through a benchmarking effort that compared human resources systems and processes inside and outside of the insurance industry. Assisting him in the benchmarking were representatives from the reengineering steering committee. Each team visited three sites: CSX Corporation's customer-service center in Jacksonville, Florida, for its customer service systems; Corning, New York–based Corning Incorporated, for its HR department's reputation for training and employee development; and San Antonio–based United Services Automobile Association (USAA) for its reputation as a state-of-the-art leader in the insurance industry.

To initiate the process of obtaining customer input, HR stressed that feedback had to begin with Met P&C's employees. In the employee-customer assessment survey form Cavanagh stated: "We want to know how you currently feel about the relationships we have and maintain with our customers. We will use this feedback to identify steps that we should pursue to make Met P&C a stronger, more customer-driven organization. I encourage you to use the comment section on this form to let us know how you would change some aspect of our current business procedures to wow the customers we serve."

The thirty-eight-question survey measured satisfaction levels in key areas such as empowerment, compensation for customer service, innovation, quality, customer relations, and continuous improvement of processes. The use of this survey marked another deviation from the normal course of events. Every three years, Met P&C usually conducts a detailed survey of employee attitudes companywide, where employees' feelings on the company, benefits, environment, and a host of additional items are gathered and reviewed to create and implement change. But this employee-customer assessment survey was the first to ask Met P&C employees how they actually felt about customer service.

More than 70 percent of the employees participated in the voluntary survey. Of the 3,735 assessments distributed 2,639 were completed, a significantly high level of response. The data was collected using scanners to read survey cards. Portable computers then scored the results and graphed levels of satisfaction by predetermined groupings.

Employees at all levels offered hundreds of suggestions for improving customer relations. Among the most common suggestions:

- Simplify customers' bills.
- Regularly collect customer feedback.
- Provide greater employee incentives for outstanding customer service.
- Integrate technology for claim service and policyholder service.
- Provide customer service training for all employees.

Customer focus groups revealed the absolute imperative that customer satisfaction was the only acceptable measure of future corporate performance. And a similarity emerged between what customers expected and what employees desired.

The reengineering effort continues. Upper management will continue its contact with the customers with a series of forums and calls scheduled for the future. A major overhaul of 800 services has been initiated to provide more service hours and increased availability for customers with inquiries. Met P&C now is considering the possibility of offering discounts for loyalty. The human resources department anticipates that more work will be required to satisfy and wow the internal employee customer. These proposals for Met P&C's internal customers' satisfaction are a high priority and are all supported by customer input. Kaplan's findings suggest that control, caring, and recognition are the three underlying values that must be ever-present in the customer relationships.

As the HR function moves to partner with the financial and operational segments of the business, what better starting point than that of addressing the gap of satisfaction between the internal and external customers Met P&C serves.

At this juncture of the reengineering and customer service focus, it's important to mention that Met P&C realizes reengineering is not process modification—it is change—and the two need to be clearly distinguished up front. Customer focus requires total commitment and support from the top down to the front line. Allow time for research and data collection. This isn't a quick-fix approach. Seek input from users, providers, deliverers, customers, and decision makers. Establish checkpoints to discuss progress and periods without progress. The key is communication throughout the entire process.[35]

Conclusion

Customer satisfaction measurement serves as a link between the organization and the outside world. It is an outstanding check on corporate success. Several elements have been identified in successful CSM systems:

- Obtain top management buy-in before moving forward.
- Determine attribute importance statistically.
- Focus on closing performance gaps.
- Use standardized data-collecting procedures.
- Establish procedures to use customer feedback in product service and process decisions.
- Assign priorities to customer feedback on different modules.
- Link customer satisfaction data to performance evaluation.

If these guidelines are followed, your CSM program should reveal some important information about your company's performance.

7

Benchmarking: Measuring vs. Other Companies

Introduction

Benchmarking is one of the tools that enables professionals to measure and identify performance gaps. Understanding the gaps allows management to better control the performance of the organization. This can provide a competitive edge over organizations that do not know how to find gaps and the resulting opportunities for improvement.

There is a constant demand to decrease cost and improve the quality of services. Corporations often view overhead as wasteful and move to minimize its cost. Benchmarking can help management to achieve true reductions in cost while improving the quality of services.

Benchmarking forces management to run the business by the numbers by:

- Regularly using analysis techniques
- Basing decisions on objective, quantifiable measures
- Improving communication of performance

In the end, benchmarking provides management with the information to make more confident decisions on such issues as:

- Staffing and skills mix
- Compensation techniques
- Systems and software purchases
- Training
- Work expectations

What Is Benchmarking?

Benchmarking is a performance measurement tool used in conjunction with improvement initiatives; it measures comparative operating performance of companies and identifies the "best practices." Benchmarking studies develop relative performance rankings using common measures of productivity and quality, then identify underlying practices driving performance.

Using benchmarking techniques, companies share nonpublic performance information to identify operational processes. Corporations measure each other's operating data, identify the best performers out of a group, then adapt the practices that make them the best. Benchmarking provides the participants with the guidance they need to make informed business decisions.

In addition to looking for areas of improvement, many managers are using benchmarking to ensure that they are doing everything that they can be doing for their organizations. Benchmarking creates a nonthreatening environment to review all possible areas for improvement.

Benchmarking Creates Value

When used as a tool, benchmarking creates value through four essential means:

- Focusing the organization on key performance gaps
- Bringing in ideas from external organizations and identifying opportunities
- Rallying the organization around the findings to create a consensus to move forward, and selling ideas that may not otherwise pass political hurdles
- Implementing ideas into operations to yield better quality products and services, and making better decisions from a larger base of facts

In addition, benchmarking allows companies to look outside their own environment to explore additional opportunities such as:

- Practices in other countries that are viewed as innovative and appealing
- Hardware and software purchases (usually so complicated that decisions are frequently made in a vacuum)

Many companies typically ask, "If we are one of the best companies, why do we want to benchmark?" The answer is twofold: First, it is not possible to know where you stand before you measure. Second, since all organizations are a mosaic of processes and functions, even the best companies can expect to find at least one area that can be improved.

Most executives probably have a good understanding of their company's bottom line results. However, high-level data can sometimes hide poor performance in one of the thousands of processes that make up today's corporation.

For example, one problem is that process performance is masked at the selling, general and administrative (SG&A) level. Figure 7-1 illustrates how a benchmarking study can drill down from SG&A expenses. You must analyze performance by breaking the area down into its functional components of accounting, legal, human resources, information systems, finance, marketing, sales, and so on. From functions we begin to identify common activities. Each function has subfunctions. For example, accounting can be further subdivided into payroll, accounts payable, general ledger, and billing. Eventually you must drill down to the individual products and services of an organization. At this level, meaningful process differences can be identified and changes implemented. For instance, the company can measure the efficiency of producing a paycheck or paycheck timelines and accuracy.

Sharing Benchmarking Information

Benchmarking is not the old-style competitive analysis that companies have done in the past. One story that continues to circulate relates to a

Figure 7-1. Using benchmarking to drill down.

SG&A: Selling, general and administrative level

company that would fly a helicopter over a competitor's plant to count the cars in the parking lot and measure the size of the building. Benchmarking analysis is far more effective than any estimates gained from competitive sources.

Today's benchmarking activities are performed in the open with all parties directly involved. Clearly, this shift did not happen overnight. Traditional barriers among companies had to come down and the success of cooperation had to be demonstrated.

Today's companies realize that in order to get information they have to give information. Most companies that benchmark recognize that sharing information with other companies is useful because readily available information, such as presentations at professional and trade associations, business articles, and financial reports, does not give enough comparative performance information on which to evaluate alternatives. The review of public information, typically called competitive analysis, is only the first step in identifying the best performers. Furthermore, comparisons from financial statements can sometimes be misleading. Different accounting practices and company situations can cause published data to lack full comparability. Comparability can only be achieved when the analysis is driven to the core process level.

While some are skittish about revealing performance information outside the corporation, most companies have come to realize that benchmarking a particular process generally does not jeopardize trade secrets. Many functions are not really strategic in nature. Furthermore, benchmarking partners can always set boundaries around topics to ensure inappropriate information is not discussed.

Benchmarking and Staff Reductions

In the early 1990s, many companies used benchmarking in connection with downsizing efforts. "Percentage" cuts ("Let's take 25 percent out") frequently do not have focus and do not improve underlying processes. "Cut the fat" has become "cut to the bone" in some well-publicized cases. Benchmarking can help tailor the sizing of an organization to its workload in order to maintain the quality of its products and services.

Benchmarking often provides a means to substitute small organizational adjustments for big cuts. By providing a continual process of fine-tuning, it frequently eliminates the need for large-scale layoffs and promotes organizational stability.

Global competitive pressures are forging new relationships among organizations. The increasingly intense competition from imports, initially based on low wage rates, has moved to create alliances among companies striving for best performance.

Without comparative information, companies in many industries fall behind as the "upstarts" and foreign concerns erode market share and profitability. If that were not the case, Wal-Mart would not have challenged Sears in the retail field and Compaq would not have challenged IBM for the PC market. If today's leaders continually improve themselves, they will be able to sustain their competitive advantage.

Benchmarking + Total Quality Management

Benchmarking, as a tool, supports quality improvement. Many organizations use benchmarking as a tool to generate data leading to process improvement.

Today, total quality management (TQM) in companies is a measurement and benchmarking focus that:

- Provides an environment for organizational change through continuous improvement and best-in-class practices and results
- Creates objective measures of performance that are driven by best-in-class targets instead of past performance
- Supports Malcolm Baldrige National Quality Award criteria
- Provides a customer/external focus
- Substantiates the need for improvement
- Establishes data-driven decision-making processes

Benchmarking Is a Continuous Process

Nike's motto, "There is no finish line," is appropriate when reviewing competition among companies. Becoming one of tomorrow's leaders requires a long-term commitment to improvement. Companies are constantly seeking higher and higher levels of performance. However, as organizations improve, competitors continue to redefine the term *best*.

As we discussed, one objective of benchmarking is to identify real breakthroughs in performance. Through the identification of practices that contribute to improvements in efficiency as well as quality, it is possible to leap ahead of the competition and establish new standards of performance.

The corporations that are benchmarking are for the most part viewing the costs as an investment in the future. If so, the benefits should outweigh the costs and produce a real payback from investment.

Ford Compares Itself to Mazda

Ford recognized that a commitment to benchmarking was long-term when it began benchmarking Mazda in 1980. A Ford Motor Company team visited Mazda in Japan (a company in which Ford has a 25 percent interest). Their mission was to make an in-depth analysis of processes. Ford measured dozens of processes and found that its accounts payable department had nearly 500 people in the United States while Mazda had only nine. A gap like this was just too hard to ignore.

This initial measure was only the beginning of Ford's research because it was not possible to unilaterally revise the number of employees. The workload was just too great and by merely cutting back, work would not get done and suppliers would not get paid. Therefore, the underlying processes needed to be changed.

From this very basic performance indicator, Ford began its search for the processes that would eliminate work that did not add value. As a first step, the Ford team identified further benchmarks impacting accounts payable performance that assisted the team in identifying three important business differences:

- Ford had more suppliers than Mazda.
- Ford captured and matched more data elements on each payment transaction.
- Ford's payments were triggered by invoices from its suppliers; Mazda's processes were not.

The differences that these measures suggested led the Ford team to look further at process differences and potential opportunities. This objective was not only to meet the competition, but also to generate ideas to exceed competitor performance. A few of the areas that they considered included:

- Instituting a supplier review
- Reengineering the requisitioning, receiving, and payment processes
- Automating the information flow between Ford and its suppliers

The timing of these efforts was critical. In the early 1980s, Ford suffered from diminishing market share and was almost on the verge of financial crisis. The organization accepted the concept that radical change was necessary for survival.

What Ford Did in Accounting, Purchasing, and Material Handling

The first thing that Ford did *not* do is automatically automate poor operating practices. The team realized that the impact of automation alone would not account for the productivity difference. Mazda did not have more automation than Ford. The Ford team realized that additional research would more fully explain the differences.

The Ford team looked into the whole process of requisitioning, receiving, and disbursements. They mapped out the basic business processes and found that Mazda was missing some steps. Japanese companies did not invoice each other—instead they paid when they received the goods.

In the United States, the practice of invoicing has developed over several generations. Originally, it was considered a prompt for payment of late accounts. After a number of years, it has now developed into a routine and required document. The Ford team realized that eliminating invoices was not a practice that would be readily accepted by its vendors. Typical accounting controls in the United States require an adequate audit trail of events leading to the payment of a supplier.

In the West, invoicing creates several tasks within accounting:

- Someone has to prepare the invoice.
- Someone has to receive and route it.
- Invoices require filing and storage.

Second, the invoice must be reconciled to all the other documents. Among the discrepancies that may exist:

- Purchased quantities can differ.
- Pricing may be inconsistent.
- Terms may vary.

Finally, since there is always a follow-up step, Ford found that employees did not always strive to maintain simple or consistent terms. It was more common that:

- Employees formulated various terms and conditions.
- Suppliers misinterpreted terms.
- Inconsistent business practices in purchasing and materials-

handling activities, with respect to pricing and receiving disciplines, required resolution in the accounting activities.

Mechanically, Ford did not have a problem eliminating invoices, but it had to change its basic processes with its suppliers. Ford decided on a program of:

- Redefining the terms of the relationship to move away from the need to invoice on a regular basis
- Standardizing payment terms on a total supplier basis, rather than by individual purchase order
- Communicating with suppliers to assure them that sufficient controls continued to exist
- Instituting disciplined receiving practices for inventory and payment control purposes
- Ensuring that all the terms and conditions were on the purchase order and understandable by all parties

Ford modified the purchase terms with its suppliers. The usual "thirty to forty-five day payment upon shipment or receipt" was changed to "all bills paid at a fixed time based on the freight on board (FOB) term" (i.e., the ownership transfer point). The result of these terms is to substitute, in writing, the same principles that Mazda used to pay its vendors. A built-in payment delay ensured that neither party would suffer or benefit from changing to the new process. The supplier would be able to eliminate the billing process and Ford would pay directly from the receiving documents and purchase order. Figure 7-2 visually describes this relationship.

After changing terms, Ford communicated to its suppliers' accounting professionals that this change did not threaten the integrity of their accounting, but instead improved the efficiency of the operations.

Some basic vendor changes were also required. For example:

- Basic information was required on the shipping document (e.g., purchase order numbers and quantities).
- Over-shipments and under-shipments would be required to be settled independently as close to the time of payment for the shipment involved.
- Vendors would electronically provide advance shipment notice so that the receiving location had information regarding material in transit to their plant.

Figure 7-2. Purchased materials flow.

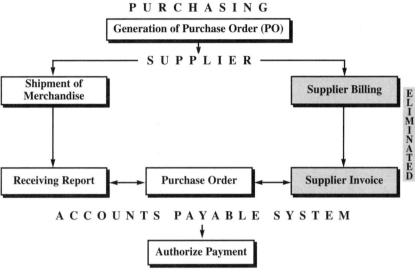

Source: © The Benchmarking Network Inc., 1998.

What They Did in Operations

Ford reduced the number of vendors by about 60 percent to 70 percent. This reduction resulted in closer working relations with each supplier and increased focus on an overall relationship that included the price, the quality of the product, and all the other factors that promote an effective relationship (e.g., delivery, availability, documentation).

How It Impacted Purchasing

In the "new" invoiceless environment, the purchase order (PO) becomes more important because it dictates the purchase price to be paid and the terms. The lack of a follow-up procedure means that the PO would have to be written with 100 percent accuracy or the wrong amount would be paid. The purchasing agents now own the whole process.

What About Automation?

Having worked out the details of the process, it could now be automated. Ford instituted electronic data interchange (EDI) between suppliers and purchasing and receiving. On this basis, automated releasing can be done and tracked from the vendor to delivery dock. Suppliers can also inquire about the status of specific orders and are able to identify when they will be paid.

The invoiceless system can be automated by using fewer data elements at each point of data capture. This cuts down the amount of time it takes to enter a transaction while improving the overall accuracy of the transaction. In a three-way match system, not tied to a specific contract at all times, it is possible to continually make errors in fields, thereby creating reconciliation problems.

Results

Ford Motor Company found that the results of benchmarking were not achieved overnight. It has taken ten years of effort for Ford to educate suppliers to change their practices. In fact, the change to two-way matching was an exercise of changing the environment, not changing internal practices, and has resulted in an 80 percent reduction in accounts payable staffing requirements. According to the Ford team that worked on the project, today Ford is as good as Mazda.

Is Ford finished? No. Ford realized that there are other ways to improve building on this success, and it has begun to explore other areas of improvement.

A Practical Approach to Benchmarking

Benchmarking is not rocket science, but it is time-consuming to do correctly. A basic twelve-step approach to benchmarking that can be modified to fit individual situations is described in the following paragraphs and illustrated by a flowchart in Figure 7-3.

1. *Develop senior management commitment.* Senior management commitment is the first step and is critical to the overall success of the benchmarking effort.

Figure 7-3. Twelve-step benchmarking methodology.

2. *Develop a mission statement.* Developing a mission statement is the second step and is done during the early selling of a benchmarking effort. To do this, list the top three or top five objectives of your effort and obtain team agreement.

3. *Plan.* Planning will initially involve defining the focus of your benchmarking effort. Each team member comes to a study with a different agenda for moving forward. Therefore, a key process early in a benchmarking study is gaining team agreement on the scope of the study. Furthermore, you will want to be able to succinctly define the scope to participating companies that might use different terminology or include different activities in the scope of the same process.

You typically will want to develop a process flowchart (see Chapter 4) to aid you in your scoping effort. A process flowchart lays out all the functions of a process. At that point, it will be possible to align the various common products and services of each organization and measurement can begin.

You will want to establish a timeline. Depending upon the complexity level of the topic, a benchmarking study can last from two months up to a year.

4. *Identify customers.* Customers of internal and external processes are the focus of all benchmarking efforts. Their perceptions are critical to defining the product and coming up with the changes to processes that will improve their perception of quality while improving efficiency.

5. *Perform research.* Library research will support the identification of best-practices information to target while conducting a study. These ideas become the focus of on-site visits and workshops. Additional information may come from six different areas: books, magazine articles, specialists, computer databases, professional associations, and vendors and suppliers.

6. *Identify partners.* Profiling partners is an important part of the decision-making process related to partner selection. Before the contact of a potential partner, you will want to get as much public information as possible in support of your partner selection. First, a preliminary call is made to see if the organization has an interest in benchmarking. Information is exchanged about the scope of the project and the partner's role. When approved, the team may decide to have each partner fill out a participation agreement regarding the confidentiality and use of the information.

7. *Develop measures.* The surveying process is directed at assessing customer needs. You will survey your customer needs in order to focus

your benchmarking efforts. You can do this using survey techniques or face-to-face interviews. After customer needs have been determined, you are in a position to develop the measures for your benchmarking activity.

When developing comparisons against other organizations, a few factors are usually considered:

- The terminology varies among companies, therefore very specific definitions of measures are required.
- The context of the process varies, since the external comparison is frequently situational.
- The measures may themselves be applied in a different manner due to the differences in the way companies operate.

8. *Develop and administer questionnaires.* We now have to develop questions to gather the measures so that we can identify the best performers. The questions should be clearly crafted so that they are not ambiguous or subject to multiple interpretations. Before sending your questionnaire to a dozen or more companies, you will want to test the effectiveness of your questionnaire with one to two organizations to work out terminology differences, identify where data may not be available, and identify other sensitivities. You will want to allow two to three months to get back all the data from partner companies.

9. *Scrub and analyze data.* When data is returned, you will want to have a data collection system in place. You may have to "scrub" the data before reporting it (i.e., analyze it for potential inconsistencies). A follow-up questionnaire is customary at this point.

10. *Isolate best practices.* Apply data-scoring techniques to determine the best performers. Keep in mind that there may not be one overall "best" company; several companies may be best in different areas.

11. *Conduct site visits and interviews.* Planning for the site visit is just as important as preparing the initial survey. It is important to get a comprehensive list of questions about how your partners do things. You will want to prepare a process comparison—a matrix that lays out the different process options between organizations. This provides a quick snapshot of the way different partners approach certain decisions. If a follow-up session is to be held among the partners, literally hundreds of practices can become the focus of discussions. You will want to prioritize issues and target the top ten to twenty ideas for discussion.

12. *Present findings/monitor results.* You will want to present findings both to the other partners and to your own management. Before doing so, you will want to take time to:

- Confirm all your statistics.
- Understand concerns about inconsistencies.
- Develop expectations when certain steps were taken and others omitted.
- Build your case from presentations.
- Present alternatives.
- Present financial projections (costs/benefits).
- Prioritize the different opportunities identified.
- Set a new performance level after changes.
- Describe how the process will be measured in the future.
- Determine next steps.

Benchmarking Policies and Procedures

While formalization of a measurement program in itself frequently does not cause a problem, many corporations struggle with policies and procedures that address contacts outside the organization. Many wonderful opportunities are passed up or poorly publicized while other areas waste valuable time and resources on inappropriate or redundant efforts. Some level of corporate control can guide employees to share only appropriate information while continuing to benefit from measurement opportunities outside the organization.

Corporations expect to receive dozens of calls from outsiders inviting them to participate in various data and benchmarking efforts. Others inside organization will be contacting outsiders to invite them into efforts sponsored by their company. Each organization will need to decide if a particular effort is worthwhile. Most are developing corporate policies to guide employees in the documentation and recording of information-gathering efforts.

Each organization needs to decide for itself how it is going to deal with the benchmarking issue. Top companies already have a coordinator to oversee efforts. Smaller organizations want to benchmark but may have to turn away opportunities just to keep up with the daily workload. Clearly, one answer does not fit all companies.

From the chief executive's perspective, there should be a set of rules for making contact with outside organizations. Many organizations have elected to develop a corporate policy on the issue and disseminate it throughout the organization.

A good corporate policy might include discussions of:

- The company's approach to benchmarking activities
- How information will be shared internally

- How to evaluate incoming requests
- Legal issues in benchmarking

Several companies also include standardized forms used to evaluate benchmarking requests and to report findings after benchmarking activities. A full example of a corporate benchmarking policy can be found in Appendix B.

Conclusion

Benchmarking is clearly a form of corporate measurement that can lead to process improvement. Though somewhat time-consuming, almost anyone in the corporation can perform and learn from benchmarking on some scale. Benchmarking is most successful as a tool for identifying large performance gaps or bringing new ideas into a process. It should, therefore, be used most heavily in the beginning stages of improvement projects.

8

Institutionalizing and Refining the Measurements Program

Introduction

The job of a measurement professional is not done when measures are established. There are three very important jobs still to do:

- Monitor the success of measures at achieving their stated goals.
- Monitor changing needs in the environment.
- Communicate successes of the measurement process and gain buy-in.

The results of your measurement program are always subject to feedback. Companies can be more or less formal when it comes to receiving and soliciting this feedback. Approximately 75 percent of the companies we surveyed employed some formal method of soliciting feedback. Most did so once a year while a few did so twice a year. The most popular methods were focus groups and employee surveys.

One company we examined evaluates satisfaction with measurement via an electronic survey (keypad on telephone) that is evaluated and compiled by a third party.

Once data had been collected, the key question was, "Did it really make a difference?" Experienced measurement specialists realize that the demonstration of success leads to the growth in the value and acceptance of the measurement process as well as an increase in the overall performance of the company.

Some of the companies we surveyed evaluated measurement effectiveness in other ways. One company correlated measurement data with business results; another company evaluated measures through management review presentations given by corporate quality.

For example, one of the most common uses for a measurement program is to motivate and serve as an incentive for high-performing employees. Therefore, the company must be able to determine that the measures in place are encouraging the appropriate behavior. Otherwise, the company will not achieve its goals and employees will become increasingly dissatisfied with a compensation system they believe to be inappropriate.

Fine-Tuning the Measurement Program

Corporate measurement is a fluid process. A company's specific needs for measurement and reporting change over time. Every company should have some feedback loop in place to determine whether the measurement program is meeting the intended mission and the most current needs of the business. Most companies present the results of the measurement program in the form of a report to senior management and process owners. Management often responds by requesting new measures or changed measures to more directly meet its current needs. While unsolicited feedback is helpful, leading companies are soliciting specific feedback to guide them in refining the measurement process. The best way to determine the need for improvement is through what is known as internal customer satisfaction measurement.

Many of the customer satisfaction measurement tools described in Chapter 6 can be easily applied to internal evaluations of the measurement group. Internal service negotiations, in particular, are designed for use within a corporation.

Internal Service Negotiation

Internal service negotiation is one of the few CSM tools designed specifically for use inside a company. It has been used effectively by accounting and finance departments. These departments' customers and suppliers are frequently located in distinctly different groups, and each group creates its own norms and sets of expectations. This has the effect of erecting "silos" around each group. Cultural bonds or lines of communication are not developed, and each group operates in its own world. With no feedback mechanism, beliefs about quality become reality. Figure 8-1 outlines the complex relationship between an internal service provider—in this case, accounting—and its internal customer. Gaps between their perceived service levels define improvement opportunities, which are then

Figure 8-1. Internal service negotiation.

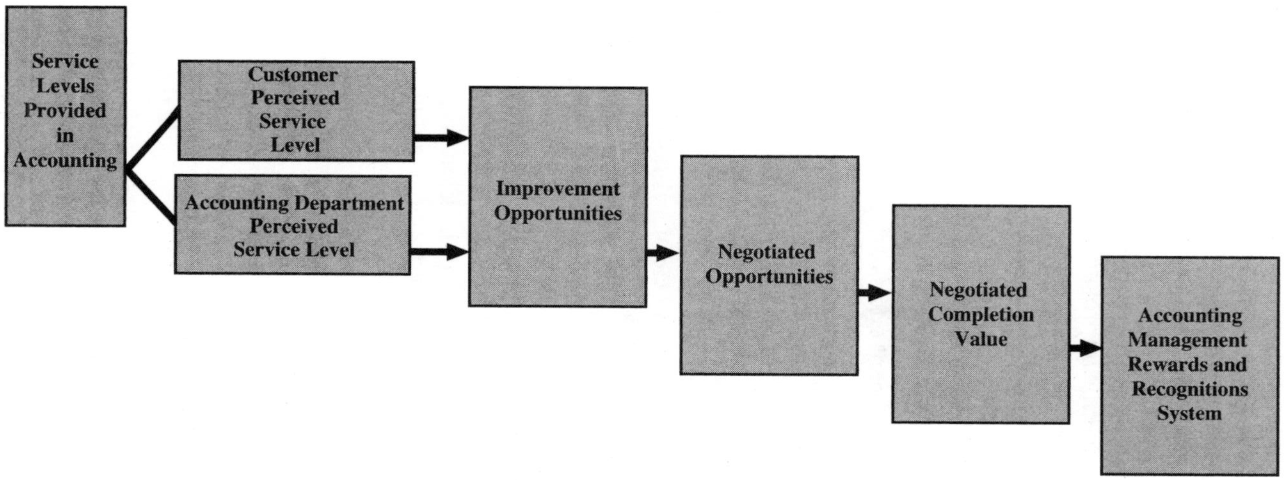

negotiated and formalized in contracts that result in rewards and recognition for fulfillment of the contracts.

The role of internal service negotiation is to construct a market where a market does not exist. True measures of internal performance become the principal point of discussion. Anecdotal information about failures is used to drive specific improvement efforts. Improvement efforts are handled in a manner similar to the way program bugs are fixed in computer software:

- The problem is first identified with the internal service provider and its user group.
- Estimates of the costs to close each gap are identified.
- All improvement efforts are gathered together into a master list of projects.
- Both the internal service provider department and the customer department develop a prioritized list of improvement efforts (some may not have a cost associated).
- Excesses in cost (over internal service provider budget) are then negotiated to be paid by the user department.
- The results of the service-level negotiation are then incorporated into the annual objectives of the managers in the internal service provider organization.
- At a predetermined date in the year, the results of the preceding year are reviewed by the customers, who score internal service provider's performance against the stated objectives.

Once the criteria of a successful mission and vision are attained, the two negotiating groups are ready to move along a commonly defined path that contains those efforts that are considered the highest value by both groups.

Some of the changes that may be proposed by internal service negotiations include:

- A redefinition of the roles of the different groups
- Reassignment of duties among the staff, while leveraging tasks down in the organization

Linking Employee Satisfaction to Hard Data

Internal customer satisfaction with the measurement program or any other program is important to gauge, but few companies have linked the measure with business results. Sears is one of the companies that has demonstrated a tie-in with business results. We spoke with the team at

Sears responsible for the measurement of employee satisfaction. Sears has an integrated employee satisfaction measurement program that marries the satisfaction of employees on various dimensions to the revenues of the corporation. In the past, such linkages were only speculative. Much of the earlier research in this area showed weak links at best between satisfaction and results. Intuitively, we all know that satisfied employees can make the customers more satisfied, but how strong is the link and how satisfied do the employees need to be?

Because Sears exists in a heavy customer interface environment, the company felt it was crucial to have the answers to that question, and to make every employee aware of just how strong an impact they had on the company. Sears has been working with a consulting firm that statistically examines employee satisfaction and predicts the resulting impact on revenues.

Piloting Measures

Of course, it would be nice to know that measures will meet business needs before they are rolled out. It isn't always possible, but one way to ascertain the success of particular measures before going to the full expense of implementing them in your measurement system is to pilot them. Common wisdom says that any new program should be tested before it is rolled out in full. Even so, you may also wish to keep testing to a minimum. Piloting a particular measure can also be time-consuming and costly. While it is important to determine the appropriateness of a measure in advance, one must always be careful not to waste resources on piloting.

The question of how measures were piloted was put to each of the companies that participated in the Corporate Performance Measurement Benchmarking Study. It was designed to determine what type of piloting, if any, is warranted. As it may be appropriate to pilot different types of measures in different fashions, we broke the types of measures into three categories: operational, statistical samples, and customer satisfaction surveys.

■ *Operational measures* are those measures that relate to the day-to-day operations of the business, excluding many statistical control measures used in a manufacturing environment. Examples might include new product time to market or sales revenue per sales representative.

■ *Statistical samples* are most typically collected in the manufacturing arena. They are continuous measures performed specifically to track performance over time. Examples from manufacturing might include scrap rates and output rates. A service company such as a public utility should also track statistical samples such as equipment failure rates. Even some consumer-products companies track statistical samples such as daily purchase behavior. But the easiest way to think of a statistical sample is anything that can be charted on a statistical process control chart.

■ *Customer satisfaction surveys* encompass a wide range of measurement activity. They could ask about operational matters or about a company's image. They could be written surveys, telephone interviews, focus groups, or collections of comments. They could involve a large or small percentage of the customer base. The key distinction is the source of information. Where the other measurements are collected directly from internal processes or through employees, customer satisfaction measurement comes from the customer.

We asked the companies to report in each category if they administered a pilot measure one time before putting it into use, tracked it over a period of time, or chose not to pilot at all.

As you can see from the charts in Figure 8-2, there was surprisingly little difference between the methods used for piloting operational measures, statistical samples, and customer satisfaction surveys. In all three cases, the majority chose to track measures over time while a very small minority didn't pilot at all. Due to the relatively small sample, it would be difficult to pull any conclusive differences between the piloting efforts.

The most noticeable difference can be found by comparing those who track operational measures over time (80 percent) with those who track customer satisfaction surveys over time (60 percent). The most likely explanation for this difference is that the associated costs are higher for surveying customers than tracking internal measures. Along with that, the customer satisfaction numbers are less likely to vary widely over time, resulting in a relatively accurate reading on one try.

Clearly, the participating companies felt it was important to pilot measures before instituting them as part of their measurement program. If you are not currently piloting your measures, it might be worth your while to check the quality of the measures you have put into place by assessing needed changes to unpiloted measures over time.

Like any kind of testing, your goal should be to do as little as possible. But most companies found piloting to be extremely important even so. This is often true because teams are unable to fully predict how people will interpret their questions or the extraneous factors that may have an effect on their data.

Figure 8-2. Piloting measures.

Operational Measure (productivity, cycle time)

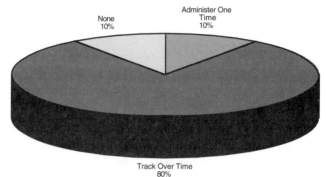

Statistical Samples (e.g., failure rates)

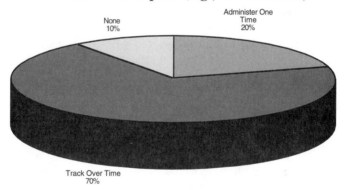

Customer Satisfaction Surveys (e.g., failure rates)

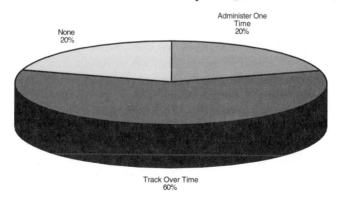

You should assess the quality of the measures you are using. If the quality is too low, step up your piloting of measures. But don't overtest. It's expensive and wastes time you could be spending implementing changes in the organization. If you can, administer only one time. If not, do a minimal number of iterations in order to receive reasonable data from tracking.

Modifying the Program in Response to Results

It will be necessary for aspects of the measurement to change as the needs in the company change. Fine-tuning also means that companies will want to look for new measures. There are frequently distortions that result in measures that don't accurately reflect reality. For example, there is more than one way to measure errors in a bill. First, you could look at errors in the dollars indicated on the billing. Another view looks at name and address misspellings. Unless you specify the types of errors in which you are interested, both categories of measures will be reported as one measure, and the usefulness and interpretability of the data will be reduced.

In a fine-tuning process, corporate measurers will anticipate the fact that the measure will initially be determined imprecisely. Fine-tuning will then seek to identify poorly constructed measures and improve the quality and wording of each measure. Fine-tuning will identify problems in the reporting and data collection process and will substitute better-formulated questions.

Therefore, the measurement group needs to come up with a series of guidelines for making changes to measures from the outset. For example, most companies want to be able to compare measures to prior periods. Therefore, measures cannot change substantially where trending is important. It would not make sense, then, to change from a five-point scale to a three-point scale. It is also problematic to change the satisfaction anchors. It would not be appropriate to move from "excellent, good, poor" to "fully satisfied, somewhat satisfied, dissatisfied." Also, major changes in the number of questions or order of the questions may affect response rates. A balance needs to be reached between consistency over multiple survey administrations and making incremental, focused changes to reflect changes in key issues or customer concerns. It is often helpful to pilot a revised survey to be sure of consistency in measurement results.

Implicit in any changes to measures are the rules for change. Frequently measures are used to motivate employees and to measure individual performance for appraisal purposes. A few rules that companies establish are as follows:

- Measures are frequently retained for multiple periods beyond which the change is made.
- The scales are frequently standardized to just a few, with common anchors that survive changes to the measures themselves.
- The change control process is administered by a central control group that pilots the new measures and ensures that the replacement measure represents the intended result.

Analyzing Measures in a Changing Environment

One of the more difficult tasks is to properly analyze trends in measures within a complex environment. For example, a company that is growing rapidly may find it difficult to determine if expenditures are tracking appropriately. The cost per unit may decrease over a period of time, but some of that may be related to increased economies of scale or changes in the economy (e.g., the price of oil). It is important to take these many factors into account, especially if employee evaluations or incentives are dependent upon these results.

Most of the companies that responded to our survey established an initial baseline against which to judge performance. They suggested several responses to uncontrollable factors that might affect the measurement process. These factors may include:

1. Unusual or unexpected events
2. A manual planning process that combines judgment on uncontrollable factors with historical analysis
3. Understanding that situational changes exist with measures

One way to establish measures based on controllable factors is to work directly with the process owners to establish a measure. Typically, the process owners have a good feel for what falls within their sphere of influence. Zircoa, a manufacturer of secondary nonferrous metals, sets an example as a company that embraces this idea. As reported in *Small Business News–Cleveland:*

> Each department and core product at Zircoa has a team. The teams develop annual recommendations in their area of expertise. These recommendations are used to create company and team goals related to departments and product lines. For instance, one of the goals was to increase sales in the amount of 5 percent through the pursuit of more sales of grain and moving into new bead markets (beads are used to mill down paint into colors and components). One team identified two new markets in the fine-grain area, a new composition that will

bring add-on business of more than 20,000 pounds, and a new bead process.[36]

Evaluating the Effectiveness of the Measurement Development Process

In order to fine-tune the measurement program, you must have a method in place to evaluate the successes and shortcomings of the program. Typically, a program should be evaluated in terms of cycle time, costs, and quality. But what connotes quality in the measurement field?

Each company that participated in the Corporate Performance Measurement Benchmarking Study was asked how the effectiveness of the measurement development process was evaluated. We suggested five ways in which a measurement development process might be evaluated:

- *Length of the measurement process.* Several dimensions of cycle time could fall into this category. One could measure the time from measurement generation to measurement use, the elapsed time required for data collection, analysis, and reporting, or any subsegment of the process.

- *Adequacy of measures.* Measurement adequacy asks if the measurement achieved the desired results. This can be found in an improvement in the measured function over time. Employee surveys can also reveal whether employees find the measure to provide adequate information.

- *Acceptance and use.* Acceptance can be determined through employee satisfaction surveys. Do the employees believe this is a good measure? Do they use the information supplied to them in reports?

- *Changes to measures.* This can be measured in terms of the raw number of changes over a given time period or in terms of time and resources spent on changing and refining measures.

- *Consistency over time.* Measures that produce erratic results are most likely being affected by other factors. A properly formulated measure should stay constant or display an explainable trend.

As you can see from Figure 8-3, the three most used categories of evaluation are adequacy of measure, acceptance and use of measures, and consistency over time (in that order). Each of these categories is used by over 80 percent of the companies surveyed.

Adequacy of measures was most popular because it gets to the heart of the need for measurement. Acceptance and use is also required before a measure can produce results. Both of these were typically determined through employee surveys that are relatively easy to administer and may contribute to the frequency of their use. Companies quickly get locked into certain aspects of the measurement process in a few areas:

Figure 8-3. Evaluating the effectiveness of the measurement development process.

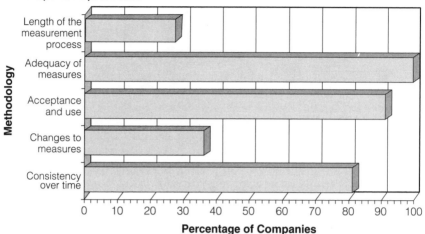

- The number and naming of performance anchors (e.g., excellent, good, fair, poor)
- Performance tied to incentives, which is a difficult factor to change over time
- Specific measures for which a trend is desirable

Length of the measurement process and changes to measures was not important to the majority of the participating companies in terms of monitoring the quality of the development process.

As always, the more measures that can be easily incorporated into an evaluation of the measurement development process, the better picture you are going to get of your successes. One criterion that should be investigated before determining what, specifically, you will measure is the ease of measurement. You don't want to spend too much time evaluating your own process and not measuring.

Clearly, most companies have found adequacy of measures, acceptance and use, and consistency over time fairly easy to measure. I would submit that changes to measures and length of the measurement process may also be important to your evaluation. They both address the productivity of your process.

Demonstrating the Value of the Measurement Process

The first step in institutionalizing a measurement program is to demonstrate value. One of the quickest ways to get employees to recognize the value of a program is for top management to get on board. An example from *Manitoba Business* follows:

> Cargill Limited, an international grain company with Cana-
> dian headquarters in Winnipeg, Manitoba, experienced this
> bandwagon effect with its TQM program. The CEO was the
> first person in the company to be trained in TQM as part of a
> companywide effort. This was done intentionally, to show the
> company's commitment to TQM. New employees also receive
> TQM training. The twenty hours of TQM training teaches
> practical, commonsense work methods, but it also clears up
> misconceptions employees harbored about the change process.
> The company's use of total quality techniques has helped it
> build a reputation as a top supplier in its field. Cargill used to
> be seen as mediocre. The company set a goal of outperforming
> its competitors. The company reduced its reject rates on malt
> barley to only four carloads in the past year. At one time, the
> rate was in the double digits.[37]

While you would probably like to try, it is very difficult to link the measurement process to specific, hard-number gains. Unfortunately, it is one of the few ways that the measurement process will truly gain organizational acceptance. With major reorganizations, it is easiest to examine the initiative after the fact. It is more difficult to show the direct impact of an ongoing measurement program.

Linking Measures to Outcomes

The first step in linking measures to outcomes is to keep corporate goals in mind when first establishing the measure. Be sure your measures track the appropriate performance so that you can demonstrate the improvements.

In addition, it might be helpful to establish some sort of incentive along with the measure. Performance on a given measure will improve somewhat because the employees will know they are accountable. However, to establish greater focus, you may need to add some incentive. The case study of AT&T Universal Card Services (presented later in this chapter) demonstrates how you can tie awards, bonuses, or recognition into the measures. This adds a higher degree of emphasis on the measure.

Nucor Corporation employs companywide performance-based compensation with no limit placed on performance bonuses. Production workers get a base pay plus a bonus for production above an established goal. Steel that is not up to quality standards has to be rerun, cutting back on a worker's potential bonus. Also, a tardy worker will lose a day's bonus pay, and an absent worker will lose a week's bonus pay.

Presbyterian Health Services Corp. (of Charlotte, North Carolina) has established financial incentives for its 6,000 employees for customer satisfaction and revenue growth. The plan splits half of all revenue beyond a budget target with its employees. Gainsharing is based on 90 percent of patients saying that they would recommend the hospital. So far, 99 percent are recommending the hospital.

Remember, just as in all measurement cases, each measure must be in appropriate balance. Otherwise, you may end up paying skyrocketing costs for quality or sacrificing quality to control costs. That is why the best-performing companies periodically revisit measures to ensure they are driving the best results.

Cost of Collecting Measures

Like any other department, a measurement department must justify its activities. We have discussed how one might measure the outcome or impact on the company attributable to the measurement program. But we must also look at the cost associated with the measurement activity. Of course, you want to achieve the maximum results for the minimum expenditure.

Of course, collecting measures is not always an inexpensive proposition. There will be various expenses to maintain the analytical talent necessary in the measurement group, but there are also other costs we have identified, including:

- Consultants
- Computers
- Data lines
- Organizational fees
- Seminar costs
- Travel for data reviews

There was quite a large range among the companies we surveyed in terms of the costs allocated to the measurement program. We asked for the allocation of human resources to get a better picture for the size of the program. Figure 8-4 shows that the total number of hours spent on measurement activities in a given company can range from under 5,000

Figure 8-4. Annual hours spent on measurement activities.

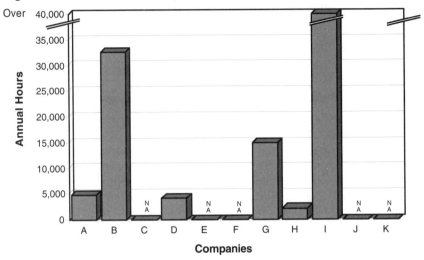

to well over 40,000—quite a range. Obviously, there is no prescription for an appropriate number of hours. Rather, you should try to match the effort to the potential benefit. The following excerpt is from *Quad-State Business Journal.*

> Mack Trucks, Inc. is an example of an enterprise that spent a good bit on improvement efforts, but achieved buy-in because it was able to quantify results. Mack Trucks, Inc.'s Hagerstown, Maryland, power train plant spent $150,000 in training time and consulting fees to implement phase one of its total quality effort. The company's investment in training led to the following measurable results: "a 70 percent improvement in product quality, a 3 percent increase in market share, a 30 percent reduction in indirect head counts, and a 45 percent improvement in direct labor. Inventory was reduced by $10 million, and lost-time accidents dropped 80 percent."[38]

Of course, the more far-reaching the program, the higher the costs associated with it, but also the higher the potential impact on the corporation. It would not be appropriate to set a target expenditure and limit activities by that expenditure. Rather, a company may wish to set a desired return on investment—that is, ratio of benefits to expenses.

Achieving Organizational Acceptance

The issue of how organizational acceptance for measures is achieved is a critical issue. Corporations engage in a variety of practices, including management by decree, simply posting measures, requesting comments on the measures, or face-to-face review and discussion of the measures. Obviously, the method of gaining acceptance for the measures could affect employee commitment to the measures, and ultimately affect the degree to which measurement data is used to implement process improvements within the organization.

Each company participating in the Corporate Performance Measurement Benchmarking Study was asked how it achieved organizational acceptance for the measures.

As you can see from the chart in Figure 8-5, organizational acceptance for measures is achieved by a variety of means. The approaches are listed below in order from most to least frequently used. Organizational acceptance for measures is achieved by:

- Distributing measures for comments (91 percent)
- Holding orientation meetings (82 percent)

Figure 8-5. Achieving organizational acceptance.

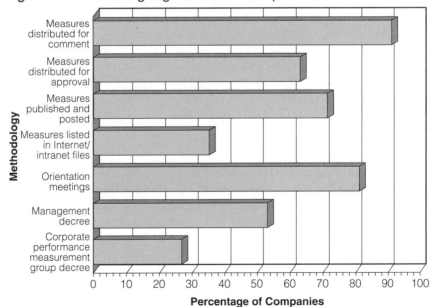

- Publishing and posting measures (73 percent)
- Distributing measures for approval (64 percent)
- Management decree (55 percent)
- Listing measures in Internet/intranet files (36 percent)
- Corporate performance measurement group decree (27 percent)

For analysis purposes, we grouped these items into three categories. The first category included approaches to organizational acceptance where input was sought on the measures from the rest of the company (distributing measures for comment, distributing measures for approval, and holding orientation meetings).

The second category included approaches to organizational acceptance where measures were posted (publishing and posting measures and listing measures in Internet/intranet files).

The third category included approaches to organizational acceptance where the corporation decreed acceptance of the measures (management decree and corporate performance measurement group decree).

The first category, where input was sought on the measures from the rest of the company, was the most frequently used approach. You will want to get input from other key people in the organization in order to gain acceptance for the measures. Ideally, giving others a chance to suggest modifications to the measures may improve the quality of the measures and acceptance of the measures. Giving others the opportunity to provide their input into a draft set of measures builds commitment and improves the likelihood that the measurement data will be used to improve the company's processes. Also, this approach is particularly recommended if your company has an active commitment to employee involvement/empowerment. Review and discussion of the measures is particularly appropriate when the corporation has made an active commitment to treat employees and their ideas seriously.

Posting measures was the second most frequently used approach. Measures should be posted so that they are available and accessible. However, an ideal approach is to combine two methods: post the measures and get input from others in the organization.

The least used approach was decreed acceptance of the measures. This is the least desirable approach and will have little positive impact in gaining commitment to the measures or encouraging the organization to use measurement data effectively.

Process Owner Responsibility for Performance to Measures

One of the best ways to gain employee buy-in is to involve employees in the development of measures. However, there are some concerns that employees involved in the development of measures will use their influence to ensure that only measures that reflect positively on themselves are included in the measurement effort. Therefore, some companies include somewhat marginalized process owners in the measurement development process who are able to provide a process perspective but are not directly responsible for performing to the measures.

The less cynical approach holds that by involving a variety of process owners to develop a mixture of measures, the self-interested motivations are pushed aside. Furthermore, better measures will result due to the direct knowledge of the process provided, while buy-in is achieved through employee involvement.

The Corporate Performance Measurement Benchmarking Study asked participants if the same process management that was involved in the process of developing measures was also held responsible for performing to the measures once established.

As you can see from Figure 8-6, the vast majority (91 percent) of the companies surveyed took the less cynical approach and held process managers who had been involved in measurement development responsible for performing to the measures when finalized. There were few known acts of blatant self-interest due to this policy.

It is clear that in a perfect world one should hold process managers responsible for performing to the measures they helped to develop. The benefits include higher-quality measures and improved buy-in. The concern of self-interest can be mitigated by making multiple process owners part of a team effort.

Figure 8-6. Process owner responsibility for performance to measures.

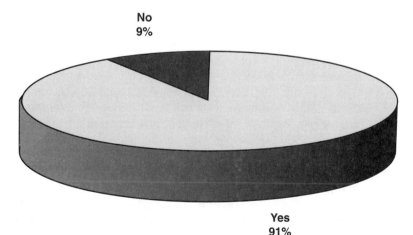

No
9%

Yes
91%

The following discussion of AT&T Universal Card Services high-lights this company's ability to get front-line employees involved in the performance of the company through self-reporting, compensation plans, and bonuses and recognition. It also points out that there is plenty of opportunity for feedback, so the measurement group always knows how the system impacts the front-line employee.

AT&T Universal Card Services

This case study originally appeared in Employment Relations Today.

The leadership team at AT&T Universal Card Services (UCS) established seven values to guide the business: "continuous improvement, customer delight, teamwork, commitment, trust and integrity, mutual respect, and a sense of urgency." One of the main business strategies at UCS is "maintaining a great work environment and a highly skilled organization." The organization is also a Baldrige winner. UCS focuses on four key issues: "Involve every employee in continuous improvement, provide a formal structure for education and training, link recognition and performance systems to quality and financial goals, and establish an approach to employee well-being and morale."

The company's Universal Card University (UCU) links training with UCS's strategic plan in order to ensure current and future competencies for both UCS and its associates. The company employs an instructional technology approach to design courses to address skill and development gaps. Training and education needs are identified by an individual through a one-on-one meeting with that individual's manager. UCU focuses on basic job skills training and management leadership, career-based skills development, quality training, and personal development. Follow-ups and training evaluation are also conducted.

The company also has a suggestion program. Employees can submit suggestions via electronic mail, voice mail, fax, or interoffice mail, and they will receive confirmation that the idea was received within no more than twenty-four hours. The company received almost 10,000 ideas last year. This rate is three times more than the U.S. industry average. Employees receive gifts or cash for ideas that are accepted. The company saved more than $600,000 in one year, and the people who submitted these ideas were given more than $42,000 in bonuses.

There are many other vehicles for employees to share ideas for improvement. Employees are also empowered to provide superior customer service. For instance, employees can initiate service guarantee certificates for $10 if they think a customer did not get appropriate service. Also, they can adjust customers' bills and grant credit-line increases without approval from management. The company also uses quality improvement teams, empowerment task forces, and self-directed teams to make empowerment a reality.

Daily quality measurements are reported by the process owner, not a quality department, so that people participate in measuring how they meet work requirements. Performance and recognition systems at the company are linked to financial and quality goals. Managers and associates mutually determine performance standards and objectives on a yearly basis. The process helps to ensure that individual objectives are aligned with departmental and corporate goals. Associates also are active in peer and upward feedback, which is used for improvement at the individual level. Associates' bonuses are based on the number of days annually that the company meets its performance standards for quality. Managers' compensation is based on quality standards, individual performance, and meeting financial commitments. Feedback on the compensation system is obtained through yearly focus groups and employee surveys. UCS also benchmarks against other companies.

Reward and recognition efforts are available for both individuals and teams. Substantial achievements are recognized and are accompanied by major celebrations and awards. Associates are involved in award development. Certificates of recognition, monetary awards, or vacation trips can be given as awards.[39]

Conclusion

It isn't enough that measurement be a one-time activity. Measurement must be an ongoing program to truly benefit the corporation. That often means a change in company culture to favor using measurement information. To change the culture, measurement activities must involve the employees—through solicitation of feedback and constant communication. Furthermore, the measurement group must stay on top of the measures to make sure they stay current with the business environment if they want to have the measures used by process owners. This means constant vigilance to refine and institutionalize measurement in your corporation.

9

Business Process Reengineering

Introduction

In Chapter 8, the need to show the impact of measurement programs was discussed. Since the goal of most measurement programs is change, one of the easiest ways to measure the success of a measurement program is through the results of specific improvement efforts that are led through measurement activities.

Our study found that the vast majority of measurement groups aid in the implementation of process improvement. Most of the companies surveyed include the measurement group in implementation, and all are somehow involved in reengineering teams and meetings. Process improvement is a logical extension for a measurement group. After all, it is the group that is most likely to understand the performance gaps in the company and can lend significant analytical and statistical experience to the teams.

Even those measurement groups that are not intimately involved with the improvement process find that their expertise and insights can be extremely helpful to process owners attempting to interpret the data. Some of the many services that surfaced in our study include:

- Aid in determining appropriate measures
- Refining measures, including providing global definitions to promote consistency
- Data analysis, including highlighting important points, causation analysis, trend analysis, and identifying abnormalities
- Presentations and reports, including summations, graphics, and best-practice sharing

Process Improvement

Traditionally, corporations have changed their way of doing business in several ways, such as:

- Automating processes as technology became available
- Moving functional groups within the organization
- Allowing organizations to evolve as new challenges presented themselves
- Downsizing through across-the-board cuts

Managing change through measures instead looks at all of these tools in concert with improved strategy and cultural change. This is at the heart of business process reengineering (BPR). BPR is the comprehensive process of reconfiguring the basic structure and relationships of individuals within an organization with the objective of:

- Discarding unneeded activities
- Taking advantage of automation opportunities
- Rewriting the basic models and expectations for each process

Let's discuss this definition in light of what it means to the business professional. By reconfiguring each process, we want to look at ourselves, not only as professionals, but also as professionals responsible to the whole organization. This global view changes the way we take responsibility for our efforts and ultimately how we interface with other organizations.

Successful efforts are generally:

- Customer driven
- Supported by top management
- Based on measurement data
- Focused on "stretch goals"
- Focused on high-value processes
- Implemented by process owners and key stakeholders

Why Is Change Important to Process?

The basic goal and intent of any measurement process is change. Change comes from a variety of learning processes. All change activities are somehow linked to knowledge of better practices. The concept of organizational learning has developed over the last few years. In concept, organizations need to develop processes for learning about practices that lead to success.

Four basic improvement processes are intertwined to provide the organization with learning opportunities. These four basic interrelated concepts and activities are total quality management (TQM), benchmarking, customer satisfaction measurement, and business process reengineering. The chart in Figure 9-1 shows the conceptual relationship between organizational learning processes.

While there are many reasons organizations implement change, the following list includes several with which most would agree. Organizations implement change to:

Figure 9-1. Corporate improvement processes.

- Increase profitability
- Increase market share
- Improve employee participation
- Lower employee turnover
- Improve quality
- Reduce operating costs
- Reduce warranty claims and complaints
- Improve customer satisfaction
- Match competitors
- Reduce supplier problems and costs
- Survive

The first item on the list, increase profitability, is often one of the most important driving factors for change. In fact, many of the other factors listed are only expected to lead to increased profitability (e.g., reduce operating costs, improve customer satisfaction).

In today's marketplace, the competition is tough, and companies are looking for ways to increase profits. Often the task that falls on marketing's shoulders is to increase sales; operations is told to increase production and improve performance; and accounting and financial managers are directed to cut costs.

The traditional way to reduce costs is to take one or more of the following actions:

- Cut overhead (usually that means training, R&D, travel, suppliers).
- Defer upgrades and routine maintenance.
- Distribute a share to all areas. Departments further subdivide budget cuts. Each unit usually solves the challenge in isolation.
- Put employees on unpaid vacation, and sell off inventory.
- Lower quality and service standards.

The problem with dealing with budget cuts using one of the above methods is that for each unit directed to make budget cuts, there are only three basic choices:

- Do fewer things.
- Do the job, but don't do it as well, as fast, or as effectively.
- Change and do your job better.

The first two choices usually result in reduced customer satisfaction and a likely drop in sales. The third choice, one that represents the essence of BPR, is the least likely to reduce customer satisfaction.

There are two expressions that come to mind when thinking about the need to change. One is, "If you always do what you always have done, then you'll always get what you always got." Perhaps more profound and certainly more eloquent was a phrase spoken by Roger Milliken, chairman and CEO of Milliken and Co., a Malcolm Baldrige National Quality Award winner. He defined insanity as, "Doing the same thing the same way, and expecting a change."

Unfortunately, reengineering also has a way of scaring employees. Often, people feel reengineering is being done to them; they fail to see it as an active leverage process that involves these individuals. It's important to remember that BPR is not the driving factor for cutting the budget or downsizing, but it will help you to meet that challenge and provide a structure for managing change.

Opportunities for improvement abound, and a company that wants to stay ahead of the market must take advantage of them. Thus, reengineering efforts should go on always, not just during a mandated project. Effective measurement can support reengineering that works.

The Texaco case study that follows illustrates how one organization approached business process reengineering. Texaco was faced with substantial overpayments in the severance tax function and found a tax difference of 15 cents per Barrel of Oil Equivalent (BOE) with "best" oil companies. It was clear that a reorganization would be required. Texaco changed the basic structure of responsibilities and instituted numerous other changes to improve communication within the tax function.

Texaco

In 1994, Texaco analyzed its severance tax return process. It was a shared function among the tax, producing, and comptrollers departments, but was not working as efficiently as possible. Generally, the tax department provided tax advice, the producing department provided volumes and values, and the comptrollers department reported and paid the tax to the state agencies on a monthly basis.

The overall weakness was found in inadequate communication and coordination among the three departments. Process weaknesses included:

- Electronic dissemination of tax advice was not being used.
- Established procedures were lacking for forwarding oil well certifications needed to justify tax exemptions.
- There was little internal review or confirmation of volumes, values, and tax dollars reflected on returns.

The ultimate result, of course, dramatically affected the bottom line in the form of tax overpayments.

A thirteen-person reengineering team was established. The only defined roles were that of champion, team leader, scribe/facilitator, and facilitator. The other nine individuals were simply designated "team members." Team members were brought in from various functional areas around the company. Each team member represented a process that was to be affected by the changes that would emerge from reengineering. They were each assigned to the team for a six-month period. For several team members, the experience served as a training ground for continued business process reengineering efforts; others returned to their functions at the end of the effort.

The team took a three-step approach. First, they defined the current severance tax return process. A high-level process model is shown in Figure 9-2. The process flowchart was drawn to identify about nine critical areas of the process. Many teams spend a lot of time creating detailed process analysis that makes it difficult for team members to get the "big picture." A quick overview allows for critical design decisions later in the process.

A more detailed model was constructed for the purpose of process investigation. That chart spanned thirteen pages when it was completed. The team members then defined the process scope through the major inputs, activities, outputs, and decision points that were identified.

Figure 9-2. Severance tax return process.

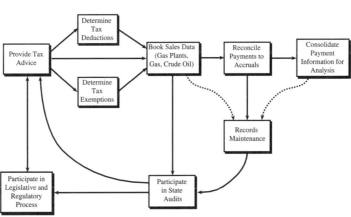

Process objectives: To report and pay severance taxes at the least cost to the company, in compliance with state law.

Source: Texaco, Inc.

Through this activity, they established project boundaries–defining what should be included and what should not.

Once the team had defined the high-level process flow, it began to drill down to the detailed elements within the process. By using an input-process-output model, the team could detail critical interrelationships in the process. An input-process-output model defines the process as the occurrences—major activities and support activities—between two points: the inputs and outputs. Figure 9-3 illustrates this concept graphically.

Analyzing the inputs requires an analysis of key workload drivers and information sources. Figure 9-4 summarizes the inputs Texaco began with for the severance tax return process.

After the inputs were identified, key processing activities were identified for the process. Figure 9-5 shows the major activities that are provided by the severance tax return group.

In addition, there were some ongoing support activities that, although they were not part of the direct processing cycle, were required to support the overall process. Figure 9-6 outlines these areas.

Finally, the team was able to identify the outputs, or end products, of the process (see Figure 9-7).

The next step Texaco took was to classify its activities. In most companies, only a few of the project efforts make up a substantial portion of the work. The team determined that the majority of the workload was in audit support. Audit support efforts were segmented into four classes by size, projected cycle time, and number of staff required to complete. Figure 9-8 shows the classification of audits by type and size.

Categorizing the work was an important factor. The team then analyzed the workload by category and by office: Bellaire (Houston), Los

Figure 9-3. Input-process-output model.

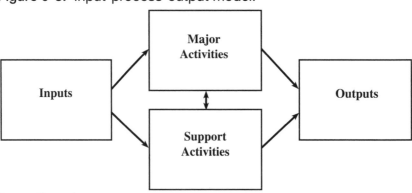

Source: Texaco, Inc.

Figure 9-4. Inputs for severance tax return process.

- Tax advice
- Field operation reports
- Field usage reports
- IRS Schedule 1s
- Run tickets
- Property Information Entry System (PIES) reports (gas allocation system)
- Producing Accounting Reporting System (PARS) reports (gas allocation system)
- Gas charts
- Handling charges
- Transportation contracts
- Liquid pricing
- Processing agreements
- Gathering charges
- Marketing cost deductions
- Certification of exemption and reduced rates
- Tax laws and regulations
- Pipeline statements
- Purchaser statements
- State administrative policies
- LPS (liquid petroleum system) information

Source: Texaco, Inc.

Figure 9-5. Major activities of the severance tax return group.

- Book sales data (oil, gas, gas plants)
- Determine tax exemptions
- Reconcile payments to accruals
- Determine tax deductions
- Consolidate payment information for analysis
- Participate in state audits

Source: Texaco, Inc.

Figure 9-6. Process support activities.

- Provide tax advice
- Monitor/participate in trade associations and legislative/regulatory process
- Maintain records

Source: Texaco, Inc.

Angeles, and Tulsa. (See Figure 9-9.) Now the team was able to identify the number of audits that drove workload in each office. Since workload is impacted by process, the team then was better able to focus on those processes that supported the different types of audits.

After the process had been defined, the team was faced with the task of generating problem and opportunity statements. Team members based their ideas on the as-is model that had already been developed, as well

Figure 9-7. Process outputs.

- Tax returns
- Tax payments
- FRS (financial reporting system) reports (accruals)
- Management reports
- Audit settlements
- Litigation

Source: Texaco, Inc.

Figure 9-8. Classes of audits.

Class	Audit(s) Defined
A	Audit initially assessed at over $1 million; will take one year to complete and one FTE to work; issues very complex (Examples: Texas Gas, Louisiana Oil)
B	Audit initially assessed $500,000 to $1 million; will take six months to one year to complete and ½ FTE to work; somewhat complex issues (Examples: Wyoming Gas, Oklahoma Gas)
C	Audit initially assessed at $250,000 to $500,000; will take three to six months to complete and ¼ FTE to work; relatively routine issues (Example: North Dakota, Alabama, Montana)
D	Audit initially assessed at $0 to $250,000; will take zero to three months to complete and ⅛ FTE to work; simple issues (Example: all other states)

FTE   Full-time equivalent.
Source: Texaco, Inc.

Figure 9-9. Audit workload by tax department (number of audits).

Audit Type	Bellaire	Los Angeles	Tulsa	Total
Class A	8	3	0	11
Class B	6	2	1	9
Class C	5	6	2	13
Class D	7	0	2	9
Total	26	11	5	42

Source: Texaco, Inc.

as other documentation that had been collected in phase one. A key driver was a comparative benchmark against competitors that showed that Texaco's severance tax expense per BOE was in the top quartile. They also conducted brainstorming sessions to generate "radical" ideas. Statements were validated through meetings conducted with process owners. Together, the team developed a laundry list of 111 statements.

The third step was to make the recommendations for improvement. The team stratified and categorized the key problems and opportunity statements. It then developed solutions that would address each area, calculating the estimated benefits from each. These were then presented in a report to management in a tabularized format that allowed decision makers to quickly see the impact of the recommendations to the bottom line.

The team's recommendations fell into three categories:

- Rapid reengineering
- Continuous improvement
- Radical reengineering

Rapid reengineering ideas are those that can be implemented quickly at little cost. The team identified sixteen areas that could be improved quickly. These included such ideas as providing quick reference sheets in the form of tax grids to field personnel and examining whether the gas plants division took applicable deductions in Oklahoma. A complete list can be found in Figure 9-10.

The majority of the ideas fell into the category of continuous improvement. These improvements are intended to add incremental benefit to the core process already in place.

The more significant continuous improvement recommendations produced by the team addressed the structure of the severance tax process. The recommendations were designed to improve communication and minimize unnecessary effort among the departments.

The team recommended that the comptrollers department assume all severance tax compliance and that the severance tax function (within the tax department) be centralized into a severance tax group. The team assessed the types of audits conducted each year and developed a proposal of four full-time equivalents (FTEs) needed to staff the centralized severance tax group. (See Figure 9-11.) Additionally, this new group would join forces with representatives of the comptrollers and producing. The responsibilities of the newly formed team would include:

- Assuming accountability for ensuring that all tax incentives are calculated in an accurate and timely manner

Figure 9-10. Rapid reengineering ideas.

- Provide quick reference "cheat sheets," in the form of tax grids, to field personnel.
- Systematically monitor tax exemptions based on production levels.
- Review all current invoices to determine if we are capturing all applicable deductions. This has not been done on a consistent basis.
- Comptrollers should formally acknowledge the receipt of certifications from production and verify that exemptions are hitting the tax returns.
- Establish a central contact/liaison within the production divisions to act as a clearinghouse for severance tax matters and facilitate a two-way flow of information.
- Make sure we are billing back our working interest owners for their share of audit assessments.
- Tax and comptrollers personnel should periodically visit field offices to learn more about their customers' business.
- Examine whether the gas plants division is taking applicable deductions in Oklahoma.
- Identify all tax incentives (exemptions/deductions) that we are not taking advantage of.
- Send out official notification that severance tax advice is provided on Bookmanager (a software package), along with brief instructions on how to access information between departments.
- Keep the production division managers informed and within the gas and oil revenue reporting loops to facilitate the flow of information among departments.
- Consistently apply the current tax policy that states that the tax department (L.A., Bellaire) should serve as a central collection point for notices of intent to audit.
- Determine who files tax returns on a state by state, commodity, and divisional basis. Provide this information to the field in the form of an organizational grid.
- Assign a tax department attorney to perform legal analysis of FERC Order 636.
- Include production departments in the preaudit and planning conferences.
- Rates for postproduction costs should be calculated annually. Consideration should be given to adjusting estimated rates to actuals.

Source: Texaco, Inc.

Figure 9-11. Full-time equivalents (FTEs) justification for proposed severance tax group.

Texas Gas Audit & Internal Review	1 FTE
Louisiana Crude Oil & Internal Review	1 FTE
AL/NM/OK/WY & Internal Review	1 FTE
Exemption/Deduction Setup & Maintenance and Internal Review	1 FTE
TOTAL FTE REQUIREMENTS	4 FTEs

Note: These positions will also share the following other functions: technical writing, policy and procedure manual format, Bookmanager maintenance, analyze/issue tax advisories and follow-up.
Source: Texaco, Inc.

- Drafting policy and procedure for internal review
- Determining the best method and format of disseminating tax advice
- Ensuring the timely resolution of all audits

Finally, the team analyzed the impact that changes to work processes would have on the severance tax return groups. Then it assigned staff based on projected staffing needs. Figure 9-11 outlines the new responsibilities of the four individuals assigned to the proposed severance tax group.

In addition, the team identified five areas that the team considered "radical reengineering" (see Figure 9-12). These were ideas that could be time-consuming or expensive, but were capable of producing the most significant benefits.

At the time of the writing of this case, the Texaco team was in an implementation stage of the reengineering effort.

Building on Strengths

Every company has strengths. It is important to recognize what those strengths are and understand how they can be used to drive a measurement and improvement program. One company may have an extremely strong product line or service that employees are willing to rally behind, such as a Walt Disney theme park, while another company may find strength in a rigorous training program. No matter where your com-

Figure 9-12. Radical reengineering ideas.

- Consolidate all severance tax functions into the tax department, including compliance, policy and procedure, and audit review. This would be similar to the Texaco Trade and Transportation, Inc. (TTTI) structure.

- Centralize the crude oil accounting functions into one location. Centralization will allow greater flexibility in the allocation of resources, better coordination of the compliance effort, and uniformity in addressing audit issues/procedures. Centralization will enhance continuity and help accountants develop a "core" base of knowledge within a particular state. Communications within crude oil accounting would improve, thus facilitating more timely responses to customers.

- Lobby for changing all state statutes to volume-based taxes, as opposed to value-based (i.e., North Dakota, Louisiana, and California). A volume-based tax has two primary benefits:
  - Ease of compliance
  - Reduction in audit carrying costs

- Consolidate tax and comptroller personnel into the appropriate business units. This would eliminate the separation of the three distinct groups (comptroller, tax, and production). These functions would then report to one manager. Other benefits would include:
  - Communications
  - Responsibility/accountability
  - Geographical proximity to the operation

- Automate to the fullest extent possible the process for the taking of exemptions and deductions. Link existing systems such as PARS (a gas allocation system) and FRS (financial reporting system) to the booking system for the purpose of automatically calculating deductions and exemptions.

  Example: Create a tie to PARS for the monthly identification of wells qualifying for reduced rates.

  Create a tie to FRS for the monthly calculation of marketing cost deductions associated with identified facilities.

Source: Texaco, Inc.

pany's strength lies, you must be aware of it and use it to drive corporate change. As an example reported in the *Journal of Accountancy:*

> Motorola disagrees with the conventional wisdom that smart companies should be eliminating redundant service opera-

tions and striving for shared services. Most of its worldwide sectors staff their own financial service departments.

Kenneth J. Johnson, corporate vice president and controller of Motorola, Inc., explains, "The shared service idea may work in some companies, but we found it's not for us. We're able to produce best-in-class results even though we maintain some redundant systems."

That's not to say Motorola rejects the concept out of hand. Adds Johnson: "We have some shared services in a few locations. But I believe that cost savings from shared services is vastly overrated. If you have common businesses, it may work, but if you have five different businesses with five different kinds of customers, it's hard to believe you'll see significant savings."

Johnson's advice: Resist jumping on the bandwagon of voguish management theories. Check fist to be sure they fit your business and management style.[40]

The case that follows is taken from the same article in the *Journal of Accountancy* and discusses an internal change that Motorola went through to improve its financial processes. There are two things to study carefully here. First, notice how Motorola executives use measurement to drive change. Second, take particular note of how Motorola uses its strength in its competitive, decentralized process to rally the troops.

Motorola's Financial Closings

In May 1995, Kenneth J. Johnson, corporate vice president and controller of Motorola Inc., revealed to an audience of management accountants at a reengineering conference in Dallas that his $22 billion company is now able to conduct its monthly closings in only two days. That's no small accomplishment considering Motorola has six operating sectors, each comprising multiple divisions scattered over thirty nations that together generate hundreds of profit and loss statements by product and as many as forty balance sheets.

After the audience of mostly CPAs absorbed the statement, Johnson added matter-of-factly that within a few months, most of the operating sectors would be doing the job in one and a half days, with a few even getting the work done in a single day. And as if that weren't enough, he told the financial managers, who were there to learn Motorola's reengineering secrets, that the final financial reports were nearly error free.

How does Motorola do it? "Our secret," explains Johnson, "is that there are no secrets. No tricks. No complex companywide management strategy. In short, no silver bullets. Instead, we look for hundreds of 1 percent improvements. It's the old-fashioned way: an awful lot of hard work."

By streamlining the closings, and through other reengineering improvements, Motorola is able to save a substantial amount of money. For a perspective on the savings, consider the history of its efforts.

Tortuous Closings

In 1987, Motorola was spending 2.4 percent of total revenue to operate its many financial departments (see Figure 9-13). That year monthly financial closings took eight tortuous working days—leaving little, if any, time for analysis. A good part of those eight days was spent finding and correcting sizable errors.

That same year the company won the prestigious Malcolm Baldrige National Quality Award for corporate excellence, and management decided that although it certainly was doing some things right, maybe it could do even more. It believed its companywide quality standards could be higher. Likewise, the financial department felt its financial reporting cycle time could be faster and the results more reliable.

In mulling over how to address this goal, Motorola's top management figured if production costs for payroll, payables, and receivables were cut by 20 percent to 30 percent, which didn't seem unreasonable, it could save as much as $35 million a year.

Listing goals is easy; accomplishing them is something else. Could

Figure 9-13. Percentage of total revenue Motorola spends on its finance operation.

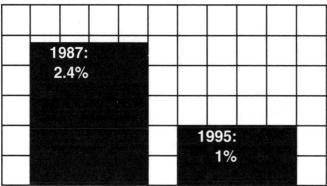

Source: Journal of Accountancy.

the corporate culture withstand a massive reengineering, which in a typical company would be planned and enforced from the top down? As one Motorola executive put it: "We have an entrepreneurial corporate setup that can best be described as a loose conglomeration of warring tribes. It may not work for others but it works well for us."

Recognizing that, management decided against imposing top-down solutions. Instead, it allowed the natural competition between the business sectors to work its magic. The logic is simple: No one wants to be on the bottom. So the manager at the bottom calls the manager at the top and asks for advice. Likewise, managers are encouraged to look at other companies with "best practices" and to adapt any world-class ideas that seem compatible with their operations.

"It Can't Be Done"

The immediate goal was to get people to stop saying, "No, it can't be done." Instead, they were inspired to look for ways to change what they were doing—not for the sake of change, but to improve it.

Each department was encouraged to look at its own functions and figure out how to do them better. No one was told how to do the job; all they were told was to get it done. For example, the corporate finance department didn't dictate what kind of accounting software to use. All that was required was that the data sent by the "sectors" (Motorola's term for an operating business unit) to corporate be compatible with the headquarters' system.

Once a hands-off management style, with a heavy dose of competition and oversight, was instituted, the goal was to figure out how this would affect the financial department. What could the department improve? Speeding up closings was easy to measure. But what about all the steps that went into improving the process?

"Errors became the clear target," says Johnson. The time spent finding and correcting errors was a major factor in slowing not just the closing but much of the work of the financial departments, which included internal audits. He figured the worst way to tackle errors was to wait until the closing, ferret them out, and correct them. Instead, he wanted either to eliminate them at the source or to make corrections as the data were prepared.

Before they could begin, some groundwork was necessary: They had to count the mistakes and determine their sources. "We decided to count errors entered into the general ledger. To do that, we needed a definition of an error: a wrong digit, a whole input, an account number? Only then could we count them and determine what was being done wrong and what could be improved."

The corporate finance managers spent a lot of time on the definition before they finally realized they just had to settle on a workable one and start the meaningful tasks. They agreed that if one wasn't working, they'd change it.

The next step was to quantify the improvements the company was seeking. Not only did each financial department have to count its errors, it also had to set a measurable goal for improvement. That's when someone with a statistical background suggested the idea for six sigma.

The Birth of Six Sigma

In mathematical jargon, the term *six sigma* indicates that a statistical sampling in an enhanced standard deviation is at its best. In other words, from a statistical standpoint, a six sigma sample is essentially free of errors—or, from a mathematician's point of view, no more than 3.4 errors per million opportunities. (When Motorola started counting errors companywide, it was recording about 10,000 a month out of about 700,000 opportunities.) The goal for the company, not just the finance department, was to achieve six sigma for its products and services. Initially, many of the sector's financial managers resisted counting errors, figuring it was a waste of time. But the corporate finance managers thought otherwise. "Unless we can count errors, we can't fix them," was the oft-repeated refrain.

Where is Motorola's finance department now? "We're at about five sigma, or 1,000 errors per two million to three million, and constantly improving," says Johnson. In one recent month the department set a record: only three errors in a closing. Today, Motorola's cost to operate its corporatewide finance activity has tumbled from 2.4 percent of annual revenue in 1987 to 1 percent.

The Low-Tech One Percent Solution

How does Motorola improve the efficiency of its financial department? "We use the 1 percent solution—hundreds of 1 percent improvements," says Kenneth Johnson.

When pressed to explain the process Motorola's financial managers use to identify their 1 percent improvements, Johnson smiles broadly and says the secret is low tech yellow Post-it notes.

"We examine a process (performed in the accounting area). Each step is listed on a yellow Post-it and the paper is stuck up on the wall. When we've flowcharted the entire operation, with maybe a hundred Post-its on the wall, we ask, 'Why is that step there? And why is that step here?' If no one can answer the question adequately, we remove the note. Each time we pull one down, it's like finding gold—less work, fewer steps. It may not be very sophisticated—but it works."

How much does Motorola invest in such cost-saving ventures? Johnson smiles again: "Nil." Then he adds, "That's not counting the cost of yellow Post-its."

For specific steps, we turned to Stephen Monaco, a vice president and controller of Motorola's land mobile product sector. For example, he explains, for years Motorola's nonexempt employees filled out time cards, which had to be keypunched into the accounting system's payroll system. Such a practice was not only time-consuming, it was prone to errors. By eliminating the paper cards and having staffers enter their own data directly into computers (supervisors checked on overtime entries), the entire keypunching cycle was eliminated. The bottom line: The payroll function was trimmed by two full days.

Billing was another area that Motorola streamlined. It recently introduced bar-coding for all shipments from vendors—virtually the only paper in the transaction is the initial purchase order, which can be eliminated if the vendor is connected via computer. When a shipment arrives at Motorola, the merchandise is recorded by "wanding it"—scanning it with a bar code reader. The signal triggers payment approval based on the price established in the original purchase order. In many cases, payment is not made by paper check, but by electronic funds transfer—another substantial savings.

Monaco says Motorola has saved a lot by reengineering its travel and entertainment process. Until recently, reimbursements occurred monthly after employees filed detailed expense reports. Now, employees are issued corporate Visa cards sponsored by the company's credit union. In addition, rather than issue separate reimbursement checks, the company direct-deposits funds into the employees' accounts.

Speedy Annual Report

Aside from saving money, these enhancements have benefited Motorola in other ways. Financial closings typically are high-anxiety times at most companies, and Motorola was no exception. Now, with closings speeded up and errors reduced, not only is there less anxiety, but the financial managers have time to focus on more important duties: analyzing trends and using that information to advise operating management.

Aside from saving money and reducing anxiety, what are the benefits of such fast closings? As a public company, it is to Motorola's advantage to get data to the marketplace as quickly as possible. In addition, operating managers use this information to determine the pace of ordering raw materials, assess excess inventory, and make decisions that affect production and marketing.

Says Johnson: "We're not yet at six sigma—but we're getting there." How fast? He replies, "One percent improvement at a time."[41]

What Motorola Did Right

The case cites several areas that contributed to Motorola's ultimate success. Specifically, the company:

- Improved the quality while cutting costs
- Identified key processes
- Employed top-down leadership with bottom-up solutions
- Measured processes
- Didn't let the status quo get in the way
- Evaluated practices for applicability
- Piloted solutions

Let's discuss each of these achievements in more detail.

- *Improved the quality while cutting costs.* Don't just look for the easy way to cut costs. Cutting overhead would not have given Motorola the dramatic reduction in errors and cycle time it achieved through reengineering. Motorola was careful to look for process improvements from many angles and not get stuck on the issue of cost cutting.

- *Identified key processes.* Motorola executives were also astute in the way they focused efforts on a process that allowed for a big impact. They recognized that it was taking an inordinate amount of resources to close the books and that even a small improvement would produce great savings for the company.

For a successful reengineering effort, one should first identify critical success factors—those characteristics, conditions, or variables that have a direct influence upon the satisfaction of customers and, therefore, upon the success of the organization. Collectively define which areas provide the highest upside, and limit the downside.

For example, to a mail-order company, the effectiveness of its phone center is paramount. To a financial institution, its sources of capital are paramount.

Don't try to reengineer everything. Your best bet is to focus on the areas that can have the biggest impact on the company.

- *Employed top-down leadership with bottom-up solutions.* There are two important lessons here. First, Motorola executives at the corporate level committed significant resources and support to the reengineering effort. They selected the process, insisted on measurement, and set "stretch goals" for process owners. It's clear the effort would not have been a success without the elevation in importance it received from corporate management.

The second important lesson, though, is that senior management did not dictate how the process was to be improved. Every reengineering effort should incorporate input from the process owners. Though Motorola management set goals and required the business sectors to work toward improvement, management did not set the procedures to be used to attain the goals. They left the real process redesign to the individuals that knew it best and let work the naturally competitive spirit among members of business sectors.

In reengineering, there is a place for strong leadership and a place for employee creativity. Motorola appears to have done an excellent job of balancing the two in the company.

- *Measured processes.* Motorola set clear measures for the process. This does two things. First, it allows employees to see trends in performance that allow them to monitor improvement efforts and even spot potential areas for future improvement initiatives. For example, the ability to count and categorize errors focused attention on the need for improvement. As the divisional improvements were recognized, the measurement of error rates allowed poorer-performing divisions to identify gaps and work toward improvement of their own processes. Second, measuring processes elevates the importance of those processes in the eyes of the corporation. By insisting that divisions count their errors, Motorola management made a clear statement about the importance it placed on error rates. It became a rallying cry for reengineering.

- *Didn't let the status quo get in the way.* There are two key examples of the way Motorola was able to get past the present and look toward the possibilities. First, it had the guts to set a goal that might have seemed unattainable at the time. Six sigma is not an easy goal to reach under any circumstances, but it certainly seems more difficult with an error rate of one in seventy (that represents a reduction of 99.98 percent). Many companies would have been tempted to set a more conservative goal—maybe reducing errors by 50 percent. Six sigma probably seemed insurmountable. Motorola is not there yet, but the goal gave its employees the needed push to make drastic reductions in their error rate—about a 72 percent reduction.

Many believe a more appropriate goal, and one that began in total quality management theories, is that of zero defects. This concept, as the name implies, states that every company should have perfection as its goal and not be satisfied until that goal is reached.

Second, Motorola made excellent use of the process flow diagrams. Although actual format varies, each has three distinctive features:

- A process flowchart of activities (each activity adding value to the process)
- A description of each function involved in a process (a sequential flow of steps with an input and a defined output)
- A listing of the products and services that result from the process

The process is the basic operations of the accounting department. In order to make effective improvement in one's processes, one needs to understand exactly what is currently being done. Merely by looking at one's methods of working, one can find opportunities for improvement. Through the use of Post-it notes, Motorola was able to establish a norm of questioning the process. Reengineering teams were expected to question each step and "throw out" those that were not needed.

- *Evaluated practices for applicability.* Every company needs to carefully evaluate the applicability of innovative practices for its particular situation. Companies need to break their paradigms and search for what may seem like "wild and crazy" solutions to their problems. Library research, benchmarking, and old-fashioned brainstorming can all help teams identify solutions. Even so, not all practices that are used in another setting are applicable to one's own. Motorola showed discretion in its choice not to centralize all accounting services. The decentralized mode worked better for it because of the distinctive nature of its business sectors.

- *Piloted solutions.* Motorola's use of business sector competition lent itself beautifully to piloting solutions. Just as you wouldn't buy a car without a test drive, it is unwise to implement a new process solution without some conviction that it will work in one's organization. By making changes at the business sector level, Motorola was able to test a solution before a corporatewide rollout. Furthermore, by not making a commitment to any one error-reduction method, there was no sense of permanency. Process owners at the business sector level could continually "test out" new techniques.

The following case, excerpted from *Mortgage Banking*, describes how James Madison successfully piloted a new process and helped it prepare for problems arising from culture change and training needs on a larger scale.

James Madison Mortgage Company

Formerly a typical, decentralized, mortgage processing company, with segments of the loan process performed in its branches and others at its corporate office, James Madison set out to streamline the loan process to meet consumers' demand for quick service and low cost.

To improve service and eliminate duplicate steps, James Madison organized around the process instead of the function and streamlined all operations so a single team could handle it. Each team member was cross-trained to individually handle all facets of a loan file, from credit analysis to closing and shipping of the loan package. The team approach took months of careful planning, scheduling, and effort to overcome skepticism. Since November of 1994, James Madison Mortgage Company has been successfully using this approach, receiving favorable response from its employees as well as from borrowers, realtors, and builders.

James Madison's change to team processing was the result of an evolutionary process that began in early 1993. James Madison initially adopted an individual development program (IDP) as part of its overall plan to modernize its traditional top-down management style. James Madison worked with a management consulting firm to conduct IDP workshops for all staff that revolved around the premise, "It is okay to make mistakes—we all make mistakes. Don't be afraid to try something different. Step outside of the box."

IDP started the ball rolling. After probing and examining the way the company did business, James Madison discovered many unnecessary steps were being performed and sometimes duplicated under the current process. Typically, a loan would bounce needlessly from department to department.

Starting at Square One

To streamline the process, James Madison started at square one—loan origination. The mortgage company wanted to eliminate the delay in receiving loan approval. When a loan officer took a mortgage application, the loan passed between the processor and the loan officer several times so that sufficient documentation was gathered before the file was eventually sent to the underwriter for the approval. The many hand-offs led to multiple opportunities for fumbles. The application process would typically take several weeks for approval.

To increase efficiency, James Madison minimized the application process by introducing the Express Approval program in August 1994. Express Approval required the loan officer to obtain as much documentation as possible from borrowers at application, getting all the needed information to make a credit decision (i.e., W-2s, pay stubs, bank statements). In addition, the loan officer would obtain an electronic merged in-file credit report via laptop, as well as supporting documents for analysis. The loan file was then submitted directly to the underwriter for credit approval.

Behavioral Changes

However, the Express Approval program forced behavioral changes among James Madison's employees. Loan officers were required to do more work up front at loan application. With Express Approval, loan application sessions typically lasted from ninety minutes to two hours. Although loan applications tended to be lengthy, the upside was that after application, the loan officer did not need to intervene in the loan process.

There is no question that Express Approval placed a burden on underwriting. Loan officers were unaccustomed to analyzing loan files and, therefore, the quality and completeness of the files varied. Because the files submitted to underwriting were not fully processed and because change in and of itself caused a loss of efficiency for a period of time, it was taking at least twice as long to underwrite a file. It became impossible for James Madison to maintain the forty-eight-hour turnaround time policy (from the time the loan reached the underwriting department). Resources from other areas of the company were reassigned to assist during the backlog, which lasted about thirty days. In addition, temporary help was hired.

To address the needs of the changing industry and be able to continue with the Express Approval program, James Madison appointed a committee in September 1994 to study the situation and find a solution that would enable loans to be processed more efficiently. The committee was composed of representatives of all aspects of the business. The committee met frequently beginning October 3, 1994. From these meetings, the committee concluded that the loan process could be divided into two segments: sales and operations. These two segments would replace what had formerly been the departmental functions of processing, underwriting, closing, and post-closing.

Planning

The committee's idea involved aggressive cultural change and required behavioral changes on the part of most of James Madison's employees.

With the Express Approval program, upper management had made decisions without consulting those that would be affected by those decisions. The result was reluctance from its loan officers and employees to adapt to the changes. Upper management had learned from its previous mistakes and wanted team processing to be a company decision.

On October 12, 1994, the committee called a meeting of the mortgage company's seven branch managers. When the proposed process was announced, it was met with negative reaction and fear. The committee listened to all the concerns. The branch managers' input and concerns became the building blocks for the committee's work going forward.

The committee met regularly throughout October. They began to attack the concerns voiced at the meeting and addressed the areas one by one. From their weeks of research and planning, the committee called a larger meeting on October 24, 1994, made up of branch managers, originators, and support staff to outline their thoughts and plans. Once again, although every concern had been addressed, there was an outpouring of emotion and continued resistance. Loan officers expressed extreme concern about removing processors from the branch and centralizing them at the corporate office. They needed to have a contact who knew where their loan was at all times. They did not want their loan files to go into a "deep hole."

"Everybody knew something needed to be done. But nobody wanted to give up control of anything," says Kathy Daubert, Frederick, Maryland, branch manager and committee member. James Madison's upper management and the committee recognized the apprehension that the team approach evoked among employees, but they believed in its importance and were going to stay the course. Michael Carr, president of James Madison Mortgage, says, "We knew the risks were great, but we had confidence in the staff and the loan officers to handle the change. The greater risk was staying status quo."

To test the proposed team approach, the committee recommended a pilot team. Management gave its approval to proceed. "The team approach was not just cooked up in a conference room by management. From the start, it encouraged participation from all in the company to be involved in the structure of the team, which was vital to its success," says Cindy Morrell, senior vice president of operations for James Madison.

The committee organized a retreat in late October for branch operation supervisors and committee members to finalize how to implement the team process and to organize the pilot team. The retreat provided a relaxed atmosphere "to get it all together" as a group. Daubert says, "After the retreat, we had almost 100 percent confidence of all involved. From the weeks of meeting, listening, and planning evolved the ninety-day pilot team—the Green Team."

It's Not Easy Being Green

The committee hand-selected the first team based on the success of the candidates, as well as their established relationships with loan officers. Fair Oaks branch office supervisor Cheryl Lockwood was chosen as team leader because of her familiarity with the branch and its loan officers. In addition to the team leader, nine team members were selected. James Madison purposely overstaffed the pilot team so as not to overwhelm its first group and to be able to document policies and procedures.

Cross-Training

The next major step the team tackled was to begin its cross-training functions. Interspersed among their day-to-day duties, all team members began to learn facets of the whole process. Loans would be assigned to team members based on the difficulty of the file. An easier loan would be handed to a member who was beginning his or her cross-training, while the more complex loans would be funneled to a team member with more underwriting experience. The team member would begin cross-training on the loan through the buddy system. If the team member was formerly a processor, he or she would then sit in with team members who had been underwriters, closers, or post-closers to be educated on the steps involved in each process. The team member would be responsible for taking that loan through to post-closing.

During the first few weeks, the Green Team experienced its share of ups and downs. In its favor, the team approach made it much easier to manage branch volume and use the resources within the team. The system sped up the loan process by at least five days and made it more efficient by eliminating unnecessary steps.

The Bottom Line

Team processing has produced its share of triumphs and tribulations. James Madison did experience fallout. Some employees chose to leave the company to seek employment with organizations that have more traditional approaches rather than to accept the new approach. However, the pros have far outweighed the cons. Under the team approach, James Madison has reaped an abundance of benefits that have affected the bottom line. Based on current retail production levels, team processing has saved the company approximately $187.50 per loan. Before team processing, the cost to process, underwrite, close, and post-close a loan averaged $462.50. These same functions now cost $275.50—a dramatic 40 percent savings. The team approach benefits James Madison in the following ways:

- The company has better control over the loan process and a shorter cycle time.
- The company was able to eliminate middle management.
- The branch structure was leveraged. Office space in the branches was made available by relocating support staff to the corporate office.
- The company successfully pooled resources. The team approach requires cross-training employees so that each employee performs all facets of a loan file from processing to closing and shipping. Team leaders can shift the team members' area of responsibility as needed.
- The new process allows for fluctuations in the market. The company now can better manage and control part-time and temporary help seasonally when volume is high.
- Miscellaneous costs were eliminated. Team processing eliminates unnecessary steps and the need for duplicating records, copy fees, faxes, and couriers.
- Job satisfaction has increased. Team members find their jobs more rewarding because they are given the opportunity to learn as well as the authority to make decisions.

Although increased productivity and efficiency have been a bonus for the company, the most rewarding outcome has been the higher quality of service James Madison can provide to its customers. Since its inception, borrowers, realtors, and settlement agents have noticed quicker approvals, timely settlements, and more efficient documentation.

In just a year's time, James Madison Mortgage Company radically changed the way it did business. The change affected a majority of its employees. It took a leap of faith on the part of many, but through constant communication and a strong commitment to service by its employees, James Madison made team processing a success. James Madison's Morrell recalls a quote from noted anthropologist Margaret Mead that she thinks sums up the James Madison employees' dedication: "Never doubt that a small group of thoughtful, committed people can change the world. Indeed, it is the only thing that ever has."[42]

Schlage Lock Company is an excellent example of a successful reengineering effort. As you read the case that follows as excerpted from *Industrial Engineering*, notice the use of the following tools and techniques:

- Process analysis interviews
- Team selection criteria
- "Blitzing" reengineering teams
- Customer satisfaction measurement

Schlage Lock Company

Retailers can now practice micromarketing, attempting to respond to consumer trends with as little delay as possible. Unfortunately for manufacturers, this kind of micromarketing means they are expected to respond with equal rapidity. Projections based on last year's sales are no longer adequate. Now production must be based on last month's or even last week's sales, and the time to get an item into and through production must be very short.

Schlage recognized that speeding up its response time would require profound changes in operations that included:

1. Implementation of a much more sophisticated information system than the one currently in use
2. Significantly greater use of automation in the manufacturing process reorganization of its marketing, sales, and administration processes
3. In order to make the preceding changes possible, retraining employees and giving them more reason and opportunity to become involved in meeting company goals

Developing the Program

The initial period, which lasted four to five months, included interviews with approximately sixty Schlage employees from the various facilities. Participants were asked to outline their responsibilities, talk about critical strategies they had developed to complete their tasks, and contribute ideas for improvements to the company's information systems.

Schlage wanted to have as many of the team members as possible hired from within the company, and the final count tallied eight existing Schlage employees and two new hires. Members were nominated either by themselves or by coworkers-workers or managers. Only when no employee demonstrated the appropriate technical proficiency in a specific area or when no qualified employee opted to participate did the company recruit from external sources. The team members were chosen based on three primary criteria:

- Expertise in one of the ten targeted company functions
- Willingness and liberty to engage in regular weekend and overtime work
- Willingness and liberty to travel to other Schlage facilities and spend significant amounts of time away from home

The team, which was selected in mid-1992, reports to a five-person sponsor group comprising the managers of the company's worldwide manufacturing and commercial business units, the company controller, and the human resources and Total Quality Management directors. The sponsor group has responsibility for interfacing between the team and senior management, which has ultimate responsibility for all actions.

Process Reengineering

Although the initial investigatory effort focused on the software programs then in use, the interviews and subsequent team discussions revealed deeper problems.

"We had a lot of custom (software) programs, in-house," explains Brent Elliott, a Schlage manager with a background in finance and accounting who was chosen to head up the reengineering effort. "And what we came up with is [that] we could actually go in and implement new systems to basically automate our existing practices. But as we were looking at where we were going strategically, we felt that just automating our current practices wasn't going to be enough for the future. We had to do something a lot more dramatic than just automating our current processes. Especially from an information standpoint."

Consequently, process reengineering became the cornerstone. It would first be applied to the information system framework and then to manufacturing.

Emphasizing the Customer

The team and its sponsors committed the company to an information systems strategy of providing centralized planning with local execution. The program devised by the team was designed to emphasize customer service and focuses on five key areas:

- Process reengineering
- Application recommendations
- Technology recommendations
- Information systems management recommendations
- Implementation plan

The plan includes communication goals, measurements, and performance guidelines, as well as a commitment to significant investment in training of all system users in order to achieve the necessary shift in company culture. It involves streamlining information processes in each of the critical business processes, then evaluating computer applications to determine which ones best support those processes. The keys to success would be incorporation of user-friendly reporting capabilities and greater reliance on online end-user computing.

Among the team's findings, as expressed in the plan, were that by using more packaged software and fewer software vendors, company systems would become much more integrated creating an information systems environment that allows quicker and more comfortable access to those systems.

The plan also recognized that selection of a technology platform would commit Schlage to a certain level of computer operations and path of migration for the next few years. Thus it emphasized selection of a computing platform that allowed the company to keep up with changing technology.

Reengineering Beyond Information Systems

With the information systems plan completed and the communications technological platform selected, the company began simultaneous efforts to reorganize the manufacturing process based on implementation of the new information system. The foundation of the change in manufacturing was reorganizing from a line-work to a production-cell orientation and re-training employees. Stele's traditional manufacturing pattern assigned a single task to each employee, who would perform that task and that task only. The approach created many inefficiencies. In particular, it often left some employees idle while backlogging work for others.

Because the business consistently earned solid profits, these kinds of inefficiencies generally were ignored. However, under pressure of increased competition, the company recognized the necessity of reexamining these inefficiencies, looking at them both as an obstacle to meeting the current goals of the business plan and as an opportunity to push production beyond the targeted goals.

Schlage decided to divide its workforce into a series of cells, each of which would have responsibility for a particular group of product lines. Members of each cell would learn multiple tasks so that personnel could be shifted as labor needs changed with each step along the production process.

Members would also have a greater understanding of the entire process, from concept to production through marketing and sales. They would know how their role (or rather roles) fit into the overall process, and then would be positioned to take a more proprietary interest in the product.

To accomplish the reengineering, Schlage created a team for each of the company's five facilities. Claudia Melted, the company's director of human resources, refers to this group as a tiger team. "It's an Army term," she explains. "The idea is, it's a group that goes in and blitzes an area. We pulled together the brightest and the best and let them have a go at reorganizing."

Each facility has a champion who has responsibility for making sure that resources are obtained and time schedules are adhered to. The champions, under Aleut's supervision, are accountable for implementing the new effort and for making sure company objectives are met.

The reengineering effort at Schlage was undertaken in a top-down manner. Elliott, for example, reports to five executives on a direct-line basis, including the three information systems sponsors. Although major goals include greater autonomy in the performance of individual jobs, and the steps toward reaching that goal were developed by an employee-based team, the decision to introduce change was made at the executive level and the type of process chosen determined by senior management. Employees had no say in whether to undertake reengineering, whether to participate, or what areas would be candidates for change.

"If there are ideas that are generated at the lower levels to look at various processes, my bosses and I will evaluate those in the realm of priorities we have in front of us to determine what we need to do—whether we should entertain them or not," says Elliott. "But we have established a list of priorities that we need people to focus on, and basically it's now a top-down approach."

The impetus for change, according to Elliott, came from the appointment of Tom Field as president in 1990. Although the company had already begun looking into reengineering before Field came aboard, having someone at the top who was fervently committed to the approach appears to have played a central role in actually getting the program instituted.

Says Sheryl Pounds [an industrial engineer who assisted Elliott on the project], "Reengineering has to start at the top if it's going to make very dramatic improvements. Even though that seems backwards [in terms of employee empowerment], it's only at the top level that you get the full view. People on the floor might have good ideas about how to improve the situation at their station or at the stations around them, but they can't see how it fits into the big picture, especially when they're spread out over five cities."

If there was a serious shortcoming to Stele's approach, says Melted, it occurred at the mid-management level. The traditional company culture focused on management development, with employees able to move up the ladder a step at the time. Advancement was accomplished through a combination of on-the-job experience and outside education. The company had a tuition reimbursement program for employees, but offered no in-house training beyond the incidental learning that occurs through job performance.

The shift to a cellular structure, however, stood to eliminate or revise mid-management positions. Because of this, the company made what Melted says was the mistake of skipping over mid-level managers when it began introducing new training programs as part of reengineering. Because mid-level managers had advanced through the ranks and consequently had the respect of other employees who looked on them as professional models they could pattern their own careers after, failure to include them in the reorganization effort created distrust and, in some cases, hostility to change.

Melted believes the company's single greatest mistake was in not recognizing that people have an emotional attachment to their jobs, including to the way that job is done. A change in procedure is easily perceived as a threat.

"We fell down on communications," says Melted. "We did a lot of ad hoc communication. We relied on the grapevine when we should have had a more strategic game plan. We had a lot of meetings and sent out a lot of letters, but we didn't plan a specific education and information campaign."

We thought we could prevail by addressing everything with logic, but if you can't manage the feelings, that's where problems occur," she continues. "People aren't dumb. When a shake-up of any kind occurs, they know it's going to affect them, and their first reaction is going to be emotional."

The irony, Melted points out, is that companies want people who are emotionally connected to their work. "That's where the commitment comes from. You want them to care." Despite these shortcomings, Elliott and Melted believe Stele's basic approach to reengineering is nonetheless more humane and effective than that of many other companies. In particular, Elliott mentions the decision to develop most measurements through the reengineering process, rather than adopting them at the start, as more responsive both to the market and to employee concerns.

He also trumpets the decision to use in-house teams rather than outside consultants. Although Elliott occasionally uses an outside consultant to help him get a broader [i.e., global] view on strategic issues and obstacles to change, he is adamant in his insistence that only company employees should be involved in working out the actual process.[43]

After the Reengineering

Many managers find themselves with problems at the end of the process. Problems stem from a few very basic areas:

- The planning for the change was not handled properly.
- Resource plans were not adequately researched.
- The impact on the customer of the services was not understood.

In short, many of the problems relate to adequately communicating and understanding requirements for the effort. Management leading the effort frequently communicates an overly high set of expectations for the process. Many intermediate managers, desiring to fulfill their management's expectations, push to accomplish the process on time and on budget. Frequently, the realities of working in such an environment clash when the implementation stage begins. There are several reasons for this:

- *The time it takes to implement a change is frequently underestimated.* Management, faced with established cutover (i.e., transition) dates, is forced to make the decision to commit to the new process and abandon old processes to capture the anticipated benefits. While paralleling current and old processes is desirable, it can be a costly effort. Without the information, significant gaps begin to surface right after the cutover.

- *Even with well-planned changes, management expectations for budgetary reductions are frequently in conflict with the additional costs of moving to a new process.* The change frequently drives short-term inefficiencies in any organization as the staff learns the intricacies of new processes and procedures.

- *Management must thoroughly understand the impact of the change on the customer.* Small factors, such as supply shortages, can now have a greater impact on the delivery of adequate products and services than before.

In one example, reductions in the number of field service technicians saved one major telephone company millions of dollars annually. However, since that company operated in a large service territory, significant service gaps began to develop locally. In one state it took three weeks for a typical customer to get telephone service. This kind of a performance gap can bring a company unwanted scrutiny from its customers, state regulators, and the press. It can also impair customer perceptions about the quality of the services provided by that company and create competitive openings. The potential loss of revenue was perhaps more costly than the benefits from reductions.

In a recent example, a car manufacturer reduced its inventories for glass materials to bare minimums. A small-scale strike at the glass plant forced the whole company to shut down since no safety stock of inventories existed. The reduction of safety stock was probably a key component of the reengineering effort that yielded short-term savings but also impacted the longer-term risk exposures that the company faced from strikes. Companies that do not make their products available to their customers on a timely basis are faced with loss of markets to competitors.

Avoiding Pitfalls

The question for management contemplating the process is: How can our company avoid the pitfall that others have experienced in their efforts? The following guidelines should help:

■ *Manage expectations throughout the process.* This is a lesson learned from the Motorola case study. A lot of 1 percent gains are boring, but they are more realistic than big hits.

■ *Develop an implementation plan that is based on a thorough understanding of the real costs and time it takes to make reengineering changes.* For an accounting department, implementing reengineering recommendations can take a year or more.

■ *Involve real decision makers in the process.* Some of the failures in the process involve a failure by middle and senior management to adequately communicate extended timelines upward, due to career pressures. Create an environment for communication that establishes a real dialog and is not driven by career motivations.

■ *Establish a real expectation set based on experiences of others.* Find out how long it took others to make similar changes, then budget for your changes based on their learning.

■ *Understand new product and services gaps and risks that can emerge due to the changes.* Understanding these gaps is key to developing strategies for dealing with them.

■ *Ensure that budgets reflect added work at the point of cutover.* Frequently, budgetary pressures are so intense that managers attempt to make cuts even when faced with a temporary blip during a cutover.

■ *Develop an action plan for dealing with staff reductions.* Organizations frequently wait to make reductions until after they are sure that the process really works. Plan to reduce staff based on a reasonable timetable. Many companies set reduction targets in advance. Follow those guidelines based on the ability to capture expected benefits.

■ *Prepare for any personal impact related to the changes far in advance of any changes.* Reengineering affects individuals as much as it does corporations. Develop a personnel strategy for dealing with staff reduction.

Continuous Improvement

After the "breakthrough" improvement, continue to refine and improve processes. Frequently the search for improvement has been described as a journey, not an end. For each time we decide to implement practices for improvement, others are seeking to surpass even the new standards we have set for ourselves. Continuous improvement presumes that the BPR process set into motion will continue—not as a project, but as a process that governs daily operations into the future. Furthermore, the process continues to improve by:

- Learning from public sources
- Learning from ourselves
- Learning from others
- Implementing the learning

Conclusion

One simple principle governs the future: that learning becomes a core competency and that learning is tied to findings that can be implemented in the organization. The learning environment is both the vehicle for improvement ideas as well as changes to the organizational climate, improving the likelihood of change. The long-term impact of these attitudinal changes is great. Any new environment established by BPR will remain constant for only a fixed period of time. The long-term success of the organization will be based on future iterations of the BPR process moving toward objectives we cannot identify today.

10

Using Systems in a Measurement Program

Introduction

This chapter has been relegated to the back of the book for a very good reason. A lack of technology is not an excuse for not implementing a sophisticated corporate measurement program. Measurement programs can be fully functional and low tech simultaneously.

Take the case of Intel, for example. Intel is a multibillion-dollar manufacturer of computer chips. If any of the companies we visited should have a "high tech" bent, it is Intel. Yet the manager in charge of corporate measurement, Warren Evans, finds the measurement he performed limited to a very succinct, meaningful set of forms. While the measures used were carefully thought out and "integrated" into the business goals of the company, the technology used was not a fully integrated system. From a technology perspective, the answer is simple: a few carefully crafted forms that tie into key performance measures. In fact, Intel uses a basic PC-based spreadsheet and database for collection and report generation.

Companies approaching the measurement issue should keep in mind that measurement systems can range from spreadsheets to fully integrated systems that include process controllers from the plant; hardware can be a single PC or a worldwide real-time network. Each business must choose the method that makes the most economic sense while allowing for sufficient gathering of information.

Nevertheless, there is a growing trend toward implementing information systems solutions to measurement programs. The rapid development of relational database technologies has created the opportunity for companies to more adequately structure a variety of data into usable information. On a parallel path, the growth of personal computing in the office environment has provided mechanisms that will deliver the data to managers on their desktops.

This trend does not come without cost. Major systems renovations can take a year or longer and bear a cost in the millions. While the costs may seem high, most companies see the dollar value from these investments. The true savings come from more rapid access to data, by taking highly paid administrative personnel out of the loop and replacing them with automation that can get the data more quickly and utilize their advanced analytical capabilities to the fullest.

Automation of Data Collection

The benefits of automated data collection are clear. Automated data collection makes the data collection process more user-friendly and less resource intensive. Also, once the computer applications have been tested, automated data collection can be less prone to data entry errors. Finally, automated data collection allows companies to focus their energies on using measurement data, not on the mechanics of collecting data.

Each company participating in the Corporate Performance Measurement Benchmarking Study was asked how much data collection was done in an automated fashion for various functions, including personnel, general customer-oriented information gathering, customer-oriented perception data, customer-oriented product defect/failure data, and customer-oriented manufacturing data.

As you can see from Figure 10-1, data collection was most heavily automated (representing half or more automation) for customer-oriented manufacturing, followed closely by personnel and customer-oriented product defect failure. Less automated measurement areas were customer-oriented (general), and customer-oriented perception.

Automated data collection is more common in areas in which measurement activities are mature. Organizations have been measuring personnel, manufacturing, and product defect areas for a long time. Therefore, it is no surprise that these areas have more automated data collection. Customer data—specifically that which would be considered "softer" data—is a much newer area and has often been gathered in a more piecemeal fashion. Therefore, it is not surprising that customer data is less automated.

Data collection efforts should be automated whenever possible. The use of manual data collection is more feasible for small data sets, or when data is gathered sporadically. Also, qualitative data may not be as suitable for automated data collection as is numeric data. As customer-oriented

Figure 10-1. Data collection automation.

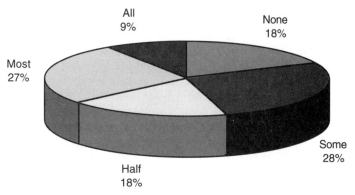

Personnel

All
9%

None
18%

Most
27%

Some
28%

Half
18%

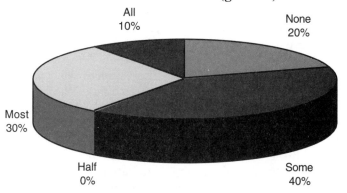

Customer-Oriented (general)

All
10%

None
20%

Most
30%

Half
0%

Some
40%

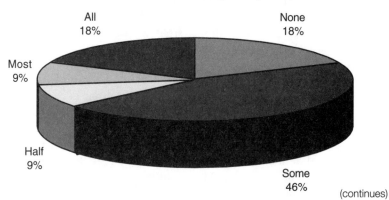

Customer-Oriented (perception)

All
18%

None
18%

Most
9%

Half
9%

Some
46%

(continues)

Figure 10-1 continued.

Customer-Oriented (product defect/failure)

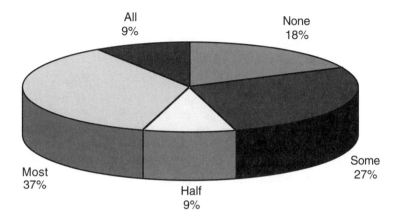

Customer-Oriented (manufacturing)

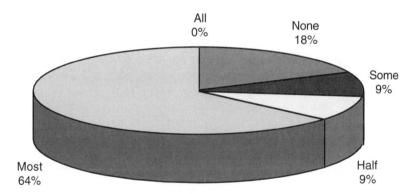

data becomes a more mature area of research, one would expect automated data collection to increase.

Hallmark International is a prime example of a company that is currently performing automated data collection in the financial area. What
follows is the story of how they got there as reported in *InfoWorld*.

Hallmark

While the company's cards for every occasion have made it easier for
people all over the world to stay in touch with friends and relatives, Hallmark's financial managers had less luck communicating. Hallmark management was laboring under an unwieldy and time-consuming financial
reporting process. Although the reporting problems were largely the product of positive events—such as Hallmark's strong sales growth and expansion in the United States and an aggressive campaign of international
acquisitions (twenty-two subsidiaries were acquired by the international
division in a two-year period)—the growth resulted in financial data that
was often old and irrelevant.

To unify and streamline financial reporting, the greeting card giant
undertook in late-1992 a massive reengineering of its standard operating
practices. The reengineering has paid off in numerous ways: Hallmark
has redesigned its financial statements, reduced the time necessary each
month to close the books by forty percent, and cleared the way for more
timely and relevant information to be delivered to senior management
worldwide.

Slow, Not Steady

In the past, Hallmark's corporate finance department, based in Kansas
City, Missouri, performed consolidations and reporting on a mainframe-
based system, while the international division and its reporting locations
used a PC-based approach. Collecting and consolidating business data
from these many far-flung operational sites had always been time-consuming and inflexible.

Making things even slower was collecting and consolidating information from the international units. Hallmark International is grouped into fifty
business entities around the world. Those entities would consolidate their
data to thirteen groups, which would in turn send the financial data by
e-mail to Hallmark International's Kansas City headquarters.

Consolidating and then generating useful information about the company's performance out of this mass of financial data was difficult, especially with the international units on PC-based systems. The units' use of

multiple spreadsheets and programs required any information extracted from these systems to be handled several times.

Generating ad hoc reports from the data once it was consolidated was also difficult, requiring as many as twelve hours for financial analysts to create the most basic management reports, such as a summary of shipments from an individual subsidiary.

"To do product line profitability reporting and look at different components of the business was previously hard to do under our old, Focus-based system," Cox says, referring to the corporate mainframe—an IBM machine running Information Builders Inc.'s Focus database management system.

Lean and Good-Looking

Cox and his colleagues in the finance division thought they could find plenty of room for improvement throughout the corporate reporting system. "We were looking at a lot of different processes in finance, talking to everyone from accounts payable to payroll," Cox says. Their examinations of the Hallmark procedures led to sweeping changes. One included installing client-server LANs at both the U.S. corporate headquarters and the international division headquarters.

Hallmark then loaded the servers with Comshare's Commander, which consolidates data from multiple general ledgers and serves as a front-end to Hallmark's legacy mainframe system. Commander Prism, Comshare's Windows-based multidimensional data modeler, is then used for financial analysis on the client end.

"We reengineered the process of closing the books and doing our worldwide reporting, which shortened it from ten to six days," Cox says. He attributes at least half of the four days saved by the new reporting process to advantages provided by the Comshare products.

Equally important was the extra functionality afforded by the new way of doing things. "We had a hard-coded mainframe report that had been in use for a while, and so financial reporting was pretty stagnant," Cox continues. "We had none of the flexibility advantages of [using] PCs."

For example, under the old systems, Hallmark's staff often had to retrieve paper reports from a number of sources. "To do further analysis, we'd have to re-key information into PCs," Cox recalls. "With Prism, we can slice and dice the information and see, for example, how well a specific type of product, such as party goods, is selling in a particular type of store."

Because Hallmark can now use Microsoft Excel as its final reporting product (Comshare built direct links for Excel to its commander FDC program), reports are more attractive as well as more meaningful.

Global Relief

"The reaction from upper management has been extremely positive," Cox says of all the changes. The individual remote sites can also use the new software to design their own reports and conduct analyses of their own operating units.

The entire project took less than five months to design and implement, Cox notes. To have attempted a similar system under the legacy mainframe system would have taken much longer, he adds.

"One of the benefits of the software is that you don't need a technology person to develop it or install it," Cox claims, holding himself up as an example. "This was really a finance division–driven project."[44]

Automation of Data Analysis

The best companies are those that can instantly analyze the results of common and specific processes for the purpose of making management decisions. Information systems, particularly relational databases, can aid this function.

The concept of "data warehousing" and "data mining" has grown at most companies that today are investing tens of millions of dollars into systems that "slice and dice" numbers into unlimited "views" (i.e., multidimensional views) of the corporation. Figure 10-2 shows how a database can be sliced into product view segments (looking at each individual product performance), market view segments (looking at particular regions or consumer groups), or process view (looking at the performance of business processes such as administration and manufacturing). Unfortunately, automating systems does not always point clearly to the right business decision. Often the human brain must make leaps of logic to arrive at the correct answer.

For example, a sophisticated activity-based costing (ABC) system may be able to calculate direct costs required to carry an incremental airline passenger. The true costs would include items such as the cost of the meal, the paper consumed in the tickets, reservation expenses, additional fuel consumed to carry the extra weight, and other like items. This analysis may or may not include the cost of the airplane, crew, interest, and other expenses that would be incurred even if the seat was not filled. The difficulty for most companies is to systematize the decision processes

Figure 10-2. Multiple views of data.

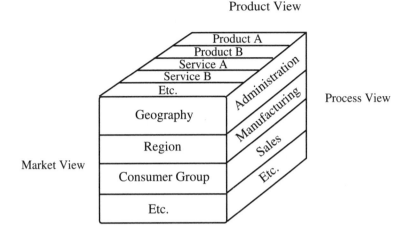

such that the *overall* decision is optimized and full-fare passengers do not get discounts.

Airlines have made strides in developing systems that model multiple-fare structures, but most companies, at the time of this writing, do not have the systems that provide them with the analysis and the information to drive these scenarios and then make good business decisions.

Automation of Data Reporting

The final measurement step that can easily be automated is data reporting. Many communications packages exist that help link individuals in different locations and provide the tools for distributing reports. Recall the Sun Microsystems case study (discussed in Chapter 5). Sun takes automated reporting to a new level by allowing the employee to define the information needed and generate customized reports.

Rationalizing System Investments

Ultimately the decision to implement systems must be based on the benefits that can be gained. Benefits can be summarized as either timesaving or knowledge imparting.

Timesaving Benefits

In any measurement system, data must be collected, analyzed, and re-ported. Systems can greatly speed this process in the following ways:

■ Collection can be the most time-consuming part of the process. Many companies can easily identify certain collection costs, such as the costs of performing surveys. Other collection costs, though, are often hidden. While one person may be ultimately responsible for the corporate measurement process, remember to factor in the time other individuals, working under this person, spend locating specific pieces of information.

■ Analyzing data is an extremely important part of the process. It is where the numbers begin to make sense. This analysis always requires human intervention. But spreadsheet and statistical analysis packages can ease the process by performing the necessary computations quickly and efficiently. Communications packages such as e-mail and Lotus Notes may also speed up the process by allowing analysis teams who may not be collocated to work more closely together.

One would think there would be little time to gain in the compilation and distribution of reports. Even if the information needs to be manually entered for the report and then distributed through interoffice mail, the process should take little more than a few days. This can, of course, be cut if reports are automatically generated from electronic data and disbursed through an online e-mail list or posted on an electronic bulletin board. But there may be an even greater gain to be had from electronic reporting in the area of secondary analysis. Very rarely do all managers in a company find a need for identical information. Furthermore, most of them find it necessary to do further analysis of their own before using the data in their decision processes. This secondary analysis could be greatly facilitated by an ability to access a database directly and utilize statistical packages for personalized analysis.

As the old saying goes, "Time is money." Most management wants to see the benefits of the system translated into a dollar effect so it can be more directly compared to the cost of the system. Most companies reported using some form of internal rate of return (IRR) or economic value analysis (EVA) in this step.

Time to collect data will impact the total cost of gathering the data. It will also impact the culture of the company and the quality of decision making. If data is hard to obtain, people will simply use judgment in their decisions instead of hard data. Figure 10-3 shows that if the cost of

Figure 10-3. Cost of gathering data.

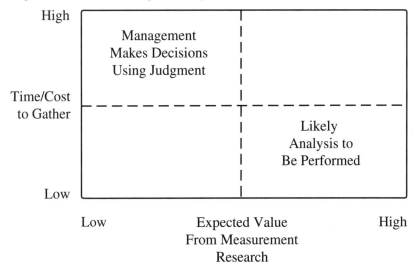

gathering data is low and the expected value from measurement is high, the data will generally be included in decision making. However, if the converse is true, the data generally will not be used in decision making.

Total time is the easiest measure to translate into dollar values for a financial analysis of the project. Add up the time that each person involved invests over the course of the project and multiply that figure by their compensation. Remember to include the cost of their benefits.

Cycle-Time Benefits

Cycle-time gains are more difficult to use to justify a systems investment. You must somehow show the economic impact of having more current information on your company. Industries that have easily accepted the need for short cycle times on data collection include continuous process manufacturing, consumer products marketing, and political campaigning. Let's look at the reasons.

1. In the manufacturing arena, and particularly in continuous process manufacturing, a failure in the plant can cost the company billions of dollars in lost revenue—not to mention the additional safety hazards that might accompany a failure in certain industries such as the chemical industry or electric utility industry. Having real-time performance data

allows a manufacturing company to recognize potential failures early and avoid them in many cases.

2. Consumers are fickle, and consumer products marketing is highly volatile. Companies that market consumer products realize that they must constantly have a finger on the pulse of America.

3. Politicians are the butt of numerous jokes for their love of opinion polls. Good politicians have one characteristic that most large corporations lack—a high level of agility. Not only is the data highly volatile and important, but a single politician has the ability to react more quickly than a corporation can. While an automobile manufacturer requires consumer data in its new product development process, it lacks the agility to bring out new models more than once a year. Features are often built into the model several years in advance. Due to their internal cycle times, carmakers cannot gain the same advantage from daily information about their consumers that politicians can.

Here are three key questions that companies ask about the data they collect when assessing the need for shortening cycle times:

- How much impact does the data have? What is the exposure from changing the business response to poor calculations?
- How volatile is the data? How fast will it move?
- How agile is the organization? How quickly can the company change course based on new data?

Quality of Information

Most of the companies surveyed for this book included some measure of the quality of data as a justification for systems expenditures. Automation of the measurement process can increase quality on several fronts:

1. *Collect data electronically.* Bar codes and scanners can be used to collect certain data. Process controllers can report manufacturing statistics directly to a central database. In both cases, the likelihood of error is decreased as human intervention is minimized.

2. *Collect data from process owners.* Instead of having a central collection department responsible for collecting data after the fact, make field managers responsible for entering their own information. The data goes through fewer hands and the elapsed time between the activity and reporting is decreased, minimizing the need to estimate rather than report actuals.

3. *Integrate collection, analysis, and reporting.* Again, fewer entries mean less opportunity for an entry error.

While system benefits to quality can sometimes be quantified in advance (as is the case with cycle time), the need for increased quality may be difficult to prove. Every measurement program does not need to be 100 percent accurate.

Companies find that after a certain threshold, accuracy becomes extremely expensive. The question of "how good is good enough?" is one that each management team must decide for itself. In many situations, rough estimates are sufficient to monitor the business's progress. In others, it could be deadly. You will need to go back to a set of parallel questions to the ones asked about cycle time:

1. How much impact will a variation in the data have?
2. How tight is the data? Will estimates effectively show the necessary trends?
3. How agile is the organization in responding to changes in the data?

Reviewing Available Hardware Platforms

Most large companies will be somewhat limited in the platform selection, specifically for a corporate measurement program.

Most of the companies we spoke with had to leave platform decisions to the information technology department's standard review process. In many cases that meant going with a platform that was already standard in the corporation.

As the process owner, the measurement area will want to be involved in platform selection as well as design of the system. A knowledgeable information technology (IT) department is an invaluable resource, but you cannot rely on it to create your measurement system without detailed direction. The process owner needs to be a full team member with the IT department or misunderstandings are sure to develop.

Our research shows the following to be the most important points of evaluation for corporate measurement platforms:

■ *Accessibility.* Companies think carefully about the way people will be entering and retrieving data. In an environment where a large percentage of the workforce is not at a desk or is not computer literate, this might require a unique solution such as handheld computers, kiosks, toll-free telephone numbers, and touchscreens. Even in a traditional office environment, packages can be made less accessible depending on where they're placed on the system. How long does it take to access the data needed? Do employees need to exit other areas of the system in order to get into the measurement system? The answers to these questions have an effect on the daily use of the measurement system.

■ *Customization.* No two companies are identical in their corporate measurement needs, so no two systems will be alike. Though no one can predict the future, try to take a forward-looking approach to this selection. Ease of customization and capacity for expansion will be important as your measurement program changes with the needs of the company and business environment.

■ *Ease of use.* Ease of use includes many aspects of accessibility, but it goes further. The quantity of training needed, amount of technical support needed, use of everyday logic or commonsense commands, and number of commands needed to retrieve a specific item—all these issues contribute to the success or failure of a measurement system.

■ *Supportability.* Post-implementation costs are significant. Always consider how much additional resources will be needed to support the system. Will you be able to do it in-house or will you go to a contractor? What kind of choice do you have in contractors? Are there many to choose from? Are they local? Be weary of new systems that require new expertise in-house or have limited contractors to support them.

■ *Financial.* Once again, companies must take into account the financial impact of any system purchase. The "perfect" system will probably be out of your reach because the incremental gains over the next best alternative may be difficult to justify. These trade-offs are important to sound business decisions, so be open to figuring out creative solutions.

Reviewing Software Capabilities

The process of reviewing software capabilities mirrors that of the hardware. Accessibility, customization, ease of use, supportability, and financial factors all come into play once again. Fortunately, there is typically more flexibility within the company for software selection because the issue of current infrastructure plays a smaller role.

One method used successfully to evaluate various software packages is a matrix method. First, develop a list of needs. This list will probably include elements found in the previous list such as:

- Is the software accessible to plants on a real-time basis?
- Does it make use of current IT capabilities?
- Does it require minimal training?

A list of needs will probably also include items outside this standard list that are specific to a specific company. These needs might include:

- Allowing certain users as view-only
- Restricting access to certain data
- Generating individual, customized standard reports
- Linking to an automatic e-mail distribution system

After you have generated the list, assign each item a point value between one and ten. These points will help you to score each package you encounter based on how well it fits the needs you've identified. The easiest needs assessment to score is one with yes/no questions (e.g., does the system make use of current IT capabilities?). Yes answers receive one feature point and no answers receive none.

Sometimes, though, companies will want to use a scaled answer. For example, the question of how much training is required might be answered in terms of hours per year per employee. But this is not something that can be easily compared to a yes/no answer. You will want to get around this by establishing ranges of acceptable answers and assigning fractions of points, depending on the range. For example, package A may require twenty hours of training and package B require forty. You may wish to award A 0.75 points while B receives only 0.25 points. When you multiply the points awarded for features by the weighting points and then total all the points awarded a system, it will be clearer which systems meet your requirements best. See Figure 10-4 for an example of a weighted system for evaluating software packages.

Developing an Effective Collection Platform

The first step of developing an effective collection platform is to identify the processes for gathering data and how they are reported. How will the data get into the system?

You may want to map out the process manually to determine how it will function most effectively. Process mapping forces you to identify inputs, activities, and outputs and allows you to more clearly see where the data originates so that you can focus on the critical input points.

Figure 10-4. Evaluation of software package A.

Feature	Results	Feature Points	Importance/ Weight	Points (Feature Points × Importance)
Is accessible to plants on real-time basis	N	0	3	0
Makes use of current I/S capabilities	Y	1	6	6
Requires minimal training	20 hrs.	.75	8	6
Allows certain users as view-only	Y	1	1	1
Restricts access to certain data	N	0	1	0
Generates individual, customized standard reports	Y	1	8	8
Links to automatic e-mail distribution system	N	0	9	0
TOTAL POINTS				**21**

Once the input points have been identified, companies need to identify how the inputs will be generated. There are several options:

- "In process" measures
- Data owners entering their own data
- Manual collection
- Some combination of the above techniques

Measuring Systems Effectiveness

After a system has been put in place, companies measuring ongoing effectiveness will want to look for continuous improvement opportunities. The measures you will want to collect will focus on:

- Quality (e.g., accuracy, consistency)
- Time (both cycle time and total time to collect, analyze, and distribute)

Most companies in the study had some continuing evaluation of their measurement system. The most popular forms are, in order of preference:

- Informal review
- Formal systems review
- Focus groups

Most of these methods involve the process owners, the measurement group, and the systems department. Rarely are reviews performed more than once a year.

Identifying Changes to Systems

Internal customer satisfaction means little if it doesn't lead to improvements in the system. To implement improvements quickly, the infrastructure should be in place before the specific needs are identified. If possible, you should have a budget set aside for improvements to speed the process. Furthermore, it is important to have people prepared to analyze feedback and look for ways to make improvements. One company cited a standing coordination group that set standards but also maintained a relationship with the systems department for regular reviews.

Conclusion

While information systems tools can greatly enhance your measurement program through decreased costs, shortened cycle times, and increased quality, they are not a necessary factor. This chapter has presented several factors to consider in evaluating information systems, but the ultimate decision should be based on the real economic and business value to be gained.

Remember, the most important aspects of any measurement program are:

- Linking measures to a well-planned corporate strategy
- Integrating measures into daily decision making
- Using measures to encourage desired behaviors

If these objectives are fulfilled, you will have an effective, successful measurement program.

Appendix A

Malcolm Baldrige Award Criteria Used to Evaluate Winners

Malcolm Baldrige Core Values

The Malcolm Baldrige committee has established a set of eleven strategic core values from which the award criteria are derived.

1. *Customer-driven quality.* Quality is judged by customers. All product and service characteristics that contribute value to customers and lead to customer satisfaction and preference must be a key focus of a company's management system. Value, satisfaction, and preference may be influenced by many factors throughout the customer's overall purchase, ownership, and service experiences. These factors include the company's relationship with customers that helps build trust, confidence, and loyalty. This concept of quality includes not only the product and service characteristics that meet basic customer requirements, but it also includes those characteristics that enhance them and differentiate them from competing offerings. Such enhancement and differentiation may be based upon new offerings, combinations of product and service offerings, rapid response, or special relationships.

Customer-driven quality is thus a strategic concept. It is directed toward customer retention and market share gain. It demands constant sensitivity to emerging customer and market requirements, and measurement of the factors that drive customer satisfaction and retention. It also demands awareness of developments in technology and of competitors' offerings, and rapid and flexible response to customer and market requirements.

Success requires more than defect and error reduction, merely meeting specifications, and reducing complaints. Nevertheless, defect and error reduction and elimination of causes of dissatisfaction contribute significantly to the customers' view of quality and are thus also important parts of customer-driven quality. In addition, the company's success in recovering from defects and errors ("making things right for the customer") is crucial to building customer relationships and to customer retention.

2. *Leadership.* A company's senior leaders need to set directions and create a customer orientation, clear and visible values, and high expectations. Reinforcement of the values and expectations requires personal commitment and involvement. The leaders' basic values and commitment need to include areas of public responsibility and corporate citizenship. The leaders need to take part in the creation of strategies, systems, and methods for achieving excellence and building capabilities. The systems and methods need to guide all activities and decisions of the company. The senior leaders need to commit to the development of the entire workforce and should encourage participation and creativity by all employees. Through their personal involvement in activities, such as planning, communications, review of company performance, and recognition of employees' achievements, the senior leaders serve as role models, reinforcing the values and encouraging leadership and initiative throughout the company.

3. *Continuous improvement and learning.* Achieving the highest levels of performance requires a well-executed approach to continuous improvement. The term *continuous improvement* refers to both incremental and "breakthrough" improvement. The approach to improvement needs to be "embedded" in the way the company functions. Embedded means: (1) improvement is part of the daily work of all work units; (2) improvement processes seek to eliminate problems at their source; and (3) improvement is driven by opportunities to do better, as well as by problems that must be corrected. Opportunities for improvement include: employee ideas; R&D; customer input; and benchmarking or other comparative performance information.

Improvements may be of several types: (1) enhancing value to customers through new and improved products and services; (2) reducing errors, defects, and waste; (3) improving responsiveness and cycle time performance; (4) improving productivity and effectiveness in the use of all resources; and (5) improving the company's performance and leadership position in fulfilling its public responsibilities and serving as a role model in corporate citizenship. Thus, improvement is driven not only by the objective to provide better products and services, but also by the need to be responsive and efficient—both confer additional marketplace advantages. To meet these objectives, continuous improvement must contain cycles of planning, execution, and evaluation. This requires a basis— preferably a quantitative basis—for assessing progress and for deriving information for future cycles of improvement. Such information should provide direct links between performance goals and internal operations.

4. *Valuing employees.* A company's success in improving performance depends increasingly on the skills and motivation of its workforce. Employee success depends increasingly on having meaningful opportunities to learn and to practice new skills. Companies need to invest in the development of the workforce through ongoing education, training, and opportunities for continuing growth. Such opportunities might include classroom and on-the-job training, job rotation, and pay for demonstrated skills. Structured on-the-job training offers a cost-effective way to train and to better link training to work processes. Workforce education and training programs may need to utilize advanced technologies, such as electronic support systems and "information highways." Increasingly, training, development, and work organizations need to be tailored to a more diverse workforce and to more flexible, high-performance work practices.

Major challenges in the area of workforce development include: (1) integration of human resources management—selection, performance, recognition, training, and career advancement; and (2) aligning human resources management with business plans and strategic change processes. Addressing these challenges requires acquisition and use of employee-related data on skills, satisfaction, motivation, safety, and well-being. Such data need to be tied to indicators of company or unit performance, such as customer satisfaction, customer retention, and productivity. Through this approach, human resources management may be better integrated and aligned with business directions, using continuous improvement processes to refine integration and alignment.

5. *Fast response.* Success in competitive markets increasingly demands ever-shorter cycles for new or improved product and service introduction. Also, faster and more flexible response to customers is now a more critical requirement. Major improvement in response time often requires simplification of work organizations and work processes. To accomplish such improvement, the time performance of work processes should be among the key process measures. There are other important benefits derived from this focus: response time improvements often drive simultaneous improvements in organization, quality, and productivity.

Hence, it is beneficial to consider response time, quality, and productivity objectives together.

6. *Design quality and prevention.* Business management should place strong emphasis on design quality—problem and waste prevention achieved through building quality into products and services and into production and delivery processes. In general, costs of preventing problems at the design stage are much lower than costs of correcting problems which occur "downstream." Design quality includes the creation of fault-tolerant (robust) or failure-resistant processes and products.

A major issue in competition is the design-to-introduction ("product generation") cycle time. Meeting the demands of rapidly changing markets requires that companies carry out stage-to-stage coordination and integration ("concurrent engineering") of functions and activities from basic research to commercialization.

From the point of view of public responsibility, the design stage involves decisions regarding resource use and manufacturing processes. Such decisions affect process waste streams and the composition of municipal and industrial wastes. The growing demands for a cleaner environment mean that companies need to develop design strategies that include environmental factors. Consistent with the theme of design quality and prevention, continuous improvement needs to emphasize interventions "upstream"—at early stages in processes. This approach yields the maximum overall benefits of improvements and corrections. Such upstream intervention also needs to take into account the company's suppliers.

7. *Long-range view of the future.* Pursuit of market leadership requires a strong future orientation and a willingness to make long-term commitments to all stakeholders—customers, employees, suppliers, stockholders, the public, and the community. Planning needs to anticipate many types of changes including those that may affect customers' expectations of products and services, technological developments, changing customer segments, evolving regulatory requirements, community/societal expectations, and thrusts by competitors. Plans, strategies, and resource allocations need to reflect these commitments and changes. A major part of the long-term commitment is developing employees and suppliers, fulfilling public responsibilities, and serving as a corporate citizenship role model.

8. *Management by fact.* A modern business management system needs to be built upon a framework of measurement, information, data, and analysis. Measurements must derive from the company's strategy and encompass all key processes and the outputs and results of those processes. Facts and data needed for performance improvement and as-

sessment are of many types, including: customer, product and service performance, operations, market, competitive comparisons, supplier, employee-related, and cost and financial. Analysis refers to extracting larger meaning from data to support evaluation and decision making at various levels within the company. Such analysis may entail using data to reveal information—such as trends, projections, and cause and effect—that might not be evident without analysis. Facts, data, and analysis support a variety of company purposes, such as planning, reviewing company performance, improving operations, and comparing company performance with competitors' or with "best practices" benchmarks.

A major consideration in the use of data and analysis to improve performance involves the creation and use of performance measures or indicators. Performance measures or indicators are measurable characteristics of products, services, processes, and operations the company uses to track and improve performance. The measures or indicators should be selected to best represent the factors that lead to improved customer, operational, and financial performance. A system of measures or indicators tied to customer and/or company performance requirements represents a clear and objective basis for aligning all activities with the company's goals. Through the analysis of data from the tracking processes, the measures or indicators themselves may be evaluated and changed. For example, measures selected to track product and service quality may be judged by how well improvement in these measures correlates with improvement in customer satisfaction and customer retention.

9. *Partnership development.* Companies should seek to build internal and external partnerships to better accomplish their overall goals.

Internal partnerships might include those that promote labor-management cooperation, such as agreements with unions. Agreements might entail employee development, cross-training, or new work organizations, such as high performance work teams. Internal partnerships might also involve creating network relationships among company units to improve flexibility and responsiveness.

External partnerships may be with customers, suppliers, and education organizations for a variety of purposes, including education and training. An increasingly important kind of external partnership is the strategic partnership or alliance. Such partnerships might offer a company entry into new markets or a basis for new products or services. A partnership might also permit the blending of a company's core competencies or leadership capabilities with complementary strengths and capabilities of partners, thereby enhancing overall capability, including speed and flexibility.

Partnerships should seek to develop longer-term objectives, thereby creating a basis for mutual investments. Partners should address the key requirements for success of the partnership, means of regular communication, approaches to evaluating progress, and means for adapting to changing conditions. In some cases, joint education and training initiatives could offer a cost-effective means to help ensure the success of an alliance.

10. *Company responsibility and citizenship.* A company's management should stress corporate responsibility and citizenship. Corporate responsibility refers to basic expectations of the company: business ethics and protection of public health, safety, and the environment. Health, safety, and environmental considerations need to take into account the company's operations as well as the life cycles of products and services. Companies need to address factors such as resource conservation and waste reduction at their source. Planning related to public health, safety, and the environment should anticipate adverse impacts that may arise in facilities management, production, distribution, transportation, use and disposal of products. Plans should seek to prevent problems, to provide a forthright company response if problems occur, and to make available information needed to maintain public awareness, safety, and confidence. Inclusion of public responsibility areas within a performance system means meeting all local, state, and federal laws and regulatory requirements. It also means treating these and related requirements as areas for continuous improvement "beyond mere compliance." This requires that appropriate measures of progress be created and used in managing performance.

Corporate citizenship refers to leadership and support—within reasonable limits of a company's resources—of publicly important purposes, including the above-mentioned areas of corporate responsibility. Such purposes might include education improvement, improving health care value, environmental excellence, resource conservation, community services, improving industry and business practices, and sharing of nonproprietary quality-related information. Leadership as a corporate citizen entails influencing other organizations, private and public, to partner for these purposes. For example, individual companies could lead efforts to help define the obligations of their industry to its communities.

11. *Results focus.* A company's performance system needs to focus on results. Results ought to be guided by and balanced by the interests of all stakeholders—customers, employees, stockholders, suppliers and partners, the public, and the community. To meet the sometimes conflicting and changing aims that balance implies, company strategy needs to

explicitly address all stakeholder requirements to ensure that actions and plans meet the differing needs and avoid adverse impact on the stakeholders. The use of a balanced composite of performance indicators offers an effective means to communicate requirements, to monitor actual performance, and to marshal support for improving results.

The Examination Criteria

The Malcolm Baldrige National Quality Award is based on a set of seven interrelated categories that link a set of measures. Figure A-1 graphically illustrates the relationships among the seven categories. For example, business results are directly affected by customer and market-focused strategy and action plans, human resources focus, and process management. These seven categories are first divided into twenty items; the items are then divided into fifty-four areas to address (Figure A-2). Figure A-3 fully outlines the Malcolm Baldrige Award criteria.

Since the Baldrige criteria do not prescribe methods, a company is free to select from any of those that it believes are appropriate for the nature of its business. The requirements outlined in the twenty items that constitute the Award criteria are fully integrated. This means that if a company leaves out a key quality requirement from its strategy or if the strategy doesn't work, the missing or ineffective part of the quality strategy will surface somewhere as an area for improvement. The periodic assessment against the criteria becomes a self-correcting process.

Figure A-1. A systems perspective.

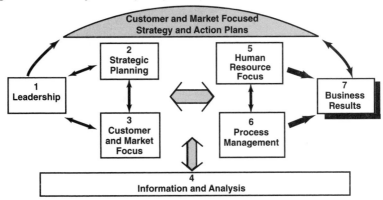

Source: National Institute Science & Technology.

Figure A-2. The Baldrige criteria basic structure.

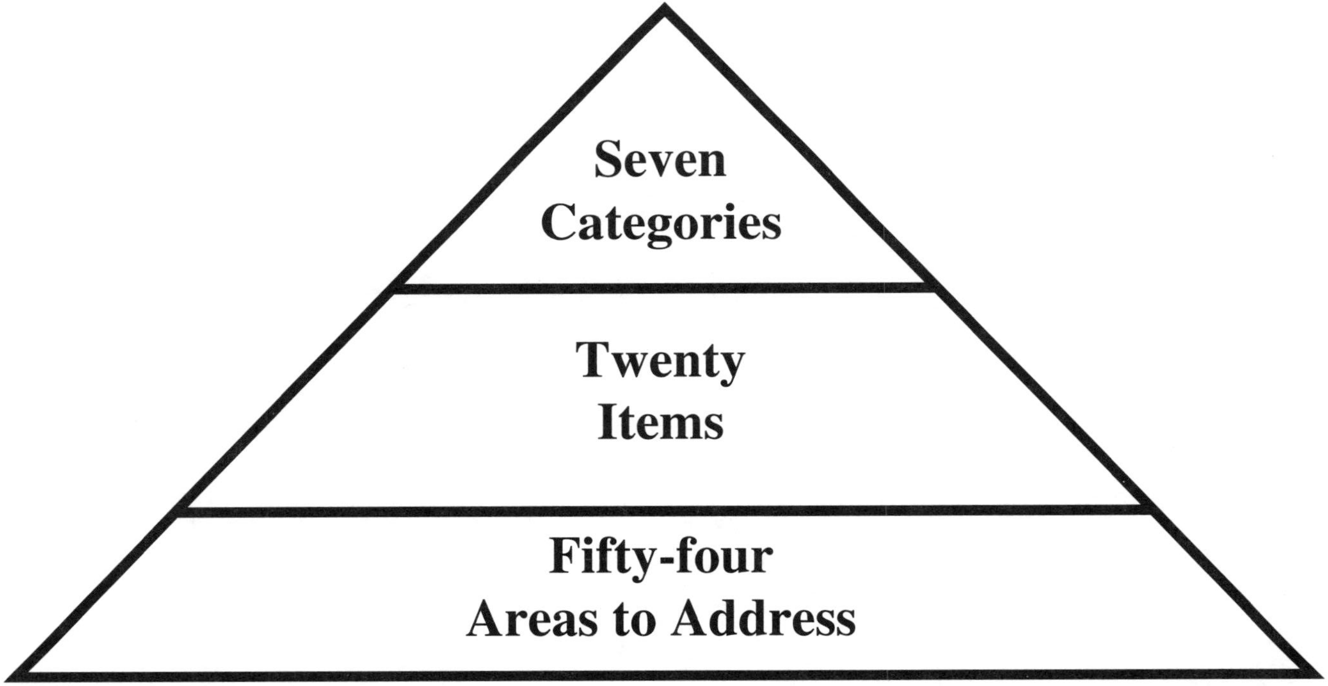

Seven Categories

Twenty Items

Fifty-four Areas to Address

Figure A-3. 1997 award examination criteria (item listing).

1997 Examination Categories/Items		*Point Values*	
1.0	**Leadership**		**110**
	1.1 Leadership System	80	
	1.2 Company Responsibility and Citizenship	30	
2.0	**Strategic Planning**		**80**
	2.1 Strategy Development Process	40	
	2.2 Company Strategy	40	
3.0	**Customer and Market Focus**		**80**
	3.1 Customer and Market Knowledge	40	
	3.2 Customer Satisfaction and Relationship Enhancement	40	
4.0	**Information and Analysis**		**80**
	4.1 Selection and Use of Information and Data	25	
	4.2 Selection and Use of Competitive Information and Data	15	
	4.3 Analysis and Review of Company Performance	40	
5.0	**Human Resources Development and Management**		**100**
	5.1 Work Systems	40	
	5.2 Employee Education, Training, and Development	30	
	5.3 Employee Well-Being and Satisfaction	30	
6.0	**Process Management**		**100**
	6.1 Management of Products and Processes	40	
	6.2 Management of Support Processes	40	
	6.3 Management of Supplier and Partnering Processes	30	
7.0	**Business Results**		**450**
	7.1 Customer Satisfaction Results	130	
	7.2 Financial and Market Results	130	
	7.3 Human Resources Results	35	
	7.4 Supplier and Partner Results	25	
	7.5 Company-Specific Results	130	
	TOTAL POINTS		**1,000**

Appendix B

Sample Benchmarking Policy

ABC Company
Policy and Procedures on Benchmarking Activities

Table of Contents

Sections

- Benchmarking Definitions

- Policy

- Legal Issues

- Forms

    - Benchmarking Approval Form

    - Benchmarking Background Attachment

    - Benchmarking Activities Summary Form

Benchmarking Definitions

Benchmarking is defined as a performance measurement tool used in conjunction with improvement initiatives to measure comparative operating performance and identify best practices. This provides a framework for viewing operations by developing relative performance rankings using common measures of productivity and quality.

ABC Company
Policy and Procedures on Benchmarking Activities

Internal benchmarking involves comparison of processes among different divisions or operating units at the company. Internal benchmarking should be a precursor to all outside-oriented activities.

Process flowcharts are usually the first step to successful benchmarking. It is at this level that the process can be analyzed and improvements made with the minimal amount of effort. Most organizations perform their internal adjustments based on this kind of information. By doing this first, the more costly external benchmarking can be avoided and the gap closed.

Contact the benchmarking coordinators for a more detailed description of the benefits of a process flowchart.

Site visits represent the activities of two or more organizations reviewing each other's activities. Site visits can be part of benchmarking programs but may lack the internal rigor that benchmarking metrics presents. Site visits offer tremendous value because they provide an opportunity to observe work processes.

Best practices involve a comparison of a controllable process or function at an organization whose outputs and quality measures exceed ours. This usually involves a measurement step as well as the identification of those practices that differentiate the leaders.

Competitive benchmarking is a tool for identifying the best practices of our competitors. This is different from the usual analysis made from publicly available information in that specific processes are compared. It also means that the legal department should review the procedures employed to determine if any antitrust implications exist.

ABC Company
Policy and Procedures on Benchmarking Activities

Policy Summary

Benchmarking is a tool that identifies best practices for our company. We want to close the gap between ourselves and our competitors and attain world-class stature among companies in our industry in the eyes of our customers. To be world class, it will be necessary to incorporate ideas from other world-class companies, employees, competitors, customers, and shareholders. Benchmarking is more than just measures; it is a total commitment to improvement in an organization. This commitment displays itself in the bottom line through increased customer satisfaction, better margins on our products, and increased profitability.

The purpose of this policy is to make our organization aware of the benefits of benchmarking and when and how to discuss our operations with outside organizations. By codifying them into the policies, each employee will have a reference guide on which to base decisions and act in the best interests of the organization.

To facilitate the sharing of benchmarking and site visit information, ABC company headquarters has created the position of corporate benchmarking coordinator.

Individuals must complete the appropriate information forms:

■ Benchmarking Approval Form

■ Benchmarking Background Attachment

■ Benchmarking Activities Summary Form

The forms are designed to record descriptions of the general areas or processes observed and to provide names of key contact people from both companies for future reference.

Page 3

ABC Company
Policy and Procedures on Benchmarking Activities

By following a standardized approach and sharing information internally, we can make our efforts more efficient and meet the goals of the organization.

Since ABC is a company with a good reputation for service and quality, we are often asked by representatives of other companies to participate in benchmarking activities. Although it is generally the company's intent to share information and expertise when appropriate, we must ensure that our interests are considered and that senior management approvals are secured when necessary.

In addition, we should be sensitive not to continually benchmark against the same companies. Since the companies typically identified as the "best" are taken from generalized lists, which include award winners and speakers at conferences, these tend to limit our world to just a few potential participants. It is important to seek diverse organizations against which to benchmark and realize that they are not necessarily just like us.

Policies and Procedures

General

This section describes roles and responsibilities of employees and management in the approval and documentation of benchmarking activities. Corporate headquarters will act in a coordinating and advisory role to ensure inbound and outbound benchmarking and site visit requests receive appropriate approvals.

Page 4

ABC Company
Policy and Procedures on Benchmarking Activities

Benchmarking Requests

All requests from other companies to benchmark against ABC must be approved by the benchmarking coordinator.

All requests to benchmark external companies must be approved by the benchmarking coordinator, who will need a clear understanding of the nature of the request.

Prior to making a formal determination of whether there is a fit with the benchmarking request, the benchmarking coordinator will consider the following:

- Determine if there is a good business reason to benchmark

- Determine if there is a potential customer relationship

- Determine if there is a reciprocity issue

- Determine whether there is another alternative to direct benchmarking

- Determine if there are sufficient resources to staff the request to benchmark

In some cases, it will be necessary to decline a benchmarking request. To determine if a benchmarking request should be declined, check with the functional areas where a current or potential customer relationship may exist. Before you decline the request, consider the consequences for the overall relationship and weigh these interests in advance of the decline.

In all cases, the request should come in the form of a formal proposal and should be screened by the legal department.

Page 5

ABC Company
Policy and Procedures on Benchmarking Activities

Legal Involvement in Benchmarking

When sharing information with outsiders, it is important that the legal department be involved from the beginning. The information can cross several lines including antitrust laws and securities laws. While conducting benchmarking studies, it will be generally necessary to document the reasons for contact, what was discussed, and the results. Generally, the issues are resolved before benchmarking begins. Questions regarding the use and distribution of proprietary and confidential information, as well as how that information may be used by others, must be addressed before the visits or activities commence. Doing so will help avoid problems later in the relationship.

Benchmarking Approval Form

Date _____

ABC contact name _____

Department _____

Position _____

Address _____

Phone _____ Fax _____

Name of company requesting to benchmark or site visit ABC

_____

Contact names _____

City _____ State _____

Primary purpose: Benchmarking ☐ Site Visit ☐

Company relationship to ABC (yes/no):

Competitor ☐ Noncompetitor ☐

Supplier ☐ Other (describe) ☐

Date of planned activities _____

Attach Benchmarking Background Form and Return to
Corporate Benchmarking Coordinator

To be completed by ABC benchmarking coordinator

Approved/date _____ Declined/date _____

Reason(s) for decline of benchmarking request _____

_____

Benchmarking Background Attachment
(Attach to Benchmarking Approval Form)

Prior to conducting a benchmarking study with an outside organization, the following information should be made available to the benchmarking coordinators:

Customers of the process

_____

_____

_____

Departments/areas impacted

_____

_____

_____

Specific area(s) to be benchmarked

_____

_____

_____

Agenda or project plan

_____

_____

_____

Names of other organizations involved

_____

_____

_____

Benchmarking Activities Summary Form
(After Benchmarking)

Date _____

ABC contact name _____

Department _____

Position _____

Address _____

_____

Phone _____ Fax _____

Company benchmarked _____

Contact names _____

City _____ State _____

Brief description   _____

                        _____

                        _____

Dates data collected   _____

                        _____

                        _____

Return this form to the Corporate Benchmarking Coordinator.

Notes

1. John H. Lingle and William A. Schiemann, "From Balanced Scorecard to Strategic Gauges: Is Measurement Worth It?" Reprinted from *Management Review* (March 1996), pp. 56–61. Copyright 1996 American Management Association. Reprinted by permission of AMACOM, a division of American Management Association, New York, http: www.amanet.org. All rights reserved.

2. Leslie Overmyer-Day and George Benson, "Training Success Stories," *Training & Development* (June 1996), pp. 24–29. American Society for Training and Development. Reprinted with permission. All rights reserved.

3. Ellen Birkett Morris, "Companies Seek to Make Job Appraisals Effective," *Business First–Louisville* (May 8, 1995), Sec. 1, p. 32.

4. Thomas Rollins and Mike Fruge, "Performance Dimensions: Competencies with a Twist," *Training* (January 1992), pp. 47–51. Reprinted with permission. Copyright 1992 Lakewood Publications, Minneapolis, Minn. All rights reserved. Not for resale.

5. Tim R. V. Davis, "Open-Book Management: Its Promise and Pitfalls." Reprinted from *Organizational Dynamics* (Winter 1997), pp. 6–20. Copyright 1997 American Management Association, New York, http: www.amanet.org. All rights reserved.

6. Rupert Booth, "Accountants Do It by Proxy," *Management Accounting–London* (May 1996), p. 48.

7. Edward Martin, "Paid to Perform," *Business Journal–Charlotte* (October 7, 1996), p. 25.

8. Overmyer-Day and Benson, "Training Success Stories."

9. Morris, "Companies Seek to Make Job Appraisals Effective."

10. Overmyer-Day and Benson, "Training Success Stories."

11. James A. Hendricks, David G. Defreitas, and Delores K. Walker, "Changing Performance Measures at Caterpillar," *Management Accounting* (December 1996), pp. 18–24. Reprinted with permission from *Manage-*

ment Accounting. Copyright by Institute of Management Accountants, Montvale, N.J., April 1996.

12. This case study has been approved by Sisters of Charity Health Care System, Houston, Texas.

13. Brian McWilliams, "The Measure of Success," *Across the Board* (February 1996), pp. 16–20.

14. Kenneth R. Stephens and Ronald R. Bartunek, "What Is Economic Value Added? A Practitioner's View," *Business Credit* (April 1997), pp. 39–42. Copyright 1997 by the National Association of Credit Management. Reprinted with permission.

15. Joel Kurtzman, "Is Your Company Off Course? Now You Can Find Out Why," *Fortune* (February 17, 1997), pp. 128–130. Reprinted by special permission. Copyright 1997, Time Inc.

16. Richard J. Schonberger, "Backing Off From the Bottom Line," *Executive Excellence* (May 1996), pp. 16–17.

17. Rupert Booth, "'Just Do It'—But How?" *Management Accounting–London* (November 1996), p. 18.

18. Kurtsman, "Is Your Company Off Course?"

19. Ibid.

20. McWilliams, "The Measure of Success."

21. Ibid.

22. "Linking the Balanced Scorecard to Strategy," in *California Management Review* (Fall 1996), pp. 53–79. From Robert S. Kaplan and David P. Norton, *The Balanced Scorecard* (Boston: Harvard Business School Press, 1996). Reprinted by permission of Harvard Business School Press. Copyright 1996 by President and Fellows of Harvard College; all rights reserved.

23. Ibid.

24. Ellen Weisman Strenger, "The Data Game," *Trustee* 50(4) (April 1997), pp. 6–10. Excerpted from *Trustee* by permission. Copyright 1997, American Hospital Publishing, Inc.

25. Laurie J. Smith, "Beyond Profit and Loss," *Best's Review* (Life/Health) (April 1997), pp. 58–62.

26. Britta Waller, "The Art of Teamwork," *Small Business News–Akron* (April 1996), p. 8.

27. Strenger, "The Data Game."

28. Alan Owen, "A Measure of Their Worth," *CMA* (July/August 1997), pp. 12–15. Reprinted with permission of The Society of Management Accountants of Canada.

29. John Teresko, "Too Much Data, Too Little Information," *Industry Week* (August 19, 1996), pp. 66–70. Reprinted with permission from *Industry Week.* Copyright Penton Publishing, Inc., Cleveland, Ohio.

30. Daniel W. Bielinkski, "Competitive Advantage," *Corporate Report Wisconsin* (October 1996), p. 8.

31. "Referring to Entergy Corporation and Its Philosophies Relative to Customer Satisfaction," *Marketing News* 30 (May 9, 1996), p. 8. The material protected by this copyright has been translated for the express purpose of this publication. The American Marketing Association cannot be held responsible for any misunderstandings caused by the translation. Reprinted with permission from *Marketing News*, published by the American Marketing Association.

32. Kaye Hamilton-Smith and Ted Morris, "Market-Driven Quality: What Management Accountants Should Know," *CMA* (May 1993), pp. 4, 23.

33. Bradley T. Gale, "Trends in Customer Satisfaction, Loyalty and Value," http://www.cval.com/Trends/Trends.html, October 1997.

34. "The Balanced Scorecard," *HR Focus* (September 1996), p. 73.

35. Mike Miller, "Customer Services Drives Reengineering Effort," *Personnel Journal* 73(11) (November 1994), pp. 87–91.

36. Jennifer A. Scott, "The Art of Teamwork," *Small Business News–Cleveland* (April 1996), p. 14.

37. Susan Podolsky, "Quality Groupies: Assessing the Total Quality Management Cult," *Manitoba Business* (July 1994), Sec. 1, p. 29.

38. Yvonne Pfoutz, "Corporate Training Officers Handle a Variety of Programs," *Quad-State Business Journal* (August 1996), p. 9.

39. Pamela Vosmik, "In Pursuit of Quality Human Resources at AT&T Universal Card Services," *Employment Relations Today* (Spring 1993), pp. 29–35. Reprinted by permission of John Wiley & Sons, Inc.

40. Zarowin Stanley, "Motorola's Financial Closings: 12 'Nonevents' a Year," *Journal of Accountancy, AICPA* (November 1995).

41. Ibid.

42. Sallie S. Anthony, "A Leap of Faith," *Mortgage Banking* 55(11) (August 1995), pp. 85–94.

43. "Changing Customer Demands Serve as Impetus for BPR at Schlage Lock Co.," *Industrial Engineering* 26(6) (June 1994), pp. 30–34.

44. Paul Karon, "Hallmark Welcomes Change in Handling Finances," *InfoWorld* 16(51) (December 19, 1994), p. 62.

Index

ABC, *see* activity-based costing
ABM, *see* activity-based management
abnormalities, 188
academia, 59
access to information, 99
accountability, 24, 65, 67, 81, 197
accountant, 38–39, 47
accuracy, 12, 14, 142, 147, 157, 163–164, 233, 237
acquisitions, 43, 87, 89, 226, 241
actionable data, 140
active accounts, 68, 71
active inventory, 108
activity-analysis program, 92
activity-based costing (ABC), 84, 90–91, 228
activity-based management (ABM), 84, 90–91
actual spending, 67
actuals, 118, 232
acute-care hospitals, 68, 71
ad hoc communication, 218
ad hoc groups, 64–65, 71, 82
ad hoc reports, 227
adaptability, 25
administrative costs, 110
administrative personnel, 223
advertising, 28, 99, 122, 149, 152
affinity diagram, 142

aftermarket parts, 112
agencies, 60, 68, 101, 114, 192
agility, 110, 112, 232
agreements, 5, 60, 100, 165, 243
airlines, 10, 91, 228, 229
Alcoa Fujikura, Ltd., xi
alignment efforts, 5–6
Allaire, Paul, 118
alliances, 159, 243–244
Alliant BEIs, 61–62
Alliant Health System, 60
allocations, 65, 91, 181, 242
Allstate Insurance Company, 60, 103
ambiguities, 141
Amoco, xi
amortization of costs, 110
Analog Devices (company), 93, 95
analysis, 157–158, 160, 177–178, 184, 188, 193–194, 202, 209–210, 214, 227–231, 233, 242–243, 250
    groups, 51, 55, 230
    techniques, 155
    tools, 84, 142
annual report, 114, 205
antitrust issues, 250, 254
appraisal-oriented measurement, 21
appraisals, 22, 60